T0265800

GAMBLING MAN

THE SECRET STORY OF
THE WORLD'S GREATEST DISRUPTOR,
MASAYOSHI SON

....

LIONEL BARBER

ONE SIGNAL
PUBLISHERS

ATRIA

New York Amsterdam/Antwerp London Toronto Sydney New Delhi

ONE SIGNAL
PUBLISHERS

ATRIA

An Imprint of Simon & Schuster, LLC
1230 Avenue of the Americas
New York, NY 10020

Copyright © 2021 by Lionel Barber
Originally published in Great Britain in 2021 by Allen Lane

First One Signal Publishers/Atria Books hardcover edition January 2025

ONE SIGNAL PUBLISHERS / ATRIA BOOKS and colophon are trademarks of Simon & Schuster, LLC

For information about special discounts for bulk purchases, please contact Simon & Schuster Special Sales at 1-866-506-1949 or business@simonandschuster.com.

The Simon & Schuster Speakers Bureau can bring authors to your live event. For more information or to book an event, contact the Simon & Schuster Speakers Bureau at 1-866-248-3049 or visit our website at www.simonspeakers.com.

Interior design by Silverglass

Manufactured in the United States of America

1 3 5 7 9 10 8 6 4 2

Library of Congress Cataloging-in-Publication Data has been applied for.

ISBN 978-1-6680-7074-1
ISBN 978-1-6680-7076-5 (ebook)

CONTENTS

PART 4: THE EMPIRE BUILDER

PART 5: HUBRIS

GAMBLING MAN

PROLOGUE

On a chilly Wednesday evening, February 2, 2000, more than two thousand people crammed into a dimly lit discotheque called Velfarre,[1] Tokyo's equivalent of Studio 54 in New York.[2] The suit-clad professionals streaming onto the giant underground dance floor were not about to twist the night away. They were waiting for a special guest. A man who embodied their hopes and dreams; a self-styled visionary with the loftiest ambitions for himself, his company, and Japan. His name was Masayoshi Son, founder of SoftBank, the global media technology conglomerate and the public face of the internet bubble.

Almost a year earlier, when dot-com stocks began their dizzying ascent, a group of young Japanese had formed the Bit Valley Association, an attempt to create a community of tech-minded entrepreneurs to interact with, help, and inspire each other. Their model was Silicon Valley in California. Every month, the group held a networking event where analysts, bankers, investors, salesmen, and traders turned up, each eager for tips on hot internet stocks. On this occasion, the gathering was held at the Velfarre disco in Roppongi, "the district that never sleeps."[3]

These were the wildest times, reminiscent of Japan's real estate bubble during the late 1980s, when stock market prices defied gravity and irrational exuberance swept through the business and financial communities. Then came the inevitable crash, a banking crisis, and years of economic stagnation known as the Lost Decade. The dot-com boom promised a return to the good times, and that night word spread rapidly that the guest of honor was indeed Masayoshi Son.

The presence of the man known to friends and rivals alike as "Masa" was by no means a foregone conclusion. Secretive and prone to last-minute changes in schedule, he'd just returned on a chartered flight from Davos, the annual gathering of the world's business elite in the Swiss Alps. All the talk was about the deal of the new century: the $165 billion merger between America Online (AOL) and Time Warner, the film, music, and publishing colossus. AOL was barely nine years old, but its frothy share price made it worth twice as much as Time Warner with less than half the cash flow. In the dot-com economy, where conventional valuations were turned on their heads, internet companies like AOL were supposed to vaporize mainstream media, leaving Masa and a handful of farsighted investors on top of the world.

In the past twelve months alone, the tech-heavy Nasdaq stock market in New York had risen 86 percent. Two weeks before the Velfarre event, the share price of Masa's online creation Yahoo! Japan had surpassed ¥100 million ($1 million), the highest price of any stock in Japanese history.[4] Intent on riding the boom, Masa was ready to announce a tie-up between SoftBank and Nasdaq. The new joint venture would create a pipeline of internet start-ups soon to go public, enriching founders and shareholders by sums unimaginable.

"The most amazing opportunities await you," Masa told the mesmerized crowd, among them Masaru Hayami, governor of the Bank of Japan. The presence of the staid central bank at Tokyo's digital rave attracted plenty of comment. Most likely, Hayami wanted to see for himself whether this was another bubble to pop, or whether the digital revolution was something genuinely transformational for Japan. Masa left the audience in no doubt where he stood.

"Japan is going through its biggest social upheaval since the Meiji Restoration. Let's make it so that a millennium from now, people will look back on our time and remember that the kind of society they're living in was created by us today."[5]

SoftBank's CEO and founder was drawn irresistibly to historical analogies. He often compared himself to the nineteenth-century samurai warrior and reformer Ryoma Sakamoto, whose rebellion swept away the old feudal order in Japan, paving the way for the restoration of the emperor's authority in 1868. In the decades that followed, Japan rapidly modernized, spawning thousands of new businesses and spurring its ascent as the leading economic power in Asia. Masa's internet evangelism was, however, about more than making Japan great again; it was a bid to revive animal spirits in a Japanese economy still semicomatose after the collapse of the real estate bubble.

"In the US, 99 percent of [internet] companies receive VC [venture capital] funding. That's money you don't have to pay back, even if your company failed," Masa intoned. "There are many entrepreneurs [in the US] who failed with four companies but on their fifth time managed to go public on Nasdaq and become a billionaire. I want you to keep challenging yourself." But, he added, people should still follow the rules.[6]

At times, in his speech, Masa sounded dangerously close to a snake oil salesman, but his "get rich quick" message resonated among Japan's fledgling start-up generation. "Young entrepreneurs are going to make ¥50-100 billion [$500 million–$1 billion]. There'll be a constant stream— in the hundreds—of the 'young rich' who are going to realize the Japanese Dream. The age of Japan as a nation of one hundred million salarymen, where executives are praised for living frugally, is over."

Four days after staging the dot-com party of the decade, members of the Bit Valley Association decided it was time to close up shop. There would be no more extravaganzas. The networking event had outlived its purpose. Masa's frothy speech coincided almost exactly with the top of the market. In hindsight, it amounted to a giant Sell sign.

On February 15, 2000, SoftBank's stock peaked at ¥198,000 ($1,850). For the next three days, including when markets were closed over the weekend, Masa was the richest man on the planet. His $70 billion paper fortune exceeded that of Bill Gates, Warren Buffett, and Rupert Murdoch. SoftBank, the software-distribution business turned media tech conglomerate he founded in 1981, was valued at $200 billion: less than Microsoft but more than ExxonMobil and General Electric, America's industrial titans.

In reality, SoftBank was heading for trouble, like a lightweight canoe hurtling toward the rapids. Just before SoftBank shares hit an all-time high, someone describing himself as a doctor falsely posted on online message boards that Masa had been hospitalized. No explanation was given for the posts, which appeared in the first two weeks of February.[7] There was no foundation to the rumors. It was one more bad omen.

In mid-March 2000, stock markets around the world experienced a savage correction. Within eleven months, as the dot-com bubble popped and SoftBank's share price slumped, Masa lost 96 percent of his paper wealth. The Nasdaq Japan venture ended up losing several hundred million dollars. Masa was forced to order a fire sale of assets to avoid being wiped out.

It was a humiliating reversal—one that for most people would be crushing. For Masa it was simply one more twist in the roller-coaster pattern of failure and success that has characterized his tumultuous life. In the decades after the dot-com crash, the diminutive SoftBank boss reinvented himself. He became the twenty-first century's ultimate conjurer of capital, masterminding a new-age, transnational tech-and-finance empire that still touches many of the most dynamic parts of the world economy. Through willpower and guts, Masa turned into a figure who embodies a gilded age of tech utopianism, benign globalization, and borderless finance.

Little known in the West, except in its corridors of power, Masa has invested or controlled assets worth $1 trillion in the past two decades. His impact on global business has been huge. He bankrolled Alibaba, China's internet colossus, before the world had heard of it; plotted with Steve Jobs to turn the iPhone into a wonder product; and financed the biggest boom Silicon Valley has seen, one that supersized hundreds of start-ups, including fiascos such as WeWork, and made the dot-com boom look trivial in the process. Along the way the superlatives have kept piling up: Masa has been both the single largest foreign investor in capitalist America and communist China; the biggest start-up funder in the world; and the boss of one of the top ten most indebted firms, continually threatening a financial implosion. He is probably the most powerful mogul of the twenty-first century who is not a household name.

This book takes you on Masa's wild ride, from the grubby offices of aspiring entrepreneurs to the modern-day temples of power. It speeds through Donald Trump's golden skyscraper in Manhattan, the royal palaces of Riyadh, and the throne rooms of China's Marxist rulers; all places where Masa has plied his unique trade. Say "Masa" to many of the world's most powerful people, and you will get an affectionate flash of recognition. Whether they admire or disdain his methods, they acknowledge he may be the most unusual person they have met: a seductive blend of humility and hubris, common sense and insane risk-taking, for whom national borders, technological frontiers, and ethical boundaries are there to be crossed.

The tale of Masayoshi Son needs telling because it captures a twenty-five-year span of hyperglobalization in which money, technologies, and ideas flowed freely. SoftBank is perhaps the most extreme manifestation of this period, which is now fading amid a new cold war and protectionism. For students of business, meanwhile, his story features a relentless quest to create a new business model adapted to this age. Masa's answer combines the federated structure of Japan's three-hundred-year-old *zaibatsu*, the speed and networked relationships of Silicon Valley, and an ethos of speculation and mercenary management cherry-picked from Wall Street and the City of London.

Most of all, for anyone interested in the human condition, Masa's story is one of personal invention: how to become somebody when you are born a nobody. Unlike the American or Chinese magnates who dominate the top of tech, Masa did not invent, control, or own a breakthrough technology. Unlike the Americans, he was not supported by the US financial system via venture capital, private equity, or the capital markets. Unlike China's tycoons, Masa does not enjoy the support that comes—or used to come—with being a card-carrying member of the Communist Party. He is sui generis, and no more so than in his native Japan.

In a place where a culture of perfection exists to the point of obsession, whether in the precision manufacturing of kitchen knives or the rituals of the Japanese tea ceremony, Masa is a maverick. He stands out because entrepreneurship is not consistent with perfection. It is about risk-taking, where failure is not merely inevitable but necessary. Born an outsider to poverty-stricken Korean immigrants in postwar Japan, he epitomizes the entrepreneur-innovator, driven to constantly stake his fortune, fate, and fame on a new idea or invention that most people can barely see yet.

For more than six decades, Masa has gone to great lengths to manicure his personal narrative and maintain his own myth. Disentangling the man and the myth requires digging to a depth even greater than the dimensions of the secret mansion in central Tokyo that serves as his home and his workplace. He resists definition, and he has wrestled with his Korean identity since his birth in a shantytown on the western island of Kyushu in the Japanese archipelago. And that is where our story must begin.

PART 1

BOY GENIUS

1

ROOTS

The first wave of Korean migrants to Japan arrived at the turn of the twentieth century. They came in search of economic opportunity. The Japanese economy was industrializing fast, education was improving, and jobs were aplenty. Compared to a life in poverty on the Korean peninsula, Imperial Japan offered attractive prospects. Among the thousands who took the eleven-hour journey across the Tsushima Strait, where a Japanese fleet of steel battleships annihilated the Russian navy in 1905, was a chippy teenager by the name of Son Jong-gyeong.[1]

Masayoshi Son's grandfather arrived in 1917 in Kyushu,[2] the western island in the Japanese archipelago that juts toward the Korean mainland as Cuba almost touches the southernmost tip of Florida. Imperial Japan was the dominant power in the region, having triumphed in the First Sino-Japanese War in 1894-95 and the Russo-Japanese War in 1904-5 and having annexed Korea in 1910, reducing its neighbor to the status of a colony. Born in 1899, the teenager lost his father when he was only four years old. Soon afterward, the Japanese military seized the family farm and turned it into an airstrip.[3]

Although Son Jong-gyeong came from a peasant's family, he claimed to belong to the Yangban class, which oversaw Korea's agrarian bureaucracy and disdained all forms of business and commerce. The more refined Yangban exemplified the Confucian ideal of "scholarly official," practicing calligraphy and traditional herbal medicine. When the Japanese annexed Korea, they abolished the Yangban class, but the Son family clung to its status. Masa's father later joked that the family's aristocratic lineage had in fact died out many years earlier. His family was more "Yaban":[4] less educated, more patriarchal, dismissive of women, and prone to vicious infighting.

Grandfather Son's first job was at a coal mine in Chikuho, a mineral-rich region known for its extreme summer humidity. As an ethnic Korean immigrant, the rail-thin teenager found himself in a legal no-man's-land. He was a subject of Japan's empire and therefore a Japanese national, but he was not entitled to the status of Japanese citizen. To blend more easily into his workplace, he followed common practice and assumed a Japanese family name: Yasumoto.

Then as now, living under an assumed identity was the easiest way to avoid discrimination. Japanese employers preferred that Korean immigrants adopt names deemed pronounceable by mainlanders. Aliases appeared regularly in newspaper reports of crime incidents or death notices.[5] But the blurring of Japanese names and Korean identity was a false assimilation. In an island nation where blood and culture cut deep into the national psyche, Koreans remained victims of systemic prejudice which at times tipped into mass violence.

On September 1, 1923, an earthquake measuring 7.9 on the Richter scale devastated Tokyo, the port of Yokohama, and surrounding prefectures. The Great Kanto Earthquake claimed more than one hundred thousand lives, many incinerated in firestorms, and led to a breakdown in law and order. When rumors spread that ethnic Koreans were poisoning the wells, raping women, and stoking the movement for Korean independence, mayhem ensued. Vigilantes rounded up the Koreans (along with ethnic Chinese and Japanese socialists) and massacred them using guns, swords, and bamboo sticks. The final Korean death toll was between six and ten thousand.[6]

By now grandfather Son, who had little appetite for manual labor, had run away from the colliery to become a tenant farmer in Tosu, a nearby railway hub. Heading toward thirty, he was an aging bachelor desperate to find a partner and start a family. He alighted on fourteen-year-old Lee Wong-jo, a Korean immigrant less than half his age. Son was a brutish character with a melodramatic streak. He threatened to kill himself unless Lee's parents consented to his plans for marriage.[7] Eventually they relented, the union was tied, and Lee Wong-jo bore two children, both girls with Japanese names, Tomoko and Kiyoko. The Japanese economy was powering ahead, and the Son family could finally look forward to a better life. In 1936, Masa's father, Mitsunori, was born, the third sibling in a family that would grow to seven children.

In the 1920s and '30s, as the world spiraled into depression and instability, Japan's leaders embarked on an increasingly frantic quest for control over the markets and resources of Asia. The Great Empire of Japan spread like a pool of blood. (On Japanese maps the empire was always colored red.)[8] Six years after the takeover of Manchuria in 1931, the Imperial Army invaded China and ran amok, committing arson, looting, rape, and the mass murder of Chinese civilians. On December 7, 1941, Japan's surprise attack on the Pearl Harbor naval base—part of a strategy aimed at seizing control of the southern reaches of Asia and the Pacific—was a monumental miscalculation. President Franklin Roosevelt finally had his casus belli, and the US entered the Second World War, with cataclysmic consequences for Japan.

During the war, Japanese authorities bribed, intimidated, and press-ganged Koreans young and old from the Korean mainland to join the armed forces. Koreans worked alongside prisoners of war and women in the coal mines. As forced labor, they were starved of food and medical treatment, left to rot in a "hell on earth." In occupied territories, Korean women and girls were used by the Imperial Army as "comfort women," a humiliating sexual slavery. The Son family, having already settled in Japan, were spared this trauma, but tens of thousands of Koreans were forcibly resettled in Kyushu, many coming to Tosu to work in the railway station's marshaling yard. This vital military staging post was the size of a football stadium; it also served as a giant casualty station where Korean workers suffered horrific injuries maneuvering the two-ton freight cars laden with coal and destined for the war fronts in Asia.

Tosu presented a rich target for American bombers. Mitsunori, then seven years old, remembered the familiar formation of ten B-29s flying overhead. "When the weather was good, they would twinkle, and the sight would be so beautiful. I would look up and marvel at them. Then they would drop bombs relentlessly, especially around the station. It was terrifying."[9]

One day, a B-29 plunged from the sky, smoke pouring from its body. Mitsunori walked several miles just to catch a glimpse of the crash site. "I remember thinking American planes are amazing, they're so big. And the window of the cockpit, the glass was so thick. I touched it with my hands and was amazed. I applauded on the spot, it was so beautiful. I came to like America after seeing that plane."

In 1945, Imperial Japan surrendered unconditionally after two American atomic bombs obliterated Hiroshima and Nagasaki. The Japanese empire, stretching across southeast Asia, shrank to its four main islands. Japan, having lost three million people, was now under American occupation, led by the imperious General Douglas MacArthur. It was zero hour for ethnic Koreans. The Son family had to decide whether to stay or leave Japan. Were they collaborators or resistance? Some Koreans had fought in the Imperial Army. Where should they go? More than a million chose to leave, fleeing to China, Europe, the US, and Korea, occupied in the north by Soviet forces and in the south by American GIs.

Between six and eight hundred thousand Koreans stayed in Japan, only to face segregation far worse than before the war. Koreans were a daily reminder of lost empire; beggars on the streets, veterans without benefits; families living in slums. Ethnic Koreans in Japan were the detritus of empire, though previously they had worked in the foundry of empire. Now the Japanese authorities encouraged them to leave en masse. Those who remained—the so-called zainichi (literally "residing in Japan")—were viewed as troublemakers and objects of suspicion. Successive postwar Japanese governments, still feeling their way after more than six years of American occupation, feared that ethnic Koreans were a fifth column, in cahoots with the Japanese Communist Party.[10]

Son Jong-gyeong was dubious about going back to Korea. He'd spent almost thirty years in Japan. It was a home, of sorts. But his wife, Lee Wong-jo, was adamant. She was worried about her children being abducted or killed by Japanese vigilantes shamed by their country's surrender and tempted to exact revenge. The Son family waited for months for a ship back to Korea, joining tens of thousands of ethnic Koreans stranded in a vast makeshift settlement at Hakata Bay in Kyushu. In 1946, they found a berth on a ship bound for Busan, the main port on the Korean mainland.

After more than two days at sea, the family arrived at their destination: the grandfather's birthplace in an old village in Daegu province. The work-shy patriarch left his wife to cope. She went begging for vegetables to sell, only to face half a dozen relatives armed with bats who destroyed her makeshift food stall. They considered themselves Yangban, not peasants hawking goods for a living. "You're Iljik Son, just like us," they cried. "How can you go begging? You're bringing shame on the family name."

The gang came every day for a week, shouting and yelling and wreaking havoc. Finally, Lee lost her will to resist. There was no option but to return to Japan. Mitsunori, then eleven, was livid. At a time of chaos, when all were in despair, he spied opportunity. A born entrepreneur, he fancied his chances of starting a business in postwar Korea, where everything felt "as poor as Africa."[11]

The Son clan waited another eighteen months for a berth for the journey from Busan to Shimonoseki in Japan. The numbers of boats crossing the Tsushima Strait had declined dramatically. Japan was a shattered land with a shattered people. The Tokyo government had no interest in taking back ethnic Koreans.

One night, under the cover of darkness, grandfather Son, his wife, and his seven children clambered aboard a smuggler's fishing boat back to Kyushu. The journey across to the Japanese mainland was perilous at the best of times, but these were the grimmest, and the Son family's luck ran out midway through the crossing as the ramshackle vessel's engine broke down and water flooded in.

When Mitsunori screamed at his father to save the family from drowning, there was no response. Son Jong-gyeong appeared paralyzed, resigned to his fate. The rest of the family took turns bailing out the water from the listing vessel. The children and their parents were adrift for two days before a fishing vessel spotted them. A second, successful attempt to cross the strait followed soon thereafter. The Son family, having smuggled their way back into Japan, finally returned to their old hometown of Tosu.

They must have prayed for a better life. What awaited them were deprivation and discrimination far worse than anything they had experienced in prewar Japan.

2

PACHINKO

In 1947, on their return to Kyushu, the Son family's new home was the equivalent of a cowshed, one of dozens of makeshift dwellings on a plot of unregistered land owned by Japanese National Railways. Around three hundred Koreans settled next to Tosu railway station,[1] a no-go area at night for local police, a refuge for the homeless and the poor, and an underworld economy of bootleggers, loan sharks, and yakuza (gangsters).[2]

Japanese railway employees routinely set fire to the Korean ghetto, ostensibly to carry out a controlled burn of company land.[3] Overnight the Koreans patched together their tin shacks with bits of discarded metal, acts of defiance that inspired Masa in later life. Everyone worked in the Son family, except for the grandfather. Doing manual labor was beneath the self-styled Yangban, "a lazy fart"[4] who turned to the bottle to block out life's daily humiliations.

The early postwar years in Japan were beyond wretched. The country was under American occupation, but everywhere there were signs of social breakdown. The press was full of stories of sensational murders. People were on the verge of starvation. Black markets were cesspools of illicit drugs, including heroin and Philopon, the stimulant used to keep Japanese pilots awake during the war.[5]

In Tosu, the Son family eked out an existence. Grandma Lee sold fish, vegetables, and scrap metal. Mitsunori, forced to leave high school when he was fourteen to help earn money, hawked liquor on the side. The old adage—"If the law doesn't respect you, then you won't respect the law"—applied to Mitsunori, who could not obtain a liquor license because he was Korean. "I started making moonshine when I was sixteen. I knew it was illegal, but I had no work," he recalled, "then I stopped caring whether what I did was legal or not. And when I got caught, I always shifted the blame on somebody else."

One night, the grandfather heard Mitsunori bragging about his moneymaking. Rising in silence from the dinner table, he fetched one of his clogs and beat his son so hard that blood streamed down the young man's face. For a Yangban, doing business was shameful enough. Boasting in public about profiteering was beyond the pale.[6]

On August 8, 1957, ten years after the Son family returned home to Japan, Masa was born in the Korean settlement near Tosu railway station, on a dirt track with no name. The baby was said to have remained silent for fifteen minutes, refusing to cry until prompted by the midwife pouring water over his face. His father claims, more implausibly, that there were signs of stigmata on Masa's back, rendering his son an infant Jesus figure. "He died before he was born," Mitsunori once joked.[7]

Masa's mother, Tamako, was born in 1936, the same year as Mitsunori. Unlike her rough-hewn husband, she came from true Yangban stock. In her early years, Tamako was known as a local beauty, often compared to a famous Japanese singer of the postwar era. One of her younger brothers, Miyata, was a talented painter, an artistic bent that Masa shared.[8]

Mitsunori and Tamako met when he came to her house to buy pigs. From that day on, he claimed he was in love and refused to leave until her parents consented to marriage. Eventually, they relented, and the marriage took place in 1955. But when her family visited the Son clan in Tosu, they were taken aback by the number of pigs roaming in and around the tin shack home, just a few feet from the main railway track. They felt sorry for their daughter, who had obviously married well beneath her station.[9]

As a *zainichi*, Masa was born with two names in Japanese and Korean: Masayoshi Yasumoto and Son Jung-eui. Both Masayoshi and Jung-eui mean "justice," signaling his parents' hope of a better life for their offspring. Masa's earliest memories were the smell of pigs and the sound of steam trains belching soot and smoke that filled his makeshift home. Locals had a saying: all sparrows are black in Tosu.[10] "We started at the bottom of society," Masa remembered, more than sixty-five years later. "I didn't even know what nationality I was."[11]

Masa's fate, along with that of all ethnically oppressed *zainichi*, stemmed from a cruel twist of history. In Asia, there was no postwar settlement on the lines of the 1945 Yalta Conference, where Stalin, Churchill, and Roosevelt carved up Europe into spheres of influence. The 1951 San Francisco treaty ended the American occupation and restored full sovereignty to Japan. But it left open numerous territorial disputes. Korea was divided between north and south along the lines of the 38th parallel. Japan was forced to renounce title to Taiwan, but the allies decided the island would not become communist China's territory. In response, China and the Soviet Union both refused to sign the San Francisco treaty.[12]

The two new Koreas did not sign the treaty either, and Korean victims of Japanese atrocities during the war were not entitled to compensation, an injustice that continued to poison relations between the two neighbors for decades. In Japan, tens of thousands of Koreans like the Son family were left in limbo, stripped of their colonial-era Japanese nationality, and noncitizens in what was once "their" country. Their fate gave the lie to the myth propagated first by the American occupiers and later by Japanese politicians that postwar Japan was a unified, homogeneous nation. The reality was that the Korean community were outcasts, forced to live a marginalized existence, confined to an underworld economy.

With both his parents working, Masa, the second of four brothers, was raised by his grandmother Lee Wong-jo. Every day, she wheeled Masa around in a black wheelbarrow, collecting scraps from local restaurants that she later fed to the five red pigs keeping the family company by the railway track. "You thought this life was normal, and you don't feel unhappy because you don't know otherwise," Masa remembered. "The pigs used to make noise in the evenings, with a bad smell, like shit."[13]

Years later, well after his first million, Masa confided to an old friend that he was plagued by a recurring nightmare, waking up in a start with the stench of pig excrement in his nostrils. When he described the experience, his friend said the dream was in fact a memory. Try as he might, Masa could not escape his past.[14]

Masa suffered hardship in those first five years, but it was nothing compared to the suffering of his parents' generation. Their sacrifice was a powerful motivating force for the young boy, leaving him with a profound sense of obligation. Whatever he accomplished in life, however much money he made, he felt he could never erase the debt he owed his parents and grandparents.[15]

By his own account, Masa enjoyed his early childhood, playing hide-and-seek in the haystacks and fishing in the local Daigi river. His first encounter with overt discrimination left a scar, both mental and physical. One afternoon, on his way home from kindergarten, Masa was attacked by Japanese kids taunting him for living in the Korean ghetto. One threw a stone that struck his forehead and drew blood. It was a moment of humiliation but also self-realization: Masa spoke Japanese, and he had inherited a Japanese name ("Yasumoto"), but he was still a pariah.

"Gradually, you start to realize that you're not a Japanese kid. You start to understand the nationality, the race—and the discrimination. And then your good old memories start to stink a little. And then you try to escape from those smells," Masa recalled.

The Son family's path out of poverty was breeding and selling hogs. Because pigs reproduce faster than cattle or sheep, and Mitsunori was working eighteen hours a day selling the animals for slaughter, the family's finances rapidly transformed. Masa's father had free family labor, free feed from restaurant scraps, and no rent because his family were squatters. It was all income, no expenses. Having set himself a target of ¥5 million ($14,000) in five years, Mitsunori ended up making ¥40 million ($111,000).[16]

Watching his father, the young Masa would have learned several things: the terrifying fear of destitution, the outsider's relentless struggle for survival, the bitter truth that no one will help you but yourself, as well as the endless corner-cutting, hustle, and reinvention required of an entrepreneur operating on the margins of society. By contrast, his mother, Tamako, was a more distant figure, absent in the literal sense (she is said to have found Mitsunori's misogyny difficult and sometimes left the family home to stay with relatives), but also in the emotional sense. Grandma Lee, ever present, always worrying about money, left an enduring impression.

More than fifteen years later, perched on a wooden armchair, Mitsunori Son, eighty-seven, reflected upon the moment he realized his second son Masayoshi was cut from a different cloth, a young boy possessed of stubbornness, self-belief, and unlimited ambition. Masa was six years old, and he was sumo-wrestling with his elder brother in the family home. Masa lost the fight, but he refused to give up. Nothing would stop him, not even when his father tried to pull him away. Mitsunori still remembered the look in Masa's eyes.

"They were like an animal's, a wolf's eyes," he chuckled. "I thought to myself: 'Wow, this bastard is not human.'"[17]

On that morning in spring 2023, shafts of sunlight pierced through the windows to illuminate a spacious living room crammed with photographs and mementos of Masa. The setting felt almost like a shrine, as if Mitsunori himself was living his life and enjoying his own self-esteem through the life of his favorite son.

At the back of the room, snapshots of the two men in baseball jackets and caps lined the mantelpiece, alongside Masa's own artwork featuring a black stallion mid-gallop against a stormy landscape. One work stood out: a self-portrait, painted by Masa when he was about sixteen years old. Everything about that picture spells defiance. The pursed lips. The thick jet-black hair swept forward in a flamboyant V-shaped curve over the forehead, casting a deep shadow down the left side of the face.

"He [Masa] would keep staring at me, with those eyes, as if they were telling me to keep calling him a genius," Mitsunori remembered, "and so I ended up having to call him a genius." Just in case the foreign visitor failed to absorb the message, the doting father added: "Because Masa is convinced that he's a genius, the good ideas follow. If you truly believe you're strong, you're a genius, then failure just bounces off you, you drive failure away through sheer willpower."

This mixture of stubbornness and inspiration illuminates the essence of Masa's character and his approach to business. Convinced of his own technocentric worldview, he truly believes he can see into the future and make it reality in the present. "Masa thinks that if something could happen, it should happen. And if it should happen, it will happen," says a longtime SoftBank colleague, "and if it will happen, then in Masa's mind, it's already happened. He's already visualized it."[18]

Masa agrees he was encouraged by his father to believe that he was exceptional. "He always said, 'Masa, you're the best, you're number one, you're brilliant.' So I had a natural belief: I'm number one. Why should I compromise to be number two?"[19]

Such praise for children was conspicuously absent in traditional Japanese families, where the atmosphere at home was more reserved, even severe. In his early years, Masa, relishing his princeling status, wasn't shy about offering business advice to his father. When Mitsunori said he'd bought a café on the fringe of town and was worried about how to attract customers, Masa, no more than eight years old, had the answer. Hand out free coffee vouchers, and the customers will come and spend money on other items. Masa was equally resourceful at middle school. Once, before being sent on a five-mile run, he worked out how to take a shortcut. To this day, he insists that he imagined the route in his own head rather than reading a map ahead of the race. When informed of this childhood tale, a former top SoftBank colleague laughed. "Masa's life is one long shortcut. It should be the title of your book."[20]

In April 1964, the Son family moved to Kitakyushu, some fifty-five miles to the north of Tosu. Nearby was the giant Yahata steel plant, where the salarymen with their monthly paychecks offered a target market for Mitsunori's new venture: loan-sharking. Customers were charged exorbitant levels of interest: a loan of ¥10,000 ($100) translated into ¥20,000, repayable on demand. This was a high-risk activity that required Mitsunori to carry a knife for self-protection. Sometimes, he thought better of taking on unnecessary risk and summoned a reluctant relative to shake down delinquent debtors.

By now, Japan's economic miracle was nearly complete. A boom in postwar construction, coupled with heavy industrialization, had restored the country to a front-rank economic power built around shipbuilding, electric power, and coal and steel production. That year, 1964, Tokyo hosted the summer Olympics, the first to be held in Asia. The two-week event was a coming-out for Japan, showcasing its spectacular technological progress symbolized by the completion of the Tokaido Shinkansen, the fastest train in the world, and a new geo-satellite allowing the games to be telecast live internationally for the first time.

Mitsunori's next business foray was into pachinko, a form of low-stakes gambling through pinball and slot machines.[21] In postwar Japan, pachinko parlors were a diversion for the older generation suffering from war trauma. For the younger generation, they were an escape from loveless homes, where wives slept with children instead of their salaryman husbands working and drinking late into the night.[22] Pachinko operated in a legal gray zone, opening a space for ethnic Koreans shut out of the traditional economy. In time, they would come to dominate an industry amounting to 4 percent of Japan's GDP, more than Las Vegas and Macau combined.[23]

In her bestselling novel of that name, Min Jin Lee describes the scene inside a pachinko hall in Yokohama in 1976: "The volcanic rush of tinny bells, the clanging of tiny hammers across miniature metal bowls, the beeping and flashing of colourful lights, and the throaty shouts of welcome from the obsequious staff."[24] Pachinko was wildly popular among men and women. Housewives would queue up early in the morning, eager to secure a place at the one reputedly lucky machine in the hall. They played till early evening, hypnotized by balls zigzagging vertically through pins en route to a hole that could spell a small fortune or a big zero. Then the husband would take over, playing game after game on the same machine, until the shop finally closed at midnight.

Pachinko was no place for fainthearts. The yakuza used the business for tax evasion, money laundering, and racketeering. Turf wars were routine in Kyushu, where rival gangs occasionally settled their differences with grenades or bursts of machine-gun fire. Undeterred, Mitsunori was set on becoming the pachinko kingpin of Kyushu. His second slot machine parlor was called Lions[25] and included a small plot of land. The total cost was ¥1.5 billion ($4.1 million), leaving Mitsunori mortgaged to the hilt. By his account, he needed five to ten thousand customers a day to keep going, five to ten times the number of customers visiting rival pachinko parlors.[26]

The level of his personal indebtedness was reckless, his financial targets insanely ambitious. After two weeks, he'd fallen well short. The gambler improvised, ordering his pachinko engineer to rearrange the pins so every customer won $100–$200. After a month, he'd lost ¥50 million ($350,000 on contemporary exchange rates), but Lions was the most popular gambling joint in town. "I was down to my last ¥50 million," Mitsunori recalled. "I was prepared to go bankrupt and make a run for it."[27]

In the third month, Mitsunori readjusted the pinball machines so he made ¥50 million, and then he went back to losing another ¥50 million in his fourth month. Mitsunori was prepared to lose everything to make a fortune. His son would be no different. Pachinko culture was embedded in his DNA.

As his gambling business turned cash positive, Mitsunori improved the net profit margin by employing members of his extended family as well as debtors from his loan-sharking business. By deducting the money owed from their salaries, he kept tight control of his profit and loss account. By the late 1970s, Mitsunori estimated the Lions business was making monthly revenue of $500,000. Over time, he expanded his Lions empire to more than a dozen parlors stretching from the port city of Nagasaki to the industrial city of Kitakyushu.

By the time Masa was in his early teens, Mitsunori was supporting up to twenty members of the extended Son family. Every weekend they would pitch up on the outskirts of Tosu in their flashy foreign cars to visit the grandparents still content to live in the Korean ghetto. This picture is far removed from later accounts of the Son family's poverty. On the contrary, the Son family's wealth provided the security for Masa's future career as an entrepreneur in Japan.

Masa's first career choice was to be a grammar school teacher. When his father told him his nationality barred him from entering the teaching profession in Japan, the precocious boy was devastated. He had assumed his life's choices would be determined by merit, not race. Suddenly the dilemma of dual identity—Japanese by name, Korean by birth—became all too real. Though he was barely twelve years old, Masa demanded that the Son family naturalize and obtain Japanese citizenship. Mitsunori refused, arguing it was a betrayal of the family's Korean roots.

"No way, Masa, no way," Mitsunori replied. "I cannot do that for you."

Ostensibly his father's opposition came down to family pride. Only "losers" abandoned their true ethnic identity, he yelled. But Mitsunori must have had concerns about the Japanese naturalization process, which invariably invited scrutiny from the tax authorities who might not look so favorably on his pachinko business. Masa fought for weeks with his father, but for once he ended up on the losing side. From then on, he confessed, he had occasional thoughts of suicide.

"I felt I was hiding something, and I always had a darkness within my heart. When I was with friends, I was carefree and had fun, but when I returned home and caught myself alone, it was like I was keeping something from them."[28]

The humiliation cut deeper when, aged fourteen, Masa was obliged to have his fingerprints taken for his "alien registration card." This was a common experience for all *zainichi*, but he felt he was being treated like a criminal or a character in a manga comic strip. What had he done wrong?[29]

Mitsunori didn't want Masa to follow him into business. At night, exhausted from working eighteen-hour days, he reached for the bottle. Then he'd start weeping. "Money is something I can make, or you can make, but that's not something you should chase. I support the family, and this is enough. To make money is sacrificing our [Yangban] pride," he told Masa. "When you grow up, you don't need money. We don't need money."

Mitsunori advised Masa to enter politics and become president of South Korea. But Masa had something else in mind. Not the shady world of pachinko, but something much bigger and bolder. He looked far and wide and alighted upon Den Fujita, by then a legendary figure in postwar Japan and the founder of McDonald's Japan, the offshoot of the US fast-food chain.

Fujita was a contrarian, brought up bilingual by his father, an engineer for a British company and an outspoken critic of the warmongers in Imperial Japan. After the collapse in 1945, Fujita, still a student, worked as an interpreter at General MacArthur's headquarters. The position gave him plenty of insider information and contacts, allowing him to set up a lucrative business as an importer of luxury Western goods. By the late 1960s, he was rich, famous, and ready for a new challenge.

Fujita found his metier during a trip to the US, where he had his first Big Mac. Using charm and guile, he persuaded the McDonald's management to let him set up a franchise in Japan. Crucially, he insisted that the restaurants had to be 100 percent Japanese. "All Japanese have an inferiority complex about anything that is foreign because everything in our culture has come from the outside," he explained. "Our writing comes from China, our Buddhism from Korea, and after the war everything new, from Coca-Cola to IBM, came from America."[30]

Fujita got his way and secured a 25 percent stake in the new venture. The first McDonald's restaurants were located in the center of town rather than the suburbs, and the English names changed to make them easier to pronounce: McDonald's became *Makudonarudo*, and Ronald McDonald would become *Donald McDonald*. Years later, Masa would adopt a similar model, selling himself to Americans as the gateway to Japan and adapting internet businesses like Yahoo! to the Japanese consumer market.

Fujita achieved cult status with his bestseller *The Jewish Way of Doing Business*.[31] The book, which Masa had read, urged the Japanese to adopt the approach of "the Jew," an American GI in Japan and moneylender par excellence. Fujita noted that "the Jew" was despised but had everyone under his thumb. It was an antisemitic trope of the worst kind, but one that Masa as an ethnic Korean in Japan took to heart.

Masa started cold-calling Fujita's office in Tokyo, begging his assistants for a meeting. Eventually, he decided a plane ticket to Tokyo was cheaper than more long-distance calls. This was a five-hundred-mile trip, his first to the capital. One day, he showed up at Fujita's office unannounced with a simple pitch:

"Tell Mr. Fujita: You don't have to look at me. You don't have to talk to me. You can keep on working, whatever you're doing. I just want to see his face. For three minutes."

Impressed that this young man would not take no for an answer, the guru agreed to a meeting. Masa asked what business he should go into. Fujita looked at him and said: "Computers! Don't look at the past, look at the future industries. The computer industry, that's the one you should focus on."

Fujita had a second piece of advice: learn English, the language of international commerce. There was only one place to go to pick up English fast. The land of McDonald's.

Masa was headed for America.

3

AMERICAN AWAKENING

In the summer of 1973, Masa set foot in the US for the first time, having signed up for a six-week language course at the University of California, Berkeley. He felt liberated the moment he stepped off the plane. Everything was so much bigger here: the supermarkets, the shopping carts, the parking lots, the eight-lane highways.[1] Compared to his "small Japan," America offered boundless opportunity.

That summer, Americans were riveted by the Watergate hearings in the US Senate broadcast live on network television, the beginning of the end of Richard Nixon's presidency. In California, "The People's Republic of Berkeley" was still recovering from violent protests against the Vietnam War. On Sproul Plaza, where a National Guard helicopter had once dropped tear gas on students and protesters, the Free Speech Movement was in full cry. Close by, drifters, eccentrics, and Hells Angels gathered on Telegraph Avenue, a central thoroughfare lined with bookshops, restaurants, and psychedelic record stores.

Berkeley was trapped in a sixties time warp, but the university ranked as one of the most prestigious in the US. Along with Stanford and other campuses in the University of California system, it was a magnet for cutting-edge scientific research and dynamic entrepreneurialism.[2] Of notable consequence was the invention of the integrated circuit containing multiple transistors. This development of the silicon chip marked a breakthrough with massive consequences for a wide range of civil and military applications. It opened the door to the personal computer, which would transform the workplace, connecting and empowering millions of people.

Masa had yet to experience the unique symbiosis between universities and entrepreneurs in California that was the foundation of the information revolution. That first day on campus something else caught his eye. Dozens of white, Black, and Asian students mixing freely, using their ethnic names, seemingly at ease with themselves and their "Americanness." Here was an equal and fair society in action, a concept at once bewildering and reassuring for Masa. Before boarding the outbound flight from Haneda Airport in Tokyo, he'd suffered a reminder of his second-class status. Despite his Japanese name, he was singled out as an ethnic Korean and told to join a separate queue for aliens.[3] In Japan, he reflected, everyone looked the same, but the invisible racism was ever present.

Half a century later, Masa recalled his emotions on setting foot in America: "I said to myself, 'What a small man I've been. I'm not gonna escape anymore, I'm gonna fight. I'm gonna prove that I'm an equally good man, not an inferior guy, okay?'"[4]

On his return home, Masa announced he intended to continue his future education in the US. His parents were stunned. Masa had switched schools regularly since Tosu; his mother, Tamako, at one point rented an apartment in nearby Fukuoka so he could enjoy a best-in-class education. Now he had barely begun his first year at the elite Kurume high school, the stepping stone to a top university in Tokyo. A family fracas erupted involving mother, elder brother, uncles, aunts, and father.

The argument wasn't about money but identity. Masa was adamant he should "come out" as an ethnic Korean. He wanted to adopt his real name "Son Jung-eui," simplified to J-U-N-G (which in American conveniently sounded like "John," one of the most common names in the English language). "I decided I'm gonna go straight, without hiding anymore," Masa remembered. "It was like Independence Day for me."[5]

But Masa's relatives accused him of being a spoiled teenager. "You cannot do that," his favorite uncle said. "What happens to all of us? We are all hiding. We are all using a Japanese family name." The only family member who kept calm was Grandma Lee. She'd never concealed her Korean identity. Indeed, she was proud of it. When Masa declared that he wanted to visit the ancestral homes in South Korea, her eyes lit up.

Grandma Lee had long been a substitute mother for Masa as both his parents were working. But the two became estranged as Masa approached his teens. Masa wanted to be Japanese, but Lee barely spoke the language.

She made regular visits to Korea, where she picked up cheap clothes and stuffed them into a knapsack for sale back in Tosu. The sight of her hawking garments was embarrassing; the sour smell of kimchi, which she ate in front of his school friends, betrayed her true origins. The entire Son family, it seemed, was living a lie. They were Korean, through and through.

The two-week trip that the young teenager took with his grandmother to South Korea turned out to be life-changing, a milestone in a long journey toward resolving the question of his identity. Back in the early 1970s, there was little hint of South Korea turning into one of Asia's tiger economies. Outside Seoul, the war's destruction was still evident. There was no electricity; poverty was ubiquitous. Masa visited Daegu, grandfather Son's birthplace, as well as Gangwon, where his grandmother grew up. People were friendly and generous, but his abiding memory was how small the apples were compared to Japan, each leaving a bitter taste in the mouth.

Masa ended his visit with several insights. He was an ethnic Korean who knew nothing about Korea: he could not speak the language, he could not read the characters, and he'd never set foot on Korean soil until then. He thought he was Korean, but he wasn't. Nor was he Japanese. And he certainly wasn't American. Then it dawned upon him that, although he was a nobody, one day he would be somebody. He was starting from zero, but he had one consolation: "At least I'm not a minus."[6]

On his return to Japan, his insistence on going to study in the US triggered another family row. Masa was violating a bedrock principle in Korean immigrant culture: he was abandoning his family, the economic entity that determined everything. Every member of a *zainichi* family was traditionally codependent, with the father or patriarch being the chief breadwinner. In the Son family, Mitsunori had made a small fortune since leaving high school early, but working eighteen to twenty hours a day had exacted a heavy toll. He was suffering cirrhosis of the liver caused by parasites from the river carp, koi, and loach he used to catch for his own father's meals, washed down with moonshine. One night, Mitsunori coughed up enough blood to fill a sink, forcing him to be hospitalized.

How can you leave your father? Tamako demanded. Look at the sacrifice made by your elder brother who's left school. His aunts and uncles piled on. Yet Masa's stricken father soon backed down when faced with his pampered son. "I thought that if I were to say no, he'd just be more willing to do anything—even bad things—to make enough money so that he could go to America on his own," said Mitsunori, "so I thought I had to say yes."

Mitsunori nevertheless set three conditions. Masa had to come back to Japan at least once a year, he would not marry an American girl, and he would not take a job to maintain himself, relying instead on regular financial support from home.

In September 1973, Masa officially transferred out of Kurume University Senior High School. He waited more than six months for a visa, which was contingent on winning a place at a local high school in California. After one of the Berkeley language-school teachers vouched for him, Masa secured a place at Serramonte high school in Daly City, just south of the city limits of San Francisco.

On the eve of his departure to the US, Masa's high school classmates sang the folk-rock group Broadside Four's song *"Wakamonotachi"* ("The Young Ones"), a big hit at the time.[7] The class president gave Masa a Japanese loincloth (*fundoshi*), the undergarment supplied to soldiers in the Imperial Army, which signified the passage to adulthood. To accept this traditional Japanese gift when about to go full Korean shows an extraordinary degree of self-control on Masa's part—or an infinite capacity to dissimulate. Maybe both.

At Fukuoka Airport, bidding farewell to Masa, Tamako broke down in tears. His mother fretted about how Americans might treat her sixteen-year-old son, imagining he was certain to face discrimination or worse.

"I am not going forever," Masa calmly replied. "I will be back."[8]

In February 1974, before enrolling at Serramonte, Masa entered an English-language school to improve his spoken and written English. The courses took place at Holy Names University, a private Roman Catholic school founded by Canadian nuns in 1868 and located in Oakland, across the Bay, east of San Francisco.

He gave no sign he could speak Japanese nor that he lived in Japan. Instead he introduced himself as "John" or "Son, from Korea." He was in fact *zainichi*, living undercover, speaking English only to his male Japanese counterparts, including a new friend and fellow student from Kyushu. One afternoon the two teenagers were sitting on a bench when Masa stretched his arms toward the sky.

"*Uwaa, kitsuka*" (Ugh, I'm tense), he let loose in a local Kyushu dialect. His friend, stunned, said, "I beg your pardon?" Realizing he had outed himself as an ethnic Korean living in Japan—a *zainichi*!—Masa said, "Sorry! I'm actually from Kyushu. . . . Tosu, even."

"Oh, come on!" replied his classmate, red with anger, asking why Masa would engage in such elaborate deception. Masa's reply was lame and made no effort to explain his troubled family history as ethnic Koreans in Japan. It was all too painful. But with the passage of time, the two boys became closer, united by their Kyushu roots and the sharing of a secret.[9]

Masa enjoyed horse riding, but most of the time he kept his nose in his books. One day, he looked up and saw a young Japanese girl with shoulder-length dark hair and a winning smile. It was love at first sight.

Masami Ono was eighteen, two years older than Masa, but he was a persistent suitor, like his father and grandfather. Soon Masami and Masa were eating ice cream together or walking around hand in hand on campus. Masami seemingly had no qualms about dating a *zainichi*. Masa was set on this Japanese girl, resolving to join her in the same entry year at college.

Within one week of enrolling as a second-year student at Serramonte high school, he asked for a meeting with the principal, a burly ex–college football player named Anthony Trujillo. "I want to go to university as quickly as possible," he said, requesting a transfer to the third year.[10]

Impressed by the young man's chutzpah, Trujillo went one better, promoting him to the fourth year. There he could sit the standardized tests for college entry: math, physics, chemistry, history, geography, and English. Masa agreed, knowing that if he failed one exam, he would have to retake them all in a year's time.

Masa breezed through the math paper, but physics, history, and English were a different matter. He had little idea what the questions meant, let alone what the answers might be, so he improvised. First, he secured a Japanese–English dictionary; then he requested an extension to compensate for his weakness in English. Trujillo checked with the exam board superintendent, who agreed to err on the side of generosity. And so was born "the Son exception," an exercise in official discretion unthinkable in his native Japan.[11]

"In Japan, it's either against the rule or not against the rule," Masa later explained. "There is no discussion of fair or unfair. They say a rule is a rule!"[12]

Masa sat his exams for three consecutive days, each lasting twelve hours as he had to use the dictionary. He finished the last paper on physics shortly before midnight. Set for the fastest high school graduation in Daly City history, he withdrew early to squeeze in another English-language school. Masa ended up as one of Serramonte High's most distinguished students; technically he never graduated.

Around this time, Masa sent a letter to each of his closest former high school classmates in Japan. He revealed he was Korean, that his real name was Son, and that henceforth he was going to live under this name. Those friends may have asked why they serenaded him with a Japanese military loincloth, but the general view was that he had done well to come clean. In Japanese terms, the affirmation of his true identity meant he had leveled with his closest friends. From that day on, their friendship could be real, not fake.

In January 1975, Masa joined Masami at Holy Names University in Oakland, where he had landed the year before at the language school. He was joined by students from Japan, Indonesia, and Mexico as well as the US. Masa stood out, not because of his quirky accent but because he made no secret that he had come to the US to make money.

His eyes initially alighted upon video games, the latest craze in Japan and the US. In the end, Masa and a student partner settled for a simpler idea: a working kitchen on campus open for two hours a day, serving stir-fried noodles, wonton soup, and other Oriental dishes. The business was popular and profitable, until the day it closed due to "creative accounting" issues. Masa blamed the snafus on his business partner.[13] Later in life, when confronted with billions of dollars of losses and negative press, Masa described himself as the captain of the ship whose duty was to save passengers and crew, going down with the ship if necessary. On this occasion, he was first in the lifeboat.

Sometime in the fall of 1976, Masa claims to have experienced an epiphany, a life-changing experience that irrevocably shaped his future business career.[14] He picked up a copy of *Popular Electronics* in his local Safeway supermarket and spotted an image of the new Intel 8080 microprocessor. He imagined he was watching a film scene or listening to a moving piece of music. "It was exactly that same feeling. I was tingling all over and warm tears were rolling down my face."

Masa's account—repeated endlessly in interviews and biographies— is almost identical to Bill Gates's story of being shown a copy of *Pop-

ular Electronics magazine in January 1975. Gates, then a second-year student at Harvard, was so blown away reading about the Altair 8800 microprocessor that he dropped out and cofounded his own company—Microsoft—in Albuquerque, New Mexico.

"I was genuinely moved," Gates recalled. "In my opinion, *Popular Electronics* completely changed the relationship between humans and computers."[15]

Whether Masa's story is true or a copycat experience is less important, perhaps, than the fact that the young Japanese student was following Den Fujita's advice and fast developing an interest in technology. It would have been strange if he hadn't. Holy Names in Oakland was only an hour's drive from the mecca of entrepreneurship and innovation, the area around San Jose in Santa Clara County known as Silicon Valley. In this unpromising terrain, where apple, peach, and pear orchards lined the highways, a period of historic technological transformation was gathering pace, driven by the tiny microchip that Masa (and Gates) had swooned over. A chance encounter with a visiting businessman, a legend in his native Japan, brought the nascent PC revolution in California alive in the young man's mind and changed his life's trajectory.

Tadashi Sasaki belongs among the elite founders of the Japanese consumer electronics industry, a giant who stands alongside Akio Morita, pioneer of the Sony Walkman, and Konosuke Matsushita, founder of Panasonic. His reputation as a world-class engineer was first established during the war. His expertise was radar technology, a skill he acquired after studying British equipment seized after the fall of Singapore in 1941. The following year, American B-25 bombers flying seven hundred miles from the carrier USS *Hornet* struck Kobe, Osaka, and Tokyo and other targets on the mainland. The damage inland was superficial, but the Americans had evaded rudimentary Japanese radar. The psychological impact on the Japanese public was devastating.

Sasaki was ordered to undertake a cloak-and-dagger mission to Germany to study superior German Würzburg radar technology. He made the hazardous trip to Germany via the Trans-Siberian Railway, a journey across seven time zones made possible only because Japan and the Soviet Union were not at war. By the time the bespectacled young Japanese engineer was ready to return, the land route via the eastern front was judged too dangerous, so he had to return home by sea.

Sasaki carried radar parts and a copy of a blueprint for the radar technology on a German U-boat to the Japanese-controlled South Pacific and finally to Tokyo. He later discovered that a second U-boat had been attacked and sunk off Singapore. Not one of the crew, including a colleague carrying a copy of the original German radar blueprint, survived.[16]

After the war, the man known as "Dr. Rocket" joined Sharp, the Japanese consumer electronics giant, where he developed the first electronic pocket calculators. Later he played a key role in the creation of the world's first microprocessor, the Intel 4004 chip, by introducing Intel's cofounder Robert Noyce to a Japanese business customer needing an advanced microchip. After that favor, Sasaki was given red-carpet treatment in Silicon Valley. He became a mentor to the next generation of American entrepreneurs driving the technology revolution, including a young man called Steve Jobs, who went on to found Apple Computer.

During one of his regular scouting visits to California, Sasaki bumped into an earnest young man who introduced himself as Masayoshi Son. Abandoning Japanese formality, Masa asked the older man: "What do you think is at the end of the universe? And where is the beginning of the universe anyway?"

The cosmic question seemed calculated to stir the older man's curiosity. Sasaki asked the young Japanese student more about his background. "He revealed to me that he was a *zainichi* Korean and that his grandparents made a living raising pigs in Tosu, Kyushu. But he also said: 'At the end of the day, I want to build a proper business. I do not want to go down the same path as my father and my relatives. That is why I came to America, to learn more.'"[17]

Sasaki later described Masa as an "alien," but something drew him to the young man, despite their age difference and disparate backgrounds. Like Tesla founder Elon Musk, another socially awkward character, Masa had an ability to persuade others that he was a genius, or at least a genius-in-waiting. His lack of social graces made him authentic and endearing, allowing him to win admiration and trust.[18]

The relationship between Masa and Sasaki continued for another forty years until Sasaki died, aged 103, in 2018 in Japan. Masa later earned the nickname "*jijii-goroshi*" or "Old-Man-Killer," referring to his knack for charming the elders of big business. Sasaki was the first of many to fall under his spell.

4

LOST IN TRANSLATION

Masayoshi Son's six years in California were marked by chance encounters with people who would shape his life for decades. He met his wife, Masami, as a precocious teenager at Holy Names University. He first encountered his longtime mentor Dr. Tadashi Sasaki on entering UC Berkeley in the summer of 1977. On campus, he met his first two business partners, one an older Taiwanese student by the name of Hong Lu, the other a middle-aged American nuclear physicist called Forrest Mozer.

Masa had secured a place at Berkeley as an economics major, having transferred from Holy Names, where he made the dean's list after barely two years of studies. The single thread connecting this period is a relentless focus on moneymaking ventures. Fellow students, professors, and computer specialists all found themselves recruited as foot soldiers in a common cause: how to make Masa his first fortune.

Masa claims he was a technology geek from day one at Berkeley, stopping off regularly at the twenty-four-hour student computer labs in Evans Hall on campus. There, using a basic Fortran programming language, he explored dozens of different business ideas, finally alighting on "talking word translator." Then he trawled through the professors/scholars phone book, searching for the best source for help with designing a prototype.

That was how Masa ended up one morning in January 1978 outside Professor Forrest Mozer's office at the Space Sciences Laboratory, a concrete complex at the top of a hill overlooking the main campus. He was wearing a suit and tie; a rare sight in Berkeley, where students usually wandered around in sandals, some sporting tattoos or pierced ears. Intrigued, the American professor asked his visitor to take a seat.

Mozer, forty-eight, was a leader in his chosen field of programming the flight of satellites; he was also an inventor who embodied the hybrid academic-entrepreneur model on university campuses in California. He had developed and patented a talking calculator for the blind, the first talking consumer electronic product to sell tens of thousands of units. Generous by nature, he kept an open door to students dropping by his lab to discuss their pet projects.

Masa, gathering himself, soon veered into the obsequious, praising Mozer as "a modern samurai." Then he got down to business. He'd heard about an exciting new product Mozer had developed: a miniaturized voice synthesizer that used a microchip the size of a thumbnail to store and reproduce spoken words.[1] Masa's idea was to put up kiosks at airports and rent pocket speech translators to arriving passengers.[2]

By the mid-1970s, the world was on the cusp of a new age of cheap travel and no-frills airlines. Masa's business application was aimed squarely—and presciently—at an emerging mass market. Mozer said he was too busy to pursue the idea, but the young student's enthusiasm and the simplicity of the speech-translator concept gradually won the older man over. He agreed to help Masa develop a prototype. Nothing was written down on paper. It was a gentleman's agreement between professor and student.

Mozer, a native of Nebraska in America's Midwest, was not prone to exaggeration. That evening he went home and told his wife: "That guy is going to own Japan one day."

By Masa's account, he took "seven or eight" computer science courses during his time at Berkeley and spent many hours programming in Evans Hall. Forty years on, however, Mozer is adamant that Masa had "zero knowledge" of coding and didn't show much aptitude for technology in general. "There were a lot of people talking about electronic translators at that time," he remembered. "The beauty of Son's idea was to sell it in kiosks. Son had no serious technical background. He was a businessman with a capital B."[3]

Whatever his proficiency or lack of it in computer science, Masa enjoyed a life of privilege on campus. He was receiving regular payments of $2,500 from his father in Kyushu—more than three times the starting salary for first-year graduates in Japan. He rented his own apartment and cruised around in a secondhand car, first a Volvo and later a Porsche. (He wrecked his first car, a Campomobile, on an inaugural trip to Los Angeles with Masami in the 7 a.m. rush hour from San Francisco.)[4] Despite these escapades, he promised his father, who had staged a remarkable recovery from his liver cirrhosis, that he would stick to his books. Once at Berkeley, his mind turned to moneymaking. Another chance encounter helped him on his way.

The Ice Creamery, on Lakeshore Avenue in Oakland, was a popular hangout for young people, only a twenty-minute drive from Berkeley. Over a busy weekend, when it stayed open until 1 a.m., the joint could serve up to three thousand customers. One day, a waitress burst into the back office to summon the night shift manager, a young student named Hong Lu, who was working part-time to help finance his civil engineering studies. A customer was refusing to pay for his milkshake unless it was to his taste. Lu, a burly man standing just over six feet tall, was baffled. Nobody refused to pay at the Ice Creamery. When he spotted the troublemaker and his girlfriend, he was taken aback: "They were both Asians," he recalled, "and Asians just don't behave like that."[5]

Lu was further stunned when he heard Masa and his girlfriend, Masami, speaking Japanese. He too spoke the language, having grown up in Japan through high school, before leaving for college in the US. Lu asked Masa in Japanese to explain himself. All he wanted was a creamy milkshake, came the reply. Lu agreed to supervise the order, and Masa himself pronounced the drink met all specifications. The seeds of a future partnership were laid.

America was the land of opportunity for young men like Lu (Taiwanese) and Masa (*zainichi* Korean). They were part of Japan's imperial legacy in East Asia when identities were fluid and borders were porous. You could be a Japanese-speaking Chinese in Taiwan, like Lu's father, or Korean Japanese in Japan, like the Son family. It was all the same: you were an outsider in your adopted homeland, with divided loyalties and a split identity.

"I did not suffer the same discrimination as Masa-san in Japan, but as an ethnic Chinese I had no prospects," Hong Lu recalled. "No big Japanese company was going to give me a job. America was my best hope."

Several months later, Lu spotted Masa on campus carrying his trademark yellow rucksack. Both realized for the first time they were fellow Berkeley students. After reintroducing themselves, they agreed to meet up again at the Ice Creamery. Several weeks later, Masa, accompanied by Masami, approached Lu during one of his shifts. He was starting his own business. How did Lu feel about joining? The older student declined. He was about to graduate. Why sign up with this baby-faced, wannabe entrepreneur?

Masa told him about the new electronic speech-translator project, which he predicted would make them both rich. Lu again refused. Masa then asked his father, Mitsunori, a regular visitor from Japan, to press his case. Masa even broached the subject at a gathering with Lu's girlfriend's parents[6]—a breach of social protocol. Finally Lu relented, only to discover that Masa had lied to him about his age.

"Masa was two years junior in classes. He thought I would never work for a younger person," Lu recalled. "My assumption was, if he was the same age, maybe he took longer because his English was weak."

Like Mozer, Lu found Masa's charm and persistence irresistible, even if his friend was flexible with the truth.

In his early days as a student-entrepreneur, Masa kept in touch with Dr. Sasaki, now head of research and development at Sharp. In early August 1978, Sasaki received a call from a pay phone in Japan. Masa said he was on a visit to sell an exciting new product: the prototype of a talking electronic translator.

Masa had written to fifty Japanese home appliance manufacturers; the response was crushing. Matsushita Electric Industrial (Panasonic) in Osaka turned him away at the entrance, and Sanyo Electric didn't even bother to listen to his sales pitch. Sharp was his last best chance, a Hail Mary pass.

On his visit to the Sharp research center in Nara, Masa was accompanied by his father, Mitsunori, who had traveled seven hours by train from the family home in Tosu. Mitsunori had invited himself along, figuring that the Japanese corporate establishment needed to see more than a twenty-year-old tyro pitching his new computer product. As the owner of several businesses in Kyushu, he carried weight. But when he met the world-famous Dr. Sasaki, the pachinko king followed Japanese etiquette, bowing formally and then pointing to his son: "Please listen to what he has to say."

Masa unwrapped the speech synthesizer that he had been carrying in a towel. It was a clunky prototype only, a black box the size of a small notebook with fat keys and a liquid crystal screen. Masa, showing no sign of nerves, demonstrated how the machine spoke English in response to clicked-on words and later translated them into Japanese on-screen.

Sasaki quickly grasped the translator's potential if combined with Sharp's range of user-friendly pocket calculators. He offered Masa ¥20 million ($200,000) on the spot, with more to come once Masa developed five language libraries, including French and German versions of the software. The package was ultimately worth $1 million (¥100 million),[7] if Masa delivered the additional language libraries.[8]

On his return to Berkeley, Masa instructed the Space Sciences Lab team to improve the prototype pocket translator as fast as possible. The idea of a diminutive Asian barely out of high school ordering around engineers and professors more than twice his age may appear far-fetched. But Masa had a presence. The humility on show during that first encounter in Professor Mozer's office had long since vanished; now the young man was strutting around the lab as if his shoes were three feet off the ground.[9]

Henry Heetderks, a tall, broad-shouldered Dutch American aerospace engineer, remembers Mozer lecturing Masa about what it took to be a successful businessman. "Masayoshi Son was listening politely, nodding at the appropriate times and saying very little. I got the strong impression that he felt he had little to learn from Mozer about 'doing business.'"[10]

Heetderks had accompanied Masa and Hong Lu on an earlier trip to Japan. That trip was memorable because he met his wife, a Japanese air hostess, on the outbound flight from San Francisco via Vancouver. He remembers Masa as superconfident when presenting to much older Japanese executives. In the one-man Masa show, he was the stage prop. "I was there just to reassure them he wasn't just blowing smoke."

On occasions, Heetderks detected a whiff of bullshit. Like when Masa handed him a batch of business cards marked "Vice President, M Speech Systems." The title applied to Mozer or someone else, the student explained, with a straight face.

Masa's single-minded focus was his greatest strength and his greatest weakness. On September 23, 1978, he set off for the Space Sciences Laboratory in his two-seater Porsche 914, mindful that this was going to be one of the most important days of his life. That Saturday was the final deadline for getting the German-language translation up and running. It was also the day of his wedding.

In the late afternoon, Chuck Carlson, a computer engineer recruited to work on the prototype, tapped on the keys and the liquid crystal display projected an English greeting. When he pressed the button marked "Translate," the screen switched from English to German. Carlson called over. "I've done it," he yelled. "It's working."[11]

Masa was elated. Then he looked at his watch and gulped. He'd been so preoccupied with the prototype that he'd lost all sense of time, even his 2 p.m. wedding appointment. Jumping into his Porsche, he roared down the hill, past the college football stadium, and toward the courthouse, some fifteen minutes away. By now it was 5 p.m. A tearful Masami was still waiting in her wedding dress. Masa bowed and scraped his way toward an apology. Then he asked an armed security guard to find the judge presiding over the ceremony. The judge was long gone, but Masa somehow wangled a date for his wedding one week later. The next Saturday Masa was back at the Space Sciences Laboratory. Once again, he was utterly focused on his work; once again, he turned up late for his wedding. Smiling politely, he asked the courthouse receptionist to ring the judge, who magnanimously agreed to let the couple tie the knot.

With the completion of the prototype, Masa devoted his time to business. He created a company called M Speech Systems Inc. (the M ostensibly standing as a tribute to Mozer's role in the project) and made another pitch to sign up Hong Lu as his right-hand man. "He said name a salary. I gave a number [$20,000 a year]. He accepted. I got the money, but the check bounced twice," Lu later recalled. "The first time, I thought he did not have the money. Second time, I thought he was totally out of money. So I confronted him: Do you have the money?"[12]

Masa assured his new partner he was solvent; he'd simply forgotten to pay. Lu gave him the benefit of the doubt, though he insisted on taking over responsibility for the company checkbook. The first company meeting took place in Masa's rented apartment on Whitmore Street in Oakland. Masa handed Lu a flowchart and instructed him to draw up a three-year strategic plan. When Lu protested he knew nothing about the new company, Masa said his job was "to do anything and everything."

Around this time, Masa, still only twenty-two, announced he wanted to be addressed in future as "Mr. Son." This struck Lu as odd because everyone in Berkeley, from professors down, addressed each other by first name. But Masa was no laid-back Californian; he was going to be the Big Boss. Lu took the hint but asked Masa why he used his Korean name in the US but switched to a Japanese name when in Japan. He had nothing to be ashamed of. He should stick to his Korean name.[13]

Lu also suggested his new partner take a break from his studies to negotiate directly with customers in Japan. Masa agreed, on one condition. He'd promised his father he would graduate from Berkeley. Would Lu be prepared to stand in for him in classes? No sane person could mistake the two young men, since Lu towered over his boss. Later, Mozer heard both men chuckling about Masa's stellar grades. To this day, Lu insists that he appeared in classes only and never took an exam on his partner's behalf.[14]

Later, Lu did Masa an even bigger favor, putting up his newly acquired home as collateral for a loan to M Speech Systems from the local branch of Sumitomo Bank. Masa repaid that debt handsomely when Lu later set up a business in China, but at the time it was a gutsy vote of confidence on the part of the older man.

After developing the prototype speech translator, the Masa-Mozer team faced three outstanding challenges. They had to complete coding the new language model, they had to find a microchip to power the device, and they had to find a commercial partner able to manufacture at scale.

In June 1979, Masa persuaded Mozer to accompany him on a weeklong trip to Japan. The professor spoke not a word of Japanese. Watching Masa perform in front of top Japanese executives, he assumed all was going well. Far from it. Canon, maker of the iconic camera range, wanted a smaller device. Casio was a straight no. Sony and Sanyo wouldn't commit. Only Sharp was ready to bite, though they wanted assurances about the supply of microchips.

To that end, Dr. Sasaki and Mozer had visited National Semiconductor earlier that year. Mozer had a long-term relationship with the US tech giant, but the American hosts treated the distinguished Japanese visitor shoddily. They claimed Sharp's real intention was not to do business but to steal the design of their chip, the "Digitalker"—a typically paranoid view of Japanese intentions held by most US tech firms at the time.

At the end of their Japan trip, Masa took Mozer to visit his family home in Kyushu. By California standards, it was a modest abode. In rural Japan, it was a small palace, with a kitchen, living room, and Ping-Pong table. Masa's parents were polite, hospitable, and visibly doted on their son. The summer humidity was stifling. Something else stuck in Mozer's mind. The Japanese name on the outside of the family home was Yasumoto, but the smell of kimchi being prepared in the kitchen was unmistakably Korean. The Son family were still living in disguise.

On his return to the US, Mozer discovered via his contacts at National Semiconductor that Masa had contracted with Japanese companies to buy National Semiconductor chips that did not exist, at prices which he'd invented. When NSC's Japan distributor heard about this unauthorized foray onto their home turf, there was an uproar. Masa was forced to fly back to Tokyo and unwind the deals. It was a personal humiliation, a lesson about the importance of written contracts that he vowed never to forget.

Forty years on, Masa insists it was all a big misunderstanding. Lost in translation, as it were. He had proposed using speech synthesizers in various products beyond dictionaries, such as elevators and alarm clocks. After suggesting he pitch to Japanese electronics manufacturers, Mozer introduced him to National Semiconductor. He assumed he had obtained permission to sell to the Japanese companies, acting as agent and distributor in Japan.

"There was no official contract [with NSC], but they said okay and were happy to see the customers. They didn't stop us. Generally I think they were okay with it," said Masa, claiming he had no idea that NSC had its own distribution company in Japan.[15]

Sitting in his Berkeley home in November 2021, Professor Mozer, ninety-two, a short, silver-haired man with a big smile, turned red with anger when recounting events. He denied introducing Masa to National Semiconductor and rejected any notion of a gentleman's agreement. "Impossible," he said. "I was the only person with contact at NSC. I dealt with them exclusively."

At the time, he conceded, Masa's get-up-and-go attitude was impressive. Having suffered his own frustrations with NSC, he joked that the lumbering American semiconductor giant should have made Masa their sales rep in Japan. But that was before he knew the full picture of what Masa was up to and the sums of money involved.

Mozer's diary entry for August 16, 1978, notes that Masa telephoned and said he had signed a contract with Sharp for ¥10 million ($75,000), according to dollar-yen exchange rates at the time. Masa cautioned there was no money to disburse because he needed to cover his expenses.[16] Mozer later discovered the total value of the Sharp contract was $1 million[17]—covering the software and the vocabulary for the pocket translator. Neither Mozer nor Heetderks received a dime.

By Masa's account, there was a gentleman's agreement between himself, Mozer, and the engineering team. Each was paid an agreed hourly rate, though in the early days of the project there was no money available. Masa says he did not disclose the size of the Sharp contract to the team because their compensation was based on an hourly rate. "In terms of time, Mozer did not work much, whereas Chuck [Carlson] put in a lot of hours."[18]

Mozer concedes he should have insisted on a written contract, but his overall verdict on Masa is damning: "I was his first business partner, and on his first business deal he lied and cheated me."[19]

After the Digitalker debacle, Masa was forced to reinvent himself once again. He held brainstorming sessions at his new home-cum-office on the second floor of a three-story building near Oakland airport. Heetderks and other engineers were invited to pitch ideas, rewarded at $1 apiece. After toying with launching a food and restaurant magazine, Masa settled on video games, the same idea he had explored earlier at Holy Names University.

Video game arcades were springing up everywhere, including gas stations, liquor stores, restaurants, and supermarkets looking for extra income. At the time, the smash hit was *Space Invaders*, developed and launched in 1978 by a Japanese game designer called Taito.[20]

Lu was initially unenthusiastic. He had an engineering degree from Berkeley; now he was being asked to set up a business little different from a pinball machine. Masa begged to differ, arguing that a consumer electronics hit in Japan would soon become a hit in the US. Buying unsold video game cabinets at a discount, he could ship them to a "fresh" American market. Instead of sending them by sea, he would choose more expensive air freight, cutting transportation time from three months to three days—a vital competitive edge when dealing with products with a limited shelf life.

When Masa offered Hong Lu a fifty-fifty split in profits and a future equity stake of 10 percent, rising to 20 percent in his new company called Unison World,[21] the Taiwanese engineer agreed. Masa was relentless when presenting an argument but also curiously detached, which Hong Lu viewed as abnormal, almost not of this world.

One day, Lu remembers, his newly hired office secretary arrived distraught and threatening to quit. As a favor, Masa had given her a lift in his Porsche. But he'd firmly instructed her not to tell anyone, having promised his wife, Masami, he would never be alone with another woman. Lu thought the episode was weird but also comic. The part-time assistant was old enough to be their mother.[22]

On campus, Masa excelled in economics, basic computer science, and physical education, but his grades in physics, math, and astronomy were middling to weak. He boasted of minimal sleep and working "stupidly hard." He was working hard—on business. Mozer watched him negotiating directly with shop owners over the installation of video game consoles in the Ice Creamery and a bustling Japanese jazz bar and restaurant called Yoshi's, both in Oakland. Masa visited the joints personally, collecting the "rent" in the form of twenty-five-cent coins inserted to play each game. His obsession with detail and his capacity with numbers were remarkable.

Within six months, Unison World had imported 350 cabinets and reportedly made a profit of $200,000. Then, as his graduation drew closer, Masa broke the news to Hong Lu: he was returning to Japan because he'd promised his mother he would come back. Masa later confessed that he felt some regret. "There was definitely a side of me that wanted to stay in America and carry on with my business, but I was determined to start all over in Japan and make a roaring success of it, making a company where my trading partner was the world."[23]

Hong Lu concluded at the time that Masa was hedging his bets. He'd committed to going home, but he'd also established a moneymaking business in the US that he was leaving to his Taiwanese partner to run in his absence. "He wanted to have it both ways," Lu recalled.[24]

A week before he was due to finish at Berkeley, Masa skipped the graduation ceremony and took a plane back to Tokyo. He'd return soon enough to America; for now, all his ambitions, dreams, and energies had turned to the country of his birth.

5

SOFTBANK 1.0

When Masa flew home to Japan in mid-March 1980, he brought with him the frontier spirit of Californian capitalism. He'd started two businesses, pitched a breakthrough consumer product, and had more than a rudimentary understanding of personal computers and microelectronics. He arrived, full of optimism, in a country that dared to dream it was destined to be the number-one economic power in the world.

That year, Japan became the world's leading car manufacturer and the top producer of raw steel. The Harvard professor Ezra Vogel's bestseller *Japan as Number One* captured the view that Japan would overwhelm the US economy. Apple's Steve Jobs, a passionate enthusiast for Japanese art and culture, was heard to exclaim: "Why can't we be more like Sony?"—a tribute to the Sony Walkman, the portable cassette player that became a worldwide consumer favorite.

In hindsight, Japan was nowhere near as strong as Jobs and others in the US feared. Vogel identified Japanese strengths: its obsessive attention to detail, consensus culture, and the just-in-time manufacturing model where space and time converged perfectly to eliminate error, injury, and waste. But along with many other Western commentators, Vogel underestimated social factors such as Japanese society's resistance to change. This was a fundamental flaw that stifled creativity, the essence of entrepreneurialism.

Despite all these barriers, visible and invisible, changes were underway in Japan which presented an opening to a techno enthusiast like Masa. After the second oil price shock in 1979, Japanese manufacturers were making great efforts to save energy and reduce the size of the cars, TVs, and high-quality consumer electronics that had powered the country's postwar success. Everything was becoming smaller and more affordable: pocket calculators, video games, and, crucially, personal computers. The arrival of NEC's PC-8001 in 1979 inaugurated the personal computer age in Japan.

Alongside miniaturization, Japan was moving rapidly toward digitization. Most consumer products such as washing machines came equipped with *micon*, the microcomputers or microcontrollers lodged in control panels that scheduled or automated machine tasks. All the talk was about the "*micon* age." Young people formed *micon* shops and *micon* clubs, eager to learn better how to program the machines themselves.[1]

The missing link in this emerging new economy was the more sophisticated software programs enabled by more powerful microprocessors. Software would turbocharge the personal computer revolution. Masa would play a lead role in this revolution, but at this stage he had no credit, no partner, and no product. Besides, he had a more pressing engagement: a second marriage ceremony with his bride Masami in Kyushu, where the Son family had first placed its roots and pulled themselves out of postwar poverty.

On March 30, more than 150 wedding guests crammed into the five-star Hotel New Otani Hakata in Fukuoka.[2] Barely three years old, the hotel was the largest in Kyushu and counted Japan's royal family among its first guests. The venue was a powerful social statement: the Son clan had arrived as a business force on the island.

This time, the bridegroom arrived punctually for his wedding. Masami wore a traditional Korean dress (*chima jeogori*) to please Masa's relatives. Months later, she was pregnant with their first child, a daughter. Masa had a new member of the family, but he had no intention of becoming the next pachinko kingpin in Kyushu.

Masami's Japanese parents would have liked their new son-in-law to take over the family medical practice in Tokyo. Masa suggested he might run a hospital, but he really wanted to go into business. A familiar dilemma arose: Should he continue using the Korean surname he had adopted in the US? Or, now that he was back home, should he revert to his Japanese alias, Yasumoto?

Masa was adamant he should choose his Korean name, Son. His family was fiercely opposed. Several members said he was crazy to ignore the reality of discrimination in Japan. He wouldn't get credit from the bank, he wouldn't be able to hire Japanese employees, and he was courting trouble with Masami's Japanese relatives. "I'm worried about you," said his favorite uncle, "you shouldn't make a mistake."[3]

Masa retorted that he wasn't a kid anymore. If he compromised, he'd be a loser, hiding and letting down all the other Koreans who suffered the same paranoia of living undercover with a false Japanese name. "I'm going to be a showcase," he said, adding with menace: "Don't try to stop me."[4]

In his first year, Masa grew a mustache, wore a double-breasted suit, and drove around town in a Mercedes. He flew to San Francisco, helping Hong Lu manage a newly acquired amusement arcade called Silver Ball Gardens. Lu remembers many long-distance phone calls kicking around moneymaking ideas, such as magazine publishing and video games.

Dr. Sasaki suggested he come to Sharp to head the research and development center in Nara prefecture, but Masa refused, saying he wanted to be his own CEO in Kyushu. After sitting around for weeks, he bought a run-down pachinko parlor. After a month, he sold it. Now he had no income and a new baby daughter. Parents and friends started to fret. "You spent years studying in the United States, and now you aren't doing anything," said his mother. "What are you going to do?"[5]

In March 1981, one year after his return, Masa launched his first business in Japan. Masa chose the name Unison World, the same as his California video game company. Unison was a marketing business set up to explore "potential opportunities in the Japanese market." Everything about it seemed rudimentary. The company was located on the first floor of a ramshackle two-story office building near a railway station in southern Fukuoka. The land and building were owned by his father. Masa was listed as a director in the articles of association, alongside his eldest brother, Masa'aki. Although the registered names were Yasumoto, Masa maintains he was using "Son" on his business card and all other documents.[6]

At this time, Masa was sifting as many as forty different business ideas, each individually rated and assembled in a stack of papers running thirty-two feet high. The key was to find a new growth market where he had a chance of being number one. Personal computers did not pass muster. Though the PC market was expanding and Japan was only one-tenth the size of the US, he knew he would struggle to attain dominance in hardware distribution. Software distribution for PCs, however, hit the bull's-eye. No single shop or catalog existed where the consumer could discover what was available. Here was a bottleneck in a market with potential for unlimited growth.

By the early 1980s, software had evolved from basic machine instructions to new products such as the spreadsheet program. Its successor Lotus 1-2-3 was followed by word processing such as WordStar and a few simple video games. All these software programs ran on external tape or floppy disks. Masa was familiar with these developments after his spell in California. His challenge as a distributor was how to find enough working capital to pay up front for inventory—a hefty commitment for an untested outsider.

Masa would go on to call his company "SoftBank"—the name encapsulating the notion of a store of value as well as the software product itself. The business was launched in the same tin-roofed office in Fukuoka, the stage for Masa's signature story, reproduced dozens of times in speeches, TV interviews, and newspaper profiles.[7] Masa recounts standing on a tangerine box and delivering a knock-'em-dead speech to his workforce, which at the time comprised one full-time employee and one part-timer:

"You guys have to listen to me because I am president of this company. In five years, profits have to be 10 billion yen, then in ten years 50 billion. Eventually I want to count profit in trillions of yen."[8]

Masa's stunt is similar to the inspiring performance by Soichiro Honda, founder of the eponymous automaker, in the early years of his company, right down to standing on a tangerine box.[9] Not everyone was persuaded. Days after his speech, Masa's two employees both handed in their notices.

His first business venture indeed enjoyed a less-than-auspicious start. Masa's mentor, Dr. Sasaki, refers to "a big failure" in Kyushu. "If you send a smoke signal in a place where no one can see it," he wrote, "the goddess of success won't smile at you."[10]

Masa took Sasaki's advice and moved to Tokyo. Unlike in Berkeley, where he would have been able to use the university as a resource, Masa had no such anchor in the capital city. He found a second-best solution in the form of Kazuo Noda, a college professor and management guru with strong academic ties in the US. Noda spoke English, was friends with fellow guru Peter Drucker, and took a special interest in personal computers, still considered something of a toy in Japan at the time.

Brash and confident, Noda was a cofounder of Japan Research Institute, a nonprofit company that specialized in consulting and training.

Masa, having attended its management seminars in Fukuoka, paid a visit to Noda's office in Akasaka in central Tokyo. After presenting a business card, he declared: "I am a *zainichi* Korean." Noda was impressed with Masa's candor and, learning that he had just graduated from Berkeley, asked why he hadn't started a business in Silicon Valley.

"Because I love Japan," Masa replied.

Japan Research Institute had just created a for-profit arm called Management Research Institute (MRI). MRI and Masa agreed to invest ¥10 million ($43,000) jointly in a new software distribution venture called SoftBank Japan. Masa moved his main business to the MRI offices in Tokyo, close to the Yasukuni Shrine. Together he and MRI held a press conference unveiling SoftBank Japan at the luxury Palace Hotel, but only a handful of reporters showed up.[11]

Within weeks Masa took a head-spinning gamble, hiring the largest booth at the annual consumer electronics trade show in Osaka, where Japan Inc. showcased its wares. Then he called all the software vendors he could find—perhaps a dozen at the time—and offered to pay all the costs of exhibiting in his booth. All accepted; all asked Masa the same question: How can you make any money?[12]

The software vendors missed the point. In a new industry, marketing, not profits, was what mattered. Intent on creating a name and a brand, Masa put up a giant sign: "Now the revolution has come for software distribution for PCs." Visitors packed into his booth. But nobody signed up for a dealership. Masa blew 80 percent of SoftBank's start-up capital and sold only $3,000 of software products. His partners at MRI were appalled and signaled they wanted to sell up.

"Many people were laughing at me," Masa recalled. "They said, that guy's really dumb. He's a nice guy, but dumb."[13]

The day after the Osaka show, Masa didn't look quite so stupid. An executive from Joshin Denki, one of Japan's top electronics retailers, contacted him. Denki had just opened a megastore called J&P Technoland in Osaka. Could Masa come and take a look? Masa was so short of cash that he begged off. His friends at Sharp were flabbergasted and ordered him to get to Osaka immediately.

That same afternoon, the Joshin Denki executive called back. The company president was coming to Tokyo the next day and wanted a meeting. When the Japanese retail boss turned up, Masa staged a sales master class. He admitted he had little money, little business experience, and no product. But he was superior in one category: business focus. Unlike Joshin Denki, which dealt in refrigerators, televisions, and VCRs, Masa promised to deal solely in PC software.

"Several months from now, who do you think will be more knowledgeable, more of a specialist in this business?" Masa asked. "If you want to be the number-one PC dealer in Japan, you have to find the number-one guy in software distribution. That's me. I have no evidence, but I strongly believe in myself."[14]

Masa, showing little regard for seniority or his own weak bargaining position, demanded that Joshin Denki sign an exclusive relationship. On this occasion, as often in the future, the older man found himself under Masa's spell. Perhaps he feared missing out on the PC revolution; perhaps it was the young man's unbridled optimism. From that day on, thanks to the Joshin Denki deal, Masa was able to negotiate from a position of strength with other Japanese department stores and retailers.

Masa's next target was Hudson Soft, the biggest software vendor in Japan. Once again, the twentysomething upstart demanded an exclusive relationship. When Hudson declined, Masa doubled down, promising to boost sales tenfold if they backed his plan. "I am a genius," he told Hiroshi Kudo, one of the founders.

Kudo agreed to Masa's proposal on condition he lodge a ¥30 million ($136,000)[15] deposit by the end of December—the equivalent of a month's sales. Masa protested that he didn't have that kind of money. Kudo, who must have known about the Son family's pachinko business, suggested he borrow the funds from his father. Masa demurred.

This was either brave or extraordinarily foolhardy. Masa needed to get his hands on $450,0000, fast. He had to cover the Hudson down payment and a stream of software orders from Japanese department stores. He was also on the hook for $130,000 to buy out MRI's stake in SoftBank Japan. Even though only three months had passed since the launch, MRI's lawyers had demanded three times the amount of the initial investment.[16] Reluctantly, Masa agreed to stump up the money. He wanted full control of his company—and to go all out for growth. But though he talked a good game, he was almost out of money.

On Christmas Eve 1981, Masa was standing at Kokura Station, the second-biggest railway hub in Kyushu. In his hand was a suitcase holding more than $200,000 in cash. In the end, he'd had to go cap in hand to his family, including his mother's sister. The family's pachinko business had come good for around half of the money he required, testimony to the phenomenal free cash flow provided by the gambling parlors. But Masa was still short of the funds needed to keep his cash-hungry company in business.

At this point Masa caught a break. He secured an appointment with Masayuki Gokitani, the suave manager at a branch of Dai-Ichi Kangyo Bank, a top-tier bank with strong ties to Korea. Masa had already tried to secure a loan from his father's local bank in Kyushu, but he'd been turned down, much to his fury. Dai-Ichi Kangyo was his last shot.

Decked out in a cool American jacket and slacks, Masa gave a brief account of his life. He described his new relationships with Joshin Denki and Hudson, whereupon he brazenly asked Gokitani for a loan of ¥100 million ($450,000). At face value, this was a crazy business proposition. SoftBank Japan was barely three months old, and Masa had no collateral or track record.

"I am not going to ask my family or my friends to cosign the loan. I will sign myself and I'll take full responsibility," Masa said. "But unless you give me the prime rate, I'm not going to take a loan from you."[17]

Many years later, Masa tried the same tactic with the crown prince of Saudi Arabia—with equal success. Back in 1982, Gokitani was so impressed by the young man that he passed the loan request up the management chain. He also called Dr. Sasaki, who not only vouched for Masa but offered his own house as collateral—an astonishing vote of confidence. The loan application went all the way to the president of Dai-Ichi Kangyo, who gave his assent.

Masa's powers of persuasion were formidable, but in this instance he owed everything to Dr. Sasaki. The bosses at Dai-Ichi Kangyo concluded that if Sasaki was putting his house on the line, Sharp Computer must be involved too.[18] The idea that Japan's legendary engineer would personally guarantee a "nobody" would have been beyond their comprehension.

During this tumultuous period, Masa still found time to visit Berkeley, where he called up Henry Heetderks, whom he'd sought to recruit as a Soft-

Bank employee. Heetderks invited Masa and Hong Lu to dinner at his home in Oakland, where his Japanese wife, an excellent cook, prepared dinner.

"Son seemed very happy and upbeat, but pretty soon I got the impression that the purpose of his visit was to taunt me for not agreeing to come and work for him in Japan," Heetderks recalled.[19]

One other thing stuck in the engineer's mind. Masa did not bother to keep his socks on or put on the slippers provided. Instead, he ran around the house barefoot. It might have been a case of absentmindedness (Masa at times was known to board planes with no shoes or socks),[20] but that night it looked more like a deliberate snub.

In early 1982, Masa scored a notable public relations coup. Thanks to an introduction via a software vendor in SoftBank's booth at the Osaka trade show, he got to know a top political reporter at *Asahi Shimbun* newspaper by the name of Masahide Kawashima.[21] Aged forty-nine, Kawashima was the lead political reporter covering the prime minister's office, a grizzled news veteran not easily impressed. But when Masa, still only twenty-four, presented him with a business card marked "CEO" and started talking about the new computer age, Kawashima took note. After several exchanges over lunch and visits to the SoftBank office, Kawashima suggested that his colleagues at *Asahi Weekly* write a profile of Japan's baby-faced entrepreneur.

The spread on February 26 featured photographs of two men—one of them Masa, the other Steve Jobs, the boss of Apple Computer. The headline was "The Vigor of the Cinderella Boys of the US and Japan who are creating a fortune with PCs."[22] This was publicity money could not buy.

Not everything went so smoothly. In May 1982, Masa launched a publishing division with two new monthly magazines, *Oh! PC* and *Oh! MZ*, to promote his software. He printed fifty thousand copies, which didn't sell. Nor did they attract serious advertising. Some 85 percent of the magazines were returned. Soon all the software business profits were wiped out. SoftBank staff were close to rebellion, but Masa insisted on staking everything on one last issue. He doubled the size of the magazine, changed the layout, doubled the print run to one hundred thousand copies, and kept the price the same. The result was a sellout. His willingness to stake all in the face of adversity marked the difference between success and failure and would be repeated time and again over his business career.

Around this time, in spring 1982, SoftBank's boss found himself feeling sluggish. Perhaps it was exhaustion due to his excessive work hours. He was working seven days a week, often demanding the same of his employees. Spending the night on an office sofa or in a sleeping bag was routine. One day, he went for one of the regular health checkups he had instituted at SoftBank. The results came in a week later. Further testing required.

On his next visit, the doctor told him the bad news: his constant exhaustion was due to poor liver function. More specifically, his hepatitis B antigens—the proteins released into the bloodstream to combat hepatitis B—were outside the normal range. When Masa visited Keio University Hospital, the diagnosis was even more serious: chronic hepatitis.

At the age of twenty-four, with a young daughter and a wife pregnant with a second child, he was told he had one or two years left to live. Maximum five.

PART 2

RISE AND FALL

6

MIRACLE CURE

In two whirlwind years, between 1981 and 1982, SoftBank grew from a three-person dog and pony show into Japan's leading software distribution company, employing seventy-five people with 75 percent of the market.[1] Masa had arrived with the right product at the right time.

The hepatitis B diagnosis threatened to kill Masa's optimism and strangle SoftBank in its infancy. There was no recognized cure for the disease eating away slowly at his liver. Masa had no successor in place, and his company was facing another cash crush, the Dai-Ichi Kangyo money having run out within months. When Masa went cap in hand, Japanese bankers said they couldn't make sense of software distribution, let alone personal computers. Masa was reduced to carrying around an issue of *BusinessWeek* containing a special feature on PCs. The response was still skeptical: "We can't possibly lend to a company whose business category is not even listed in the Yellow Pages," said one baffled banker.[2]

For all its promise as Japan's leading start-up, SoftBank was still in a precarious position. The idea that someone would discover that Masa was chronically ill was terrifying. "At night I would cry on my own in the hospital room—the treatment [to reduce inflammation of the liver] was really horrible. I kept on asking myself why I had to die at a time like this," he said. "If word got out about me being sick, the bank would pull funding, which is why I'd sneak out of hospital and turn up at meetings—we had to keep up the facade at all costs."[3]

Masa spent the next three and a half years in and out of the hospital. Hong Lu flew in from San Francisco and went with Masami to visit Masa, who was lying prostrate in bed. Lu was shocked at the state of his friend. But to his surprise, Masa appeared curiously unemotional and detached. Rather than dwelling on his illness, he was eager to talk about business, starting with the future of SoftBank.[4]

Masa said he was no longer strong enough to travel back and forth to the US. Lu should return to Japan and take charge of SoftBank. The tall Taiwanese American was normally as willin' as Mr. Barkis, the dutiful coachman in *David Copperfield*, but this time he shook his head. His wife spoke no Japanese, and his children were settled in the US. This was no time to move his family.

"Why not buy me out?" said Masa, referring to his 74 percent stake in Unison World, their jointly owned US business. Having shifted from video games to calendars and greeting cards, Unison was in a less volatile, more profitable line of business. But Masa's asking price was way beyond Lu's means.

On the way back home, Lu noticed Masami was weeping.

"Why are you crying?" he asked.

"The doctor told me, 'You may not be able to see your husband's thirtieth birthday,'" she replied.[5]

Masa wanted ¥142.5 million ($540,000)[6] for his stake in Unison World, a handsome return on his initial $28,000 investment but one likely to attract substantial capital gains tax. He therefore came up with an elaborate scheme to access enough cash to support SoftBank while minimizing his own tax liabilities. Sketched out in minute detail with flowcharts, boxes, and names, the plan offers a rare insight into the mind of a sick man living on the edge; it also highlights the shady connections and practices that a stricken Masa felt obliged to consider to ensure SoftBank survived.

In October 1982, Masa arranged to meet with Hong Lu in the New Otani in Tokyo, a favorite watering hole for politicians and Cabinet members located near the Japanese parliament. He placed on the table a piece of paper outlining a rough loan agreement between himself and a certain Manabu Matsushita, the Japanese alias for Park An-nam, a Korean academic and business adviser in Tokyo whom he had met several months earlier.

"I will help your children and your children's children," Masa told Park, who was sixteen years older but willing to come to the aid of a fellow *zainichi* who represented the next generation of Koreans in Japan.[7]

Under the complex scheme, Masa would sell his Unison World shares cheaply to Lu to avoid capital gains tax. Park, meanwhile, having loaned the desired sum (¥142.5 million) to Masa, would be repaid with interest for services relating to a fictional "Japan Project" in the US set up by Unison World. The Japan project was allocated a padded cost of ¥181 million ($680,000), to be repaid in monthly ¥3 million ($11,000) installments over a five-year period, allowing Park to pocket ¥39 million ($140,000) in fees.

SoftBank does not deny the existence of the scheme but maintains that Masa called off this circular financing scheme after consulting with lawyers and accountants. He paid the tax owed before the reporting period.[8] Ultimately, therefore, there was no tax avoidance. Beyond doubt is that Masa's start-up was burning cash. SoftBank was short of working capital, it had one major bank lender only (Dai-Ichi Kangyo), and its founder was mortally sick. These were desperate times.[9]

Masa's other pressing issue was how to find someone to run Soft-Bank while he was undergoing treatment in the hospital. Once again, he turned to Sasaki. By chance, his mentor was due to have dinner with a businessman with an impeccable pedigree: Yasuhiko Omori, a former Nomura Securities executive trained at Goldman Sachs in New York. Omori had completed more than one hundred initial public offerings of Japanese companies. He was Mr. IPO.[10]

Masa joined the two men at a dingy bar called Elmy in the basement of the New Otani, where he had previously struck his unorthodox financing deal with Park An-nam. Masa, twenty-eight years junior to Omori, wore his best suit and tie. Omori was impressed by the young man's enthusiasm but instinctively cautious about joining the start-up. Days later, Masa turned up in his office carrying a copy of SoftBank's accounts. What would he advise on the best way forward? Masa had the answer. Omori would succeed him as SoftBank CEO while he switched to the titular role of chairman.

In Japanese corporate culture, the plan turned best practice on its head. Masa was still a corporate minnow running an unquoted business employing fewer than one hundred people; Omori was vice president at Japan Patrol Security, a publicly listed home alarm and security business employing six thousand people with ¥3 billion in capital stock.[11] Omori turned down Masa several times, including during a visit to his hospital bed. But something about Masa appealed to the older man, a cold character with a vain streak symbolized by the precise parting in his dyed jet-black hair. In his earlier career as a banker, he'd played the financial markets. Now, aged fifty-three, he was cocooned inside Japan Inc., a few years off retirement. Joining a start-up reminded him of his time as Mr. IPO, when he'd helped young companies like Japan Patrol Security grow into giants. Why not take the risk? he said to himself.[12]

But then a last-minute hitch appeared. Omori's departure from high-profile Japan Patrol Security (now known as Secom) to join a software start-up was bound to attract headlines in the Japanese business press, potentially embarrassing for his employer.

Dr. Sasaki came up with a solution. Omori resigned from his post and registered with a headhunting agency, whereupon he was approached and hired by SoftBank. This avoided any suspicion that an upstart had "poached" a senior vice president of a prestigious Tokyo Stock Exchange–quoted company. Sasaki's scheme also protected his own employer, Sharp, which had an important commercial relationship with Secom. The Japanese media swallowed the story, with the exception of one reporter from *Asahi Shimbun*. He asked Masa whether he was too young to step down as SoftBank CEO.

"No, it's okay. In the US, [the] chairman is more important than [the] CEO," said Masa, with a straight face. In fact, the opposite was true, and he knew it.

On May 27, 1983, Japan's corporate elite celebrated the Son-Omori partnership at a glittering party hosted by the CEO of Nomura Securities, the Japanese investment powerhouse. On the eighth floor of the Tokyo Chamber of Commerce building, there was a breathtaking view of the Imperial Palace. Around one thousand top executives came, including those from Sanwa Bank, NEC, Fuji Xerox, IBM Japan, and Dr. Sasaki. Even the boss of the jilted employer Secom turned up, ensuring nobody lost face.[13]

Yet at this moment of triumph, a mortal threat to SoftBank appeared in the form of an alliance between Bill Gates and representatives from the fourteen largest computer and home appliance manufacturers in Japan. Gates said he wanted to end the balkanization of Japan's computer industry, where each model ran its own software and operating system specifications. Masa was taken aback. He too favored standardization, but Microsoft's move undercut his hard-earned position as intermediary-in-chief between software buyer and seller in Japan.

Bill Gates was the global face of the computer industry. But he was also a geek with a ruthless streak. In the late 1970s, he spotted the potential in the mass market in Japan. The key was to find the right partner. In Microsoft's case, that partner initially turned out not to be Masa but a university dropout by the name of Kazuhiko Nishi who had launched Japan's first computer magazine, *ASCII*, later adopted as the name of his own company. Soon afterward, Nishi cold-called Gates when Microsoft was a modest start-up in Albuquerque, New Mexico, with only eleven employees. "I will make you a success in Japan," he promised.

Thanks to the *ASCII* partnership, Microsoft's software sales in Japan soon grew to be as big as its turnover in the US. Gates visited Japan four or five times a year, always sleeping in the same hotel room as Nishi and taking calls through the night. Japanese business, Gates remembered, featured copycats and "quality fiends."[14] While there was a ton of engineering prowess and plenty of entrepreneurial spirit, companies were less concerned with maximizing profit because they always had an eye on lifetime employment. But they were always open to new ideas, and their commitment to quality left many American companies in the dust.

"There were long dinners, with some guy with a salary of $30–40,000 doing multimillion dollar deals with you. It was crazy. We would turn up late and the guy would say: 'I'm going to be fired because you are late,'" Gates remembered fondly, "but the Japanese were so demanding on quality. Zero defects. IBM Japan revolutionized our quality control. We were a bit sloppy, and our Japanese customers were so demanding."[15]

Gates was still tied with Nishi when he met Masa in the early 1980s, but the SoftBank boss stood apart from the pack. "A lot of us had drunk the Kool-Aid that the personal-computer industry was going to change the world, and he was one of those. But he saw down the end of the line, how the technology would be adapted," Gates remembered. "He believed these markets would grow, and he always wanted to do more. He was very flamboyant, energetic, and understood Western things, and there were very, very few people in Japan who could do that."[16]

On June 16, 1983, Bill Gates and Nishi unveiled their plans for standardization under a system called MSX. From now on, software written in Microsoft's BASIC programming language could run on computers produced by any hardware manufacturer that paid the relevant license fee and built the PCs to agreed specifications.

Five days later, Masa, still only twenty-five, rose from his hospital bed and held a press conference, flanked by his own manufacturing allies led by Sharp and Sord, which had the second- and fourth-largest market share in the Japanese PC market. Masa said SoftBank would offer its own rival standard with a much lower license fee. He attacked MSX, arguing that it was a monopoly rather than an open standard for software developers and hardware manufacturers.[17]

After a tense late-night meeting with Nishi, at one point involving Matsushita playing peacemaker, the two rivals called a truce. Microsoft agreed to lower the license fee for PC manufacturers and to make hardware specifications available to developers without charge. The Japanese press declared an end to the ten-day war between "the genius who creates" Kazuhiko Nishi and "the prodigy who sells" Masayoshi Son.[18] Evidently, mainstream media in Japan were not yet ready to accept his father's label of Masa as a genius.

The compromise was much-needed relief after a series of terrifying health setbacks, potentially devastating for his business career and his family. If Masa's chronic hepatitis B progressed and developed into cirrhosis of the liver, the next stage was cancer. Masa began to plan for the worst, racking his brain for ways to make money fast to provide for his young family. He reverted to the family comfort zone: pachinko.

From his hospital bed, Masa produced an encyclopedic analysis of the industry, including real estate plays, parking lots, tennis courts, swimming pools, and golf courses.[19] Each activity would be handled by a separate company in the Unison group. Unison Development would manage the construction of the stores and the surrounding land; Unison Sales would stock and sell the pachinko machines to company affiliates. His brother Masa'aki would handle Unison Sales, his father, Mitsunori, would manage Unison Development, and Masa would direct the overall group from the hospital.

While Masa was plotting his pachinko empire, Omori was remaking SoftBank in his own image. Stiff and aloof, invariably dressed in a dark suit, white shirt, and tie, he embodied the old way of doing business. There were endless meetings but few decisions. Omori disdained SoftBank's start-up culture and had little time for the younger employees. Hong Lu, who dined with Omori a couple of times in Tokyo, left unimpressed.

"He hired his own people and made a lot of dumb decisions and spent too much money," he remembered. "It was painful for Masa to watch. He had lost control."[20]

Toward the end of 1983, with no sign of remission in his hepatitis, Masa became desperate. Laid up in the hospital, he devoured articles written by liver specialists in scientific journals and scoured the newspapers for sources of encouragement. One day, Mitsunori arrived with some promising news. He'd spotted a newspaper article describing a groundbreaking treatment of hepatitis, pioneered by Dr. Hiromitsu Kumada, a physician at Toranomon Hospital in Tokyo.

The traditional treatment was to keep patients on a course of corticosteroid to treat inflammation and slow progression of the disease. Kumada proposed temporarily suspending the treatment and allowing the affected parts of the body to grow worse before the immune system fought back to get rid of the antigen. Kumada's counterintuitive approach lit a public controversy in Japan—which is how Masa's father read about it in the newspaper.[21]

The young patient listened intently as Dr. Kumada explained that, based on his antigen count, he was heading for full-blown cirrhosis of the liver within five years. Aside from his antigen count, however, the young patient appeared to be perfectly healthy.

"Will the treatment work?" Masa asked.

"I give it a 70 to 80 percent chance," Dr. Kumada replied.[22]

The therapy began on March 17, 1984. After a short course of corticosteroids, Masa went "cold turkey." For the next three months, he waited, prayed, and badgered Dr. Kumada on whether the treatment was working. The doctor, a portly figure with a kindly face, said the prognosis was good but it would take time.

Masa tried to contain his impatience, reading many books, including a favorite from school days: a historical novel on the life of Ryoma Sakamoto, the low-ranking samurai and reformer who was assassinated at age thirty-three on the eve of the Meiji Restoration in 1868. Masa was mesmerized by Ryoma's story. He too was a Japanese modernizer, inspired by America and destined for greatness. But his life was about to be snuffed out, depriving him of a legacy like Ryoma's. Many years later, he would hang a giant portrait of the samurai in his private office at SoftBank headquarters in Tokyo.

On May 5, 1984, almost four months after he had begun his treatment, Masa's antigen levels dropped to near-normal levels. He'd come back from the near dead. Still, it took two more years for Masa to recover fully. During his time in hospital, he started a new magazine publishing company, independent of SoftBank, called DataNet. But having borrowed money from the bank and thrown in his own savings, he watched as his company piled up losses. "I had to invent something new," he recalled. "I could be lucky or unlucky, but I had to give it a shot."[23]

His next move was into the telecoms market. At the time, the Japanese government was tentatively embracing Anglo-Saxon-style deregulation, forcing the incumbent giant NTT to compete against "new common carriers." Masa's new idea was a tiny computer device capable of automatically finding the best rate for users. It was called the NCC Box.

Having filed a patent, he had to find an engineer to build a prototype. Proving that life is stranger than fiction, he happened to meet an engineer in Toranomon Hospital who was also suffering from chronic hepatitis. The patient, Sakano, said the idea looked promising. When Masa asked how long it would take to make a prototype, the answer was two months.

"I don't have two months," said Masa. "Make it three weeks."

The two men met regularly in their pajamas in the hospital ward to check on progress. Near the three-week deadline, after fiddling with numerous wires, Sakano shouted: "Son-san. I got the prototype working." A year or so later, progressively weakened by disease, he died.

The NCC Box ultimately earned handsome royalties, allowing Masa to clear his personal debts from the DataNet failure. But by the autumn of 1985, SoftBank itself was racking up losses. Omori was making expensive hires, and costs were running out of control.[24] Then came an intervention from the US which inflicted lasting damage on the Japanese economy.

The Plaza Accord, signed on September 22, 1985, was a joint agreement signed at the Plaza Hotel in New York between the US, the UK, France, Germany, and Japan to engineer a depreciation of the dollar against the pound, franc, deutsche mark, and yen. Ostensibly, Plaza showcased international economic cooperation, avoiding a repeat of the mistakes of the 1930s, when countries unilaterally devalued their currencies, triggering a wave of protectionism that contributed to the Great Depression. In fact, Plaza was a deft piece of American arm-twisting by the US treasury secretary, James A. Baker III, to deal with American industrialists and politicians baying for protection against Japanese manufacturing exports, especially cars, machine tools, and semiconductors.

The Plaza intervention in the currency markets was dramatic. In the space of several months, it pushed the yen to appreciate against the US dollar from ¥250 to around ¥160, roughly a 56 percent increase. The impact on the export-oriented Japanese economy was hugely deflationary, but the Tokyo government was powerless to resist the Americans. Professor Dan Okimoto, the world-renowned Japan expert at Stanford University, labels the Plaza Accord "the single most devastating sanction against Japan."[25]

In a fateful decision, the government turned to stimulus to keep the economy going. The trouble was there were only a limited number of viable projects on which it could splurge fiscal spending, because infrastructure such as roads and railways was in excellent shape thanks to the postwar construction boom in Japan. Meanwhile, monetary stimulus triggered an asset price bubble with property prices spiraling out of control.

In the middle of this slow-burning crisis, Masa began plotting how to topple Omori. His chance came when the SoftBank board, prodded by Omori, decided to close the loss-making magazine publishing division. Masa considered magazines to be sacrosanct, declaring: "No parent would ever hate his own child."[26]

Masa's next move was to call for a maximum age limit of forty for all directors of the board. At fifty-six, Omori was way out of time. Preserving face, however, was paramount. SoftBank may have considered itself to be a US-style start-up, but it had unmistakable Japanese characteristics. An emergency board meeting agreed that Masa come back as CEO—a belated confirmation that his earlier protestations that power resided with the chairman were pure fiction. Instead, Omori was shunted upstairs to chairman.

In his new role, Omori was given a monthly $10,000 salary, a 30 percent stake in SoftBank, and a company car and driver. The charade went on for three years until Omori resigned on May 20, 1989, with his 30 percent stake bought out for several million dollars. Briefly retained as a "special adviser," he went on to run a semipublic internet service provider, KNet, and an antiaging business running clinics and selling vitamin supplements. Both went bankrupt.[27]

Aged eighty-one, Omori was tracked down by a Japanese reporter outside his modest Tokyo apartment. He was immaculately dressed in a navy suit with red tie, pocket square, and green cuff links. Asked about his time at SoftBank, he quoted General Douglas MacArthur, the supreme commander in postwar Japan later fired for insubordination by President Harry Truman: "Old soldiers don't die, they just fade away."[28]

Omori was not the first nor the last to be charmed, used, and discarded in Masa's drive to be number one. That day, the old Japanese corporate adventurer showed no bitterness toward his younger boss. If Masa had a weakness, he said, it was his failure to lay the groundwork, work behind the scenes, and bring people on board.

"I suppose that's the thing with geniuses, but it doesn't really fit the Japanese corporate custom," he said. "He operates at high speed, and there aren't many who can catch up with him. I just hope he takes care not to find himself looking behind him and finding no one there."[29]

7

MR. GATEWAY

In November 1986, Masa flew to Las Vegas to attend Comdex, the eighth annual trade fair for the computer industry, featuring 1,200 exhibitors and eighty thousand attendees. Eager to impress, he took a suite at Caesars Palace with a giant hot tub in the middle of the room. That hot tub—as well as the three Japanese men in suits waiting to greet him—was the first thing Bobby Kotick noticed when he turned up for his appointment.

A squat New Yorker with curly black hair and a deadpan humor, Kotick belonged to a new generation of American software developers-cum-entrepreneurs. In junior high school, he had his own business cards. In high school, he made money renting out Manhattan clubs on off nights. In 1983, Kotick dropped out of the University of Michigan on the advice of Steve Jobs, who was impressed by the young man's coding skills for the Apple II. Focus on building your own company, said Jobs, a fellow college dropout.[1]

Kotick went to see Masa on the advice of another powerful mentor, Bill Gates. What struck him was how Masa never stopped smiling—or talking. The Japanese spoke English with such self-confidence, it defied belief that he was Japanese. Kotick later discovered he was ethnic Korean, but that was beside the point. Masa's enthusiasm was infectious. When he talked about the infinite potential of the software business, it was hard not to pay attention.

"He always made it seem like you were missing something," Kotick remembers. "From that very first meeting I knew Masa was something special."[2]

Back in the early 1980s, Kotick produced a new graphical interface for computers with a mouse which could manipulate images and text, like the Apple II. This was a game changer for PC users. (Kotick had "borrowed" the idea after seeing a prototype of the Lisa, the earlier model developed by Jobs.) Intrigued by the mouse feature, Masa agreed on the spot to take Kotick's product. His willingness to take a punt on a stranger left an indelible impression on Kotick, even though the software ended up not working. In a homogeneous society, Masa stood out because he was comfortable with risk and disruption. He had no time for consensus-building; he wanted on-the-spot decision-making. His three favorite words were: "Let's do it."[3]

Kotick was keen to crack the Japanese market, knowing the prize was access to more than one hundred million consumers with a fair chunk of change in their pockets. Yet the barriers to entry were formidable, in many ways more cultural than commercial. Most Americans spoke no Japanese. They had little grasp of Japan's culture or history beyond the surprise attack on Pearl Harbor and a Pacific war which cost 111,000 American lives and more than a quarter of a million wounded. Most had little idea that Japan lost three million lives—and an entire empire.

An educated minority in the US nevertheless remained fascinated by Japan and its commercial potential. Many worked in technology. Bill Gates, who first visited Japan in the 1970s, still remembers how baffling the experience was and how useful Masa proved to be as a cultural interpreter and commercial middleman.

"Whenever you've been three or four days in Japan, and have had nothing but polite things to say to each other, invariably through an interpreter . . . then there's a guy who speaks perfect English. It's such a relief. Masa was easy to talk to. He was an insider but an outsider too."

Crucially, Masa had figured out the complex network of wholesalers in Japan, the proverbial "black box" where everything depended on special relationships impenetrable to Westerners. He effectively controlled the sales outlets, and he owned the PC magazines that advertised the latest computer hardware and software. Together these channels allowed him to maintain focus on volume, giving him overwhelming superiority in the domestic market.

But consumer software and PCs were like pop songs: they could be a smash hit one year, but the next everyone was looking for the sequel. SoftBank needed a new album. In this case, the title was "localization"—not exactly snappy but critical because it involved customizing US software so it could run on different Japanese PC models.

Most of the grunt work, such as translation from English into Japanese, was carried out by an army of workers operating inside Masa's grandly titled SoftBank Research Institute.[4] Breaking down language barriers and tackling diverging standards was vital to grow a market in constant flux. In the mid-1980s, Japanese corporations were switching to mass use of computers using "enterprise software," bringing together data from multiple sources to improve efficiency dramatically. Once again, US software developers were in the lead, headed by Lotus and, naturally, Microsoft.

Masa grasped that the software business had reached a turning point. All the innovation was happening in the US rather than Japan. He couldn't be in two places at once. He needed eyes and ears in the US, someone with enough technical expertise to understand the software revolution unfolding. In 1986, he discovered Ted Dolotta, a computer industry veteran.

Dolotta was born in Warsaw in 1934. His father was a lawyer, and his mother ran her own printing and translation business. When the Nazis invaded Poland in 1939, the Dolotta family fled, along with thousands of fellow Jews. Aged five, Dolotta spent the next few months on the run, at one point hiding in a nunnery disguised as a girl.[5] After the war, the family stayed in France for five years, where Ted went to high school. In 1951, the Dolottas immigrated to the US, where Ted attended graduate school at Princeton. After a spell teaching on the faculty, he transferred into the computer industry, working at the world-renowned center of scientific excellence Bell Laboratories, based in Murray Hill, New Jersey.

By the time Masa met him, Dolotta was fifty-two, living in Santa Monica, California, and working for Interactive Systems, one of a new breed of companies serving and developing the PC market. Interactive specialized in Unix, the operating system of choice for corporate customers developed by AT&T's Bell Labs in the 1960s. Unix was not only reliable, it was scalable and capable of handling a heavy workload inside a big company. By chance, when Masa was looking for someone with specialist Unix knowledge, Dolotta's name came up. Masa promptly called him on the phone. There was something important to discuss. Could Dolotta please come to Tokyo? Tomorrow?[6]

Dolotta stonewalled, though he did let slip he was about to fly to Australia. Masa, who seemed in perpetual motion and never bothered about time zones, proposed a stop-off in Tokyo. A week later, the two men met in the foyer of the five-star Palace Hotel opposite the Imperial Palace. The older man found himself seduced, though in truth he did not need too much persuading. His life had been packed with thrills, at times too many for comfort. Why not take a chance on the baby-faced Japanese entrepreneur with the big mouth?

Dolotta was a reassuring presence with a touch of the academic about him. He taught his younger Japanese boss any number of tricks, such as the art of negotiation and American table etiquette. Masa referred to him as "Dad," an evergreen source of wisdom and advice. Dolotta viewed Masa as a brilliant if unruly teenager: impulsive, prone to losing focus, and leaving others to deal with the ensuing chaos. When he stepped down, some ten years later, Dolotta offered a tip to his successor, a genial South African computer industry executive by the name of Ron Fisher:

"Get a shovel."[7]

When Fisher asked him to elaborate, Dolotta referred to the circus. "When the elephants leave town, there's a guy with a shovel to clear up the mess."

By the late 1980s, Masa had one goal in mind. SoftBank had to become a public company listed on the Tokyo Stock Exchange (TSE). This involved the nontrivial act of skipping the junior over-the-counter market (Jasdaq), just as he had jumped a year in high school in the US. But Japanese regulators were not programmed like Anthony Trujillo, the head of Serramonte High School. They stuck to the rules because the alternative was regarded as chaos.

Few Japanese start-ups like SoftBank had ever gone public, let alone followed the path to the Tokyo Stock Exchange trodden by industrial giants like Mitsui, Mitsubishi, Nomura, and Toyota. Nor was SoftBank ready in terms of its accounting or profits track record. Besides, the business was under threat from yet more disruptive change, this time in the enterprise software market where Bill Gates was determined to establish its new Windows system as the industry standard.

The wild card was Novell, based in Provo, Utah, a company populated by hard-selling Mormons and headed by Ray Noorda, a third-generation Dutch American and ex–GE engineer. Novell's technology allowed personal computers to talk to each other, sharing access to files and printers within a local area network (LAN). Novell's "netware" provided a fast alternative to the workhorse mainframe computer, but it also put the Utah company directly in Microsoft's line of fire.

Of the many rivalries in the PC industry, the one between Microsoft and Novell was one of the nastiest. Noorda resented Microsoft's dominance, while Gates called his older rival "the grumpy grandfather" of technology. Masa soon grasped the significance of netware. Alarmed that Novell might team up with a Japanese retailer, he called Ted Dolotta in Los Angeles and asked him to book a flight to Salt Lake City.

When Masa passed on his flight number from Tokyo, Dolotta realized it was an emergency. Masa kept his travels to the US secret (a habit he would maintain for the rest of his life. His calendar is known to only a tiny handful of SoftBank colleagues). When Dolotta asked why his boss was flying to Utah, Masa said he needed to see Ray Noorda.

"Okay. When are you meeting him?" Dolotta asked innocently.

"What are you talking about, Ted? You're the one who's going to make the appointment with him."

The meeting in Utah with Noorda, by then heading toward his seventies, was bumpy at the outset. But Masa secured an agreement to explore the idea of a joint venture in Japan. He then contacted NEC, Fujitsu, Toshiba, Canon, Sony, and his other business connections, asking for capital investment. Impressed by Masa's speed and ability to raise funds, Noorda signed up.

The joint venture with Novell in Japan transformed SoftBank's position. At a stroke, it moved from being a software distributor and magazine publisher to a networking business. "Once we had this new technology, customers treated us differently," said Ken Miyauchi, Masa's top telecoms executive, who for more than three decades has faithfully executed his boss's strategy, turning dreams into reality. "The Novell deal suddenly changed the way we were seen by foreign and Japanese companies."[8]

Despite teaming up with Novell, Masa continued to butter up Bill Gates, who had since had a spectacular falling-out with Nishi over his reluctance to focus on software rather than hardware. Masa jumped in, securing an interview with the Microsoft boss in his own magazine in Japan. Microsoft chose SoftBank as their distributor (though not on an exclusive basis). Sun Microsystems, Lotus, and IBM soon followed suit.

Another partner was Phoenix Technologies, based in Campbell, California, and run by the previously mentioned Ron Fisher. A devout Jew, Fisher had grown up in apartheid South Africa before earning a degree at Columbia University in New York. Blessed with abundant patience (SoftBank colleagues likened him to the biblical character Job), Fisher joined Ted Dolotta at Interactive Systems in 1986. When Dolotta was about to move to SoftBank, he suggested that Fisher and his wife, Lisa, meet "a crazy guy from Japan" for dinner. Masa stole the show with his tale of SoftBank's launch, when he stood on a tangerine box and told his two employees that SoftBank was going to take over the world. Fisher's wife was impressed.

"He's the single most energetic and impressive person I have met in my life," she told her husband.[9]

Masa wanted to become Phoenix Technologies' distributor in Japan. He also had his eye on Phoenix's stable of PC magazines, where Japanese publishing rights would give him an extra marketing edge in Japan. Fisher agreed, selling the magazines to Softbank for $30 million. The deal was useful but hardly decisive. In the world of computer magazine publishing, there was really only one name that mattered: Ziff Davis, based in New York.

Run by William Ziff, the family patriarch, the company had been a leader in consumer publishing since the 1920s. After the Second World War, Ziff launched car and photography magazines, later diversifying into computer publishing. Ziff's titles like *Popular Electronics*—the magazine that had made such an impact on Masa and Bill Gates at the start of their careers—produced reviews that could make or break the launch of new products.

After a ten-minute meeting with Masa at Ziff's headquarters on Fifth Avenue in New York, Ziff agreed to allow SoftBank to publish Japanese-language versions of *PC Week*. *Computer Weekly* soon followed. On the flight back to Tokyo, Masa confided to a Japanese colleague that he intended to buy the whole US publishing business one day. The idea sounded crazy. Ziff's price tag was around $1.5 billion, way beyond SoftBank's reach. But Masa sounded strangely confident that one day he would pull it off.

In April 1990, Masa gave the strongest signal to date of his company's global ambitions. SoftBank Japan became simply SoftBank. Five months later, Masa took a second momentous step, naturalizing himself as a Japanese citizen. For seven long years he'd been fighting the Japanese bureaucracy, which insisted the price of citizenship was changing his name from Son (Korean) to Yasumoto (his Japanese alias). This was too much for Masa.

"It was a matter of family pride," he explained. "If you give up your family name then you are losing everything. You are denying your ancestry and surrendering [the cause of] all the children born in the same circumstances. It's like a betrayal."[10]

Yet Masa recognized that he had Japanese employees and Japanese customers whom he could not afford to alienate. "I did not want to make any excuses [about being Korean]," he said. "I could not be a foreigner in my own country. I was born in Japan and am a citizen of Japan."

Searching for an answer, he turned to his wife, Masami. She had taken his family name, Son, when she first married in the US in 1978 and later Japan in 1980. But her own Japanese family name, Ono, was the name in the official family register in Tokyo. Masa asked his wife if she would mind altering her officially registered name from Ono to Son.

"What do you mean?" she admonished her husband. "I am already Son, and my two daughters are Son. Even the nameplate at the entrance of our house is Son."

Masami agreed to change her name in the official registry. For the last time, Masa went back to the bureaucrats and asked to become a naturalized Japanese citizen, with his Korean name intact. "I was the first guy," he said in an interview thirty-three years later, "I was truly the first guy that broke that rule."

It wasn't exactly true, but Masa believed it to be so.[11]

He simply had to be number one.

8

PAPER BILLIONAIRE

I n the summer of 1989, as communist regimes in central and eastern
Europe drew their last breath, Japan was trapped in an asset bubble
that had inflated real estate and stock prices to dizzying peaks. Tokyo
property values were 350 times higher than the same space in Manhattan. The Imperial Palace and its surrounding park were worth all the real
estate in California.

The boom in real estate and the stock market was widely seen as a mark
of Japan's economic prowess. Japan retained its manufacturing power and
quality, while its banks had access to seemingly unlimited funds. At the
peak, the ten largest banks in the world by market value were all Japanese;
Japan's banks were making 20 percent of all international loans. Japanese
investors gobbled up prized US assets, including Columbia Pictures in
Hollywood and Rockefeller Center in New York. The coming "Pacific century" seemed to be Japan's for the taking.[1]

The bubble economy was in fact driven by excessively lax monetary policy, the Japanese government's response to the strong yen inflicting daily
pain on its export-driven economy. The yen's surge followed the 1985 Plaza
Accord, which the Reagan administration had engineered to weaken the
dollar and boost US competitiveness. Ideally, Tokyo's response would have
been to open the Japanese economy to foreign competition, but instead the
authorities chose the path of easy money.

In this make-believe world, investors at home and abroad kidded themselves that the stock market had reached a permanently high plateau. In Tokyo, the Japanese business elite succumbed to hubris. Black limousines sat
double-parked in the swish Ginza district until the early hours, while white-

gloved chauffeurs waited for their drunken masters to stagger out of their favorite bars or whiskey joints. At the peak of the boom, "no panties cafés" and bars sprang up, with waitresses wearing short skirts with no underwear. These were the scandalous *no-pan shabu-shabu*, where the women earned tips from well-heeled customers, operating under a "no touch" policy.

In Osaka, a restaurant owner became an overnight sensation on account of her seemingly unerring ability to pick winners in the stock market and on the racecourse. In 1988, near the peak of the bubble, Japanese banks lent Nui Onoue ¥227 billion ($2.3 billion), making her the single biggest investor in the country. Only later, after she had helped bring down the Industrial Bank of Japan, then one of the largest banks in the world, was she discovered to be a fraudster.

Throughout this period of collective delusion, Masa tried to keep his feet grounded. His goal was to create a tech business of scale and take Soft-Bank public on the stock market. But as the distortions in Japan's economy grew, and his fame and wealth rose, schemers and con artists began to be attracted to him—a phenomenon that became more pronounced in later years. In this case, the point of vulnerability was his father Mitsunori.

By 1989, Mitsunori had sold his pachinko empire and staked his chips on the real estate and stock market. That same year, he borrowed $13 million from a single bank, using the family's large wooden home outside Tosu, known as "The Palace," as collateral.[2] He splurged the money on numerous investments, the last in a remote town 125 miles northeast of Fukuoka City called Tamagawa. Masa was eventually forced to step in to rescue his family.

The story begins with a wheeler-dealer named Takeo Furukawa, a senior executive at Fukuoka Bank.[3] He had approved the loan for Mitsunori's original pachinko business, later becoming his personal account manager. Three decades on, local bigwigs asked the two partners if they could help put run-down Tamagawa back on the map. Furukawa, limited in imagination if not financial ambition, suggested a golf resort and hotel. Later, he added a "computer academy" to lend a respectable veneer. Furukawa and Mitsunori then approached Masa, who agreed to lend his name to the venture.

In 1990, Masa landed by helicopter in Tamagawa.[4] Still only thirty-two, he was greeted by local dignitaries, including the town mayor, who rolled out the red carpet. Like most things in the bubble economy, appearances deceived. Furukawa had partnered with a newly incorporated company called Santas, whose chairman was none other than Mitsunori Yasumoto, still operating under his Japanese alias. Fellow board members included Masa's eldest brother, Masa'aki, and his younger brother, Masanori. They were joined by the cronies of a notorious figure in the bubble era, a corrupt ex–finance ministry bureaucrat named Hiromi Tokuda.[5]

In Tamagawa, Masa came face-to-face with the old-school world of Japanese business, featuring cronyism, debt, and manipulation. In his own mind, this dubious setup embodied everything that he wanted to transcend with his California-tinged technocentric optimism. Yet despite his protestations, Masa was hardly immune to the temptations of debt and speculation. He had more in common with his father than he cared to admit.

The Son family's Tamagawa venture took shape at the top of the market, forcing Mitsunori to pay a premium for a thirty-two-acre golf development. Like every other investor, he believed land prices would continue to rise. After all, real estate in Japan had not dropped in value since the end of the Second World War, except briefly in 1975. The stock market told a different story. The Nikkei peaked at ¥38,915 on the last day of trading in December 1989. From then on, successive central bank interest-rate rises punctured the euphoria. The real estate market slumped, accentuated by the central government imposing new restrictions on property lending. The Japanese economy thereafter entered a prolonged period of deflation and low growth, dubbed "the lost decade."

Much of the weakness came down to the fragile state of the Japanese banks. Having lent reckless sums on real estate, many were sitting on a mountain of toxic assets. Making matters worse, the debt was carefully hidden, covered up by dubious accounting techniques and other opaque arrangements. Banks parked their bad loans in their own off-balance-sheet companies, a technique known as *tobashi* ("skipping").[6] Regulators turned a blind eye, afraid to speak the truth for fear that the entire Japanese financial system might collapse.

For three years, Japan's powerful Ministry of Finance sat on its hands, fearful that a bank bailout would provoke public outrage. Their inertia ended up creating "zombie banks" incapable of lending and unable to restore the economy to growth. Meanwhile, the price of inaction rose. The lesson was not lost on Tim Geithner, a young US diplomat stationed in Tokyo at the time. Twenty years later, during the 2008 global financial crisis, Geithner, by then president of the New York Fed, backed plans for a speedy recapitalization of the banks to avoid a repeat of the Japanese disaster.

Compared to the devastation in Japan's banking sector, the software and personal computer industry largely escaped intact. Several firms went bankrupt, but their failure owed more to a saturated PC market and subsequent pressure on margins. Masa's challenge was how to deliver reliable profits ahead of SoftBank's planned IPO. To propel growth, he needed more revenue streams, and that meant expanding his network in the US.

One key relationship was Businessland, America's largest computer retailer, which had one hundred stores nationwide and more than $1 billion in sales. Having coaxed Businessland to come to Japan and form a joint venture, Masa persuaded Canon, Fujitsu, Sony, and Toshiba to jump on board. The consortium plan failed to take off, but Masa agreed to compensate all parties for their financial investment. His response was instructive. Always fiercely protective of his own financial interest, he was still ready to sacrifice short-term gains to buy long-term goodwill. His reputation as a reliable middleman spread.

Masa's next move was more audacious. He wanted to address head-on Japan's failure to develop a US-style start-up culture. In a society where failure spelled humiliation, would-be entrepreneurs like Masa were deemed either crazy or criminal. But Masa believed he could effect change by importing US management techniques and the venture capital mindset, thereby placing himself in the vanguard of an economic revolution.

His new business—SoftBank Venture Capital—set out to invest in start-ups specializing in software and PC accessories. Masa also partnered with the Japan Associated Finance Company (JAFCO), the largest venture capital fund in Japan, set up by Yasuhiko Omori, the Nomura banker drafted in to run SoftBank. Though Masa's venture fund was relatively small at $300,000 (¥30 million), and JAFCO's stake was only 5 percent, this baby step in venture capital was propitious.[7] Three decades later, Masa set up the SoftBank Vision Fund in a bid to disrupt the global VC industry.

Masa's call to create and fund a new class of start-ups attracted media attention in Japan. Even *The New York Times* took notice. "It's so difficult to start [in Japan] unless you are the son of a rich family," Masa complained to its business correspondent in Tokyo.

This was disingenuous. The Son family had been relatively rich for years, only to watch the patriarch Mitsunori squander millions on real estate. In one instance, he'd used rented land next to one of his pachinko parlors as collateral. (When Masa found out, he was furious. He agreed to make the third party whole but banned his father from similar wild bets.)[8]

On another occasion, Mitsunori secured $100 million (¥10 billion) in financing from a North Korea–affiliated bank and stuffed it into Tokyu Corporation shares, the parent of Tokyu Railway.[9] The stock turned into one of the bubble's biggest scandals, involving affiliates of Nomura Securities and Nikko Securities lending $360 million to yakuza to buy up shares. This was standard fare as Japanese financial institutions flush with cash tried to find investment outlets, but when the story came to light, Tokyu Corporation stock crashed. Along with other investors, Mitsunori lost a fortune.

In the market euphoria, the excesses of high rollers like Mitsunori remained hidden. But as the legendary US investor Warren Buffett remarked: when the tide goes out, you soon discover who is wearing bathing trunks. Mitsunori was fully exposed. His financial difficulties posed a material risk to SoftBank's plans to go public, assuming Masa as the major shareholder was prepared to bail him out. As lead underwriter, Nomura Securities was starting to ask awkward questions. In the autumn of 1992, Masa quietly shelved his plans to go public on the Tokyo Stock Exchange. Instead, he opted for a quotation on the over-the-counter market later known as Jasdaq, with a tentative date set for 1994. Something serious had gone wrong.

At their peak, Mitsunori's businesses were said to be generating around $100 million (¥10 billion) in annual revenue. The pachinko king owned thirteen gambling parlors in Kyushu, each producing a high turnover, if not handsome profit. In addition, Mitsunori owned several Korean barbecue shops, and a consumer-lending business and was managing multiple golf courses. The Tokyu Corporation Railway share collapse cost him $44 million alone, according to a local who spoke to him.[10] But beyond these losses, the slump in real estate prices reduced the value of the collateral he'd put up to support his personal borrowing. Now he and his own company were on the hook for tens of millions of dollars.

The reckoning with the banks came in 1993. The Son family properties were seized, one by one, and put up for sale. These included the oldest brother Masa'aki's house and later the family home in Tosu. Mitsunori was out of money, forced to turn to his favorite son for a bailout. It was a humiliating loss of face for the patriarch, etched in the family consciousness during a final showdown with Mitsunori's partner, the dodgy banker Furukawa.

The meeting took place inside "The Palace," then facing foreclosure. For Masa, it was a poignant moment. He admired his father for lifting the entire family out of poverty after the war. Mitsunori had left school at fourteen and worked all hours to make his fortune in pig breeding, loan-sharking, and pachinko, all so that the next generation could have an education and a better life.

Masa would be forever in debt to his parents' sacrifice. But he too had made his first fortune—and more. He'd naturalized as a Japanese citizen and come out as an ethnic Korean. Now he had the best of both worlds. The family showdown in Tosu was a reminder of how his own kin were still living in the shadows, still using a Japanese alias. Masa wanted nothing to do with that marginal existence, but he could not entirely escape it.

"The review [by Nomura] is extremely severe," he explained to Furukawa, who was pleading to revive the Tamagawa project, "I cannot support my father now. If you want to go ahead with the project, you can do it yourself."[11]

After SoftBank successfully pulled off its IPO, he confronted his father: "I will take care of your personal debts, but I won't lend you any money. As for your business debts, you deal with that."

Later Masa would be even more direct: "You're past it. Your business instincts don't cut it anymore."[12] When the family home was eventually put up for forced sale in October 1996, it was repurchased by Masa through a private company of his called MAC.[13]

Sitting in that same wooden house, thirty years later, Mitsunori, eighty-seven, claimed he had enough money at the time to buy back "The Palace" and send the bailiffs packing. Presumably safe in the knowledge that his favorite son was a billionaire, he made light of the dressing-down he received and made no apologies for living life on the edge. "Having money is fun," he said, "but making it is even more fun."[14]

In the early 1990s, the software business was once again changing fast. Developers were increasingly tempted to cut out the Masa-style middleman and deal directly with the retailer. SoftBank no longer enjoyed pricing power. A new approach was needed.

When SoftBank started out, software was dispatched in packaged boxes. By the early 1990s, the new thing was the CD-ROM, a prepressed compact disc that contained multiple demo versions of software. Masa distributed the CD-ROMs through SoftBank's computer magazines. If customers wanted the full version, they contacted call centers that could remotely enable the software. A host of new service companies sprang up advising customers how best to amend or upgrade existing software. This was the business known as telemarketing.

The US was more advanced in telemarketing than Japan. Masa was alert to the opportunity, though the painful Son family rescue and the stagnant domestic economy acted as further incentive to look overseas for growth. In the summer of 1993, he paid $7 million for a 49 percent stake in a Monterey, California–based telemarketing company, Alexander & Load. Sealing the deal over breakfast at the Marriott Hotel in Santa Clara, Masa pulled out his napkin, wrote down a list of numbers, and asked everyone around the table to initial the deal. When he asked the Alexander & Load boss if he was happy, the latter answered in the affirmative.

"Well, that's good," said Masa, "because I've just wired one million dollars into your account [as a down payment]."[15]

Masa pulled the same napkin trick when he hired Ron Fisher two years later to head his US operation. Masa wanted to show he was a man of his word. Fisher warned him that he couldn't trust people simply by looking them in the eye; one day, he would be dealing with rougher types.

"That's their problem, it's not my problem," Masa replied. "I'm not going to change how I work."[16]

Masa loved adopting the dramatic gesture to disarm would-be allies and potential enemies. But his charm came with a certain credulousness. Having watched his family escape poverty, he was by nature an optimist who wanted to believe the best of everyone. This would cause him no end of trouble in the future, when the sums were greater and the size of ego somewhat larger.

SoftBank's next move in the US was on the East Coast. Upgrade Corporation, founded by Jordan Levy and Ron Schreiber, was a fast-growing telemarketing business based in Buffalo, a few miles from the Canadian border. Levy and Schreiber were rugged types used to winter temperatures dropping as low as minus-twenty degrees Celsius. When Masa turned up in mid-1994 with a takeover bid, his reception was suitably frosty.

"I said, 'Who the hell are you? You're not going to buy my company!'" Levy recalled.[17]

Masa would not go away. For nine months, he pestered and flattered the thirtysomething founders with the same pitch: "I really admire your company, but SoftBank is the number-one software distributor in Japan. *You would be crazy to turn me down.*"

When Levy and Schreiber finally agreed to sell, they discovered Masa intended to buy only 60 percent of the company. The deal was unusual because Masa didn't push for 100 percent control, and he forfeited his right to voting stock. When Levy asked why the young Japanese tycoon wasn't worried about exercising his voting rights as majority shareholder, Masa's matter-of-fact reply took the New Yorkers aback:

"Why would I want to vote? You are the ones running the company!"

Masa invited Levy and Schreiber to Tokyo, where he produced a stack of charts and decks that laid out a three-hundred-year vision for SoftBank. Along with the napkin trick, Masa was beginning to develop a business persona—a mix of beguiling innocence, strut, and swagger that, for a while, would make him the world's most consequential tech investor. Levy and Schreiber were left befuddled by this high-minded commitment to corporate longevity. Three hundred years? Hell, they were happy to make it past next week.

When Masa discovered Levy was a fellow golfer, he invited him to play at the Privileged Club, one hour's drive from Tokyo. It was the only club in the area that Koreans were allowed to join, and the membership fee was an astronomical $2 million. As the two men rode out in separate cars, Levy noticed something unusual: "Our driver was never allowed to go as fast as his."

Masa was sensitive to his status as the Big Boss, the title he would later adopt and use for his personal email; he was always capable of the unexpected, magnanimous gesture. When SoftBank later merged Upgrade with Alexander & Load, Levy said they would honor the original terms of the SoftBank deal, even though the respective valuations had changed. "We had been brought up as good Jewish boys," he explained, "we had shaken hands on the deal."[18]

Masa's response left him speechless. He gave Levy and Schreiber $1 million of his own SoftBank stock and an extra $750,000 in cash to cover their tax liabilities and expenses. "With that one million dollars, he bought us for life," says Levy, ruefully noting he could have been a millionaire many times over had Masa followed through on all his other promises in their business partnership.

By temperament, Masa was a combination of cherry-picker and fast follower. He had no interest in developing proprietary software like Microsoft nor investing in the next generation of personal computers like Apple. He was drawn to adjacent businesses like computer magazines or trade shows such as the annual Comdex trade fair in Las Vegas. This was all part of the software services business, what Masa called "infrastructure." His joint venture with Novell was the first step to establish himself in this new tech ecosystem. His next step was to approach the biggest infrastructure player of all: Cisco Systems, based in Silicon Valley.

Cisco had cracked the core problem of the coming age of the internet: how to get computers to talk to each other using networking hardware and software. Masa was introduced to Cisco by Gary Rieschel, a former Intel executive he had met on yet another golf course in Japan. That same day, Masa invited Rieschel to his home to meet his young family. Aware that Cisco was desperate to break into the Japanese market, Masa insisted he was the natural partner. He spoke English and Japanese, he had the contacts, and he knew how the system worked.

Cisco was struggling to penetrate the walled garden that protected Japanese companies from foreign competition. Electronics and telecoms giants like NTT operated their own protocols, the set of rules that determine how data is transmitted between different devices in the same network. Under threat from foreign interlopers like Cisco, the Japanese incumbents reacted with arrogance and complacency. Their motto was simple: we are leaders, not followers.

In the summer of 1994, Cisco gave up and chose SoftBank as its Japanese partner. Within months, Masa achieved the seemingly impossible. He persuaded Hitachi, Fujitsu, Toshiba, and other corporate giants to join SoftBank in a consortium led by Cisco to unify the fragmented network-router market. The new joint venture—Cisco Japan—was a case study in Masa's creativity. Traditionally, the Japanese model was "copy and compete," but Masa persuaded the big companies to sink their differences in the interest of importing cutting-edge technology to Japan. "So I said: 'Hey, don't try to copy and compete, you can be an equity investor together. We will create a joint venture.'"[19]

Masa persuaded his Japanese elders—the leading lights of corporate Japan—to invest $37 million for a combined 26 percent stake.[20] Cisco retained the balance of equity, while SoftBank made only a token down payment for its own minority stake. The result was a US-Japanese company that yielded hundreds of millions of dollars of value in the years to come. Masa's reward was a seat on the Cisco board, a "sentry position" in Silicon Valley.

Shortly after pulling off the Cisco Japan coup, Masa achieved his lifelong dream of turning SoftBank into a public company. True, he had to settle for a quote on Jasdaq rather than the prestigious Tokyo Stock Exchange. True, Japan Inc. and certain parts of the government still viewed SoftBank as a Korean rather than a Japanese company. True, Masa was still viewed as something exotic, to be treated with a degree of suspicion.

But the initial reaction among investors to Masa and SoftBank was unequivocally positive. On July 22, 1994, SoftBank shares rose 70 percent above the asking price, making Masa one of the richest men in Japan.[21] Aged only thirty-six, he was worth $2 billion. A four-page profile later appeared in *Gekkan Keieijuku* magazine, headlined "The Ambitions of Son Masayoshi, the Bill Gates of Japan."

Underneath the editors published a photo of Masa with a caption that, by Japanese standards, came close to breathless: "Son Masayoshi, CEO of SoftBank, who is also known as 'The Boy Genius.'"[22]

9

WHAT DOES IT TAKE TO WIN?

Just before SoftBank's stock market debut, Masa received an urgent fax from Ted Dolotta that the privately owned Ziff Communications publishing empire was up for sale. He'd long coveted Ziff, the largest computer magazine publisher in the US, with $1 billion in revenue and a growing online business. Full ownership would give him a swanky office on Manhattan's Fifth Avenue and an entrée into the top tech companies in the US.

"What does it take to win?" Masa asked his investment banking adviser, Morgan Stanley's Jeff Sine.[1]

"You have to bid," replied Sine, a laconic lawyer from New Jersey, who went on to be Masa's personal banker. A week later, Masa and his chief financial officer, Kobayashi Toshishida, showed up at One Rockefeller Plaza, headquarters of Lazard Frères bank in New York.

Neither Steve Rattner nor Peter Ezersky, the two lead advisers to Ziff, had heard of Masayoshi Son. Neither would forget that first encounter. Masa presented each banker with a pair of exquisitely engraved chopsticks. Then came his life story, delivered with his now-trademark blend of innocence and bravado: growing up dirt-poor, going to study in America, making a fortune with his pocket speech translator, returning to Japan, becoming the number-one software distributor. No detail was spared. Kobayashi, poleaxed by jet lag, remained semicomatose throughout.[2] After half an hour, the meeting was over. Masa had barely got around to mentioning the business at hand.

Ziff hoped to fetch up to $2 billion for the entire business. Rattner was skeptical whether Masa had that kind of money. A former business reporter at *The New York Times*, Rattner had seen all sorts of flaky people turn up at auctions, and this dude from Japan was the flakiest of the lot. *He talked too much, and he didn't make a lot of sense.* Besides, a credible buyer had come calling: Teddy Forstmann, the playboy-philanthropist-private-equity-tycoon. Ruggedly handsome, with an immaculately coiffed thatch of silver hair, Forstmann's passions were hockey, gambling, and beautiful women. Known as "the buyout king," he was the showman and public face of one of the earliest and most respected names in private equity, Forstmann Little.

"Teddy would always turn up with a suitcase full of cash," says one veteran Wall Street investment banker. "He was a force of nature."

Private equity involved buying companies with money borrowed against the value of their assets. Forstmann paid the loan interest from the acquired company's cash flow, reengineered the business, and either put it up for sale or took it public on the stock exchange, (usually) making a handsome return on its initial investment. Forstmann had no interest in hanging around for an auction; he put a $1.4 billion cash bid on the table and set his own deadline, which happened to be several hours ahead of Ziff's stipulated time at 5 p.m., October 27, 1994. Lazard agreed. With one week to go, Masa signaled he couldn't match an all-cash offer.

Back in Japan, where word had earlier leaked of SoftBank's ambitions in the US, the press reaction to Masa's retreat was astonishment, followed by a sense of injustice that Forstmann had preempted the auction, leaving SoftBank high and dry. Masa claimed to have secured a $1 billion commitment from Wall Street banks, including Bank of New York, Chase Manhattan, and Citicorp, but that risk-averse Japanese banks were unwilling to put up the kind of money needed to land a big deal in the US. He wasn't entirely wrong, but the view in Japan was that if SoftBank was serious about expanding in America, its bigmouthed boss needed to wise up.

But all was not lost. On the very day that Ziff slipped away, a consolation prize appeared. The Ziff empire comprised computer magazines, a trade show arm (Interop), and an online portal, later branded ZDNet. Because Forstmann wanted only the publishing business, Masa was free to bid $200 million for Ziff's trade show.

"I came here for shopping," he told Rattner and Ezersky. "Now at least I don't go home empty-handed."

Dirk Ziff, the eldest son, then aged thirty, was charged with wrapping up the trade fair deal in Tokyo. He stepped off his New York flight and headed into a meeting at SoftBank's headquarters in the Sego building. This time, the jet-lagged Americans fell asleep. Ziff Jr. dimly remembers a samurai sword in Masa's office. Something else stuck in his mind: Soft-Bank's final offer was marginally above the asking price of $200 million, at $200,072,000. Where did the stray $72,000 come from?[3]

Breaking down the financial aspects of the bid, SoftBank paid $120.7 million. Masa's private company MAC, of which we will hear much more, put in $81.3 million. Then an extra $72,000 was thrown in. It was a coded message. A few months earlier, Masa had shot par—72—at one of Tokyo's most prestigious golf courses. Now he thought 72 was his lucky number— and he had a point to make.

Unbeknownst to Dirk Ziff, Masa had long been eyeing a separate target in the trade show space in the US: Las Vegas–based Comdex, owned and run by Sheldon Adelson, a sixty-one-year-old multimillionaire casino operator reputed to be the roughest businessman in the West.

One of four children, Adelson was born at the onset of the Depression. His father was a cabdriver, with Jewish Ukrainian and Lithuanian ancestors. His mother emigrated from England and worked in a knitting shop. In the family's two-room apartment in the Dorchester section of Boston, the parents slept on a mattress and the children on the floor.[4] Adelson often joked that his life was a rags-to-riches story, except his family was too poor to own rags.

In his younger days, Adelson fought prejudice, squaring up with Irish roughnecks in a neighborhood notorious for its antisemitism. Business was more rewarding. Aged twelve, he borrowed $200 from an uncle and purchased a license to sell newspapers in the city. He went on to candy vending machines, toiletry kits, and De-Ice-It, which marketed a chemical spray that cleared ice from car windshields. By his mid-thirties, Adelson had twice made and lost a fortune.

One of Adelson's boyhood heroes was Bugsy Siegel, the Brooklyn-born gangster who helped build the first Las Vegas strip. Adelson too traveled west, launching a Las Vegas computer trade show in 1979 called Comdex. As the PC business exploded, Comdex became the most popular venue for tech entrepreneurs launching new products. By the 1980s and '90s, Comdex was the nation's top computer exhibition, drawing up to ten thousand attendees and giving Adelson the cash to expand.

He went on to buy the Sands Hotel and Casino, the Frank Sinatra Rat Pack hangout, to which he added a convention center.

Adelson kept his rivals close, and his bodyguards even closer.[5] He was always driving for dollars, complaining that tech geeks attending his computer trade fair didn't drink and they didn't spend enough time at the tables. His solution was to make all companies pay for conference booths one year in advance, on top of the current year's booking fee.

"It was so expensive. Those guys had it so monetized, they pushed it to the limit," says Bill Gates, a regular visitor. "Every year the companies would say: 'Are we going to fuck these guys and set up a competitor show?'"

Nobody fancied taking on Shelly Adelson. So nobody set up a rival trade fair.

On November 15, 1993, the opening day of Comdex, Masa turned up with his Japanese entourage. He strutted around like he owned the place, briefly scanning the exhibits while checking out which tech big shot was loitering in the vicinity.

"I am going to buy Comdex," he suddenly blurted out. "I am sorry, but I have to leave now to talk to the board."

Stunned, the Japanese executives turned to SoftBank's finance director Kobayashi. He too assumed his boss was joking.[6] In the meeting with Adelson and his team, Masa was charming and direct. "I like the computer industry. I want to make it bigger," he said. "Why is Comdex only in Las Vegas? If I get Comdex, I will make it global; I will take the conference all over the world."[7]

"Have you got the money?" Adelson inquired.

Masa admitted he didn't have the money. Adelson started laughing. "Come back when you've got the money," he said.

After the meeting, Adelson ordered his people to check out whether Masa was for real. Then he admitted to his partner Jason Chudnofsky, a fellow Bostonian, that he'd driven Comdex's admission charges to the limit. Maybe it was time to sell the business. He wanted $325 million.[8]

A few months later, Masa, desperate to grab control of a marquee brand offering an entrée into Silicon Valley, came back with $500 million, supplied via a syndicated loan from Japanese banks. Adelson, sensing he could play his Japanese visitor, asked for more. In the end, he settled for $842 million. "Masayoshi Son was so keen, he would have paid a billion for the business," says Chudnofsky.[9]

Adelson used the Japanese cash to assemble the largest casino empire in the world. He refurbished the Sands in Las Vegas and built a new generation of mega-casinos in Macau and Singapore. Toward the end of his life, he was worth anywhere between $20 and $40 billion. He never forgot what he had gained from the deal with Masa. One day he would repay his debt handsomely.

The idea that he'd overpaid for Comdex never occurred to Masa. At a stroke, the young man from Japan was a player. He wasn't "one of the small guys standing in a two-hour line with a badge waiting to get into the convention."[10] Soon he would be high-fiving onstage with Bill Gates and Steve Jobs. He didn't care about short-term profits or cashing out like Sheldon Adelson; he was cementing SoftBank's place in the US, the land of cutting-edge high-tech innovation.

"Sheldon played checkers," says Chudnofsky. "Masa played chess." *The New York Times* agreed, headlining their story on Masa's forays into Las Vegas "A Japanese Gambler Hits the Jackpot."

Back in Japan, the reaction was a lot more skeptical. SoftBank had paid top dollar for Comdex. The consortium of fourteen Japanese banks extracted a high price for providing the syndicated $500 million loan covering the bulk of the Comdex acquisition. In the future, SoftBank would need prior approval from every single bank if it wanted to make an acquisition of more than ¥8 billion ($80 million). Far from being an intrepid Japanese investor conquering the world, Masa looked like a tethered goat.

"SoftBank is chasing after Microsoft and Intel at ten kilometers an hour while they are running at a hundred kilometers an hour," he complained. "If we do nothing for seven years until we pay off our debt, we will be left behind forever by rapid global growth. It would also mean the end of SoftBank."[11]

Masa needed to find someone who shared his global ambitions, someone unafraid to challenge the risk-averse Japanese financial sector to unlock the capital necessary to drive SoftBank's global expansion plans. That person was Yoshitaka Kitao, a top salesman at Nomura Securities, the powerful Japanese investment bank and broker-dealer.

A rare Japanese extrovert, with thick dark glasses, short hair, a protruding belly, and a padded double chin, Kitao, forty-four, was a man in search of a new challenge.[12] In the mid-1980s, he worked in Nomura's New York office, selling Japanese stock with an intensity matched only by his passion for food. Every month, he earned the firm almost $600,000 in commissions. One day, an admiring Wall Street banker, himself a Jew, told Kitao that he must be Japanese Jewish. "No," replied Kitao, "I am a Jewish Japanese."[13]

Kitao was of cosmopolitan heritage. His father came from a family of merchants based in Osaka who distributed books, newspapers, and foreign magazines. His mother was born in Hong Kong and grew up in occupied Tianjin, now communist China. Kitao's father also worked for Nomura, including a spell in Sumatra, where he spent time as a prisoner of war. On his return to Japan, Kitao Sr. turned down an offer to rejoin Nomura because the firm would not reemploy his old wartime colleagues. Kitao Jr. had fewer scruples about signing up.

After graduating from the prestigious Keio University in Tokyo, Kitao joined Nomura Securities in their General Planning Division. During a company medical, he discovered he suffered from chronic high blood pressure, which resulted in dizzy spells. Undeterred, he applied to Nomura's study-abroad program, winning a place at Christ's College, Cambridge University, in the UK.

Kitao was following the same path as Masa: studying abroad, speaking English, exposing himself to a world beyond Japan. Back in Tokyo, Kitao chafed at Nomura's hierarchy. In July 1994, he was assigned to the SoftBank IPO, a successful placing that led Masa to invite him to join the company as chief financial officer. After ten days, in which he read everything published about SoftBank and its mercurial founder, he accepted the offer.[14]

Kitao was attracted by Masa's ambitions to grow bigger and faster in the US. When he heard about the terms of the $500 million Comdex loan, he was shocked. The rational approach, he argued, was to repay the loan and raise the funds on the capital markets. But when he asked the prestigious Industrial Bank of Japan to manage SoftBank's proposed bond issue, they turned him down; so did all the other Japanese banks. Kitao was a smart guy—an American colleague once said he had something of the mafia about him. Convinced the banks were colluding, he dreamed up a scheme that would disrupt the entire bond market, untethering Masa and giving him free rein to pursue acquisitions.

It went like this. In 1993, the Japanese Diet approved a revision to the Commercial Code, part of the government's cautious moves to liberalize Japan's financial markets at a time when the post-bubble banking sector was sinking under a mountain of nonperforming loans. Thanks to Japan's "Little Bang,"[15] companies could issue corporate bonds by nominating a financial agent, cutting out the banks as intermediaries. When the Industrial Bank of Japan and others learned that Kitao was about to take advantage of the new rule, they panicked and contacted Masa, then on a business trip to the US.

"Kita-yan [his nickname], what in the world is going on?" Masa asked his new finance director.[16] On hearing his explanation, Masa ruled it was time for a meeting of the newly formed SoftBank board, where the majority of the twelve directors were loyal SoftBank executives. Kitao later said he was ready to be sacked if the financing plan did not work out. But his self-sacrifice proved unnecessary because, having convened the board, Masa declared, "I rely on Kita-yan five hundred percent."

With his boss's blessing, Kitao invited his old firm Nomura Securities to act as fiscal agent, cutting out the major banks. After fierce lobbying from all sides, the Ministry of Finance sided with SoftBank and Nomura in favor of liberalization. At a stroke, the fee structure for corporate bond issuance was reduced by 90 percent. In September 1995, SoftBank issued twelve-year debenture bonds at 3.9 percent interest and raised the $500 million needed to pay back the bank consortium's syndicated loan.

The once-all-powerful Industrial Bank of Japan sued for peace. They proposed that SoftBank move from a "main bank" system to a "core bank" arrangement where several banks would make competitive bids for its services. Masa agreed and listed SoftBank's core banks: Dai-Ichi Kangyo, Fuji, Sanwa, Toyo Shintaku, Tokyo-Mitsubishi, Sumitomo, Sakura, and Industrial Bank of Japan. Then he added a key condition: in the future, SoftBank would operate a ranking system, evaluating each bank according to its willingness to accommodate SoftBank's financing demands.[17] On this basis, Dai-Ichi Kangyo and Fuji were rated the best, while the original troublemaker, the Industrial Bank of Japan, was ranked last.

At a stroke, Masa and Kitao had disrupted the deep state of Japanese finance in a way hardly anyone had managed before. He had stared down the banks and the regulators, shifting the balance of power decisively in favor of the borrower. But this breakthrough was not without cost. SoftBank would become one of the most indebted firms in the world, propped up by those same Japanese banks. This weakness was later compounded by Masa's taste for financial engineering involving complex, multiple layers of leverage in the pursuit of higher returns.

In Masa's defense, he took full advantage of Japan's ultra-low-to-negative interest-rate policy, which was a feature of the next twenty-five years. Drastically lowering the cost of borrowing was aimed at reversing Japan's economic stagnation, but it was also especially helpful to a Japanese businessman like Masa looking to expand overseas. From the autumn of 1995 onward, Masa could borrow cheaply and directly through the domestic bond market to finance acquisitions and investments in the US. A strong yen helped, peaking at ¥79.75 to the dollar in April 1995.[18] Masa was able to pay prices for US assets that his more risk-averse compatriots could only dream of.

In the summer of 1995, Ron Fisher flew to Tokyo. Having received an offer from Masa to head the fledgling US operation, the South African wanted to take the measure of SoftBank's headquarters in Japan. His first experience was an all-employee meeting, some one thousand people, addressed by Masa, who strutted the stage, half huckster, half force of nature. Masa declared that he wanted SoftBank to provide $500 million of operating profits in the next five years. It sounded absurd. Only a few years before, Masa had talked up the idea of SoftBank achieving $500 million in *revenue*, never mind profits. But showmanship left employees enthralled.

"He divided the workforce into groups of five to seven people," Fisher recalled. "Everyone in the group stood up and said how they would contribute to the goal. It was wild."[19]

Masa picked the best twenty presentations and announced he was giving them stock options from his own portfolio.[20] When one of the visitors asked incredulously whether Masa had just handed out $30 million, the answer came in the affirmative. When Fisher got home, he told his wife he had a change of plan. He was taking the SoftBank job. Don't worry, he said. Masa is based in Japan, and we are in the US. Maybe we will do four or five deals a year. Then the genial South African let loose a bombshell: he was going to invest the Fisher family's entire liquid net wealth—between $8 million and $10 million—in his new role as Masa's partner.

"Are you out of your mind?" said his wife, Lisa.

Her plea fell on deaf South African ears. The next Sunday, the telephone rang. "I want to meet Teddy Forstmann," said Masa, revealing that Ziff Davis was up for sale again.

Forstmann had quickly soured on computer magazine publishing, with profits failing to match his expectations. Masa, haunted by his earlier failure to come up with the money, immediately declared he was going big this time. He was ready to pay between 80 and 90 percent of the Ziff purchase through debt. Everyone in his team thought he had gone mad. Fisher remonstrated that taking on such a hefty slug of debt was high-risk, but Masa pointed to Japan's near-zero interest rates. "You don't understand: in Japan, money is free."

Masa arrived in New York at Lazard Frères' headquarters, fully briefed on how to negotiate with Teddy Forstmann, thanks to his advisers at Morgan Stanley. "He didn't listen to a word of our advice," one of the team remembered. "He got eaten alive."[21] Masa shelled out $2.1 billion.

Teddy Forstmann thought he'd made out like a bandit, flipping Ziff for a $700 million profit inside twelve months. Yet Masa was looking like he'd pulled off the deal of the century. It made no sense.

But Masa saw the strategic value of the Ziff deal. He was now the owner of a bunch of highly rated, high-tech assets that no one else in the world possessed, even less in Japan. These were not patents or promises; they were real operating businesses to be bartered or sold at an even higher price in future. And he was in charge of the most popular computer-industry trade show in the world.

He was ready for his next act.

10

YAHOO!

asa turned heads in Japan and the US after his acquisition of the
Ziff computer publishing empire. He'd forked out $2.1 billion, not
as much as Sony paid for Columbia Pictures ($3.4 billion) but more
than Mitsubishi paid for Rockefeller Center ($1.4 billion). Another news
snippet of long-term significance for SoftBank largely escaped public notice: thanks to a prescient Ziff investment, Masa inherited a stake in a
business with one of the goofiest names in Silicon Valley: Yahoo![1]

The name stood for "Yet Another Hierarchical Officious Oracle," an
irreverent moniker for a new online portal linking users to other searchable websites. Yahoo!'s cofounders were Jerry Yang, a twenty-four-year-old
Taiwan-born Stanford graduate with a mop of jet-black hair and a toothy
grin; and David Filo, twenty-eight, an introverted, slightly zany Midwest-
erner whose desktop computer was named Konishiki, after the champion
sumo wrestler from Hawaii. Together the two young men had formed one
of the most iconic companies of the internet age.[2]

Masa prided himself on being able to visualize the future, but he
arrived relatively late to the internet party. Amazon, AltaVista, Excite,
InfoSearch, Lycos, Netscape, and ZDNet, the new generation of online stars, were up and running by 1995. Whether Masa fully grasped
that he'd bought a publishing business that was about to be massively
disrupted by the internet is also doubtful.

Despite his time at Berkeley and regular visits to California, Masa
never truly absorbed the culture of Silicon Valley, with its mix of academia, entrepreneurship, and innovation. He was never deep into "Big
Science," unlike Robert Noyce, the physicist who cofounded Fairchild

Semiconductor, or David Packard, cofounder of Hewlett-Packard. Nor did he contribute tens of millions to his alma mater, like Noyce, Packard, and many others who were deeply involved in the mission and goals of the university. Then as now, Masa was an interloper, who only collected his Berkeley degree ten years after graduation.[3]

One man who did understand the shape of things to come was Eric Hippeau, a French native whom Masa had inherited as Ziff's CEO. Hippeau wasn't shy about pressing his case for investment in the internet. Born in Paris and schooled in England, Hippeau trained as a journalist in Brazil before taking up a business career in New York. He loved his time as editor of an English-language newspaper in Rio de Janeiro, though his tenure featured one notorious schoolboy error. The day after the lunar landing, on July 21, 1969, his front page celebrated Neil Armstrong's giant leap for mankind with the headline: "Man Lands on Mars."[4]

Hippeau identified the best route into the internet as "search"—how best to discover content in the infinite galaxy of cyberspace. One day, one of his junior executives, a prolific reader of Ziff's business magazines, came up with an answer: Yahoo! cofounders Yang and Filo had grasped the importance of the "Netscape Moment," the birth of the eponymous web browser that made access to the internet friction free. Until then, consumers were obliged to use dial-up via CompuServe and AOL, a process so cumbersome and prone to failure that, Jerry Yang joked, it caused brain damage.[5]

Other investors were hunting for opportunities in Silicon Valley. Among the shrewdest was Michael Moritz, a dapper, bespectacled Welshman who had arrived in the US as an Oxford history graduate student. His first job was as a reporter for *Time* magazine, where he covered Silicon Valley, later tapping sources to write a book on Steve Jobs and his fabled return to Apple Computer after being ousted in a boardroom coup. Having joined the venture capital firm Sequoia in 1986, Moritz had reached out to Masa after his successful Cisco Japan deal in 1994. The Welshman went on to make a host of brilliant bets on tech companies like Google, PayPal, and Stripe to become a billionaire.

Moritz visited Filo and Yang on Stanford's campus and quickly figured out their business model. Fainter hearts saw huge risk in backing a search business with a seemingly free service. Moritz grasped that Yahoo! could become a go-to directory for digital information, a platform with a potentially mass audience that in turn could attract online advertising dollars. No one to date had imagined such a virtual business world could exist.[6]

In the spring of 1995, Moritz convinced his partners at Sequoia to invest $975,000 in the start-up, taking 32 percent of its equity. Filo and Yang, who had until recently treated Yahoo! as an amusing distraction from their PhD theses at Stanford, each retained 25 percent of the company. The balance of the shares was reserved for staff.

On November 15, 1995, Masa gathered his top executives in a suite on the twenty-ninth floor of the Las Vegas Hilton. Ted Dolotta, Ron Fisher, and Masa's chief of staff, Masahiro Inoue, were present. Thanks to the Ziff acquisition, SoftBank had inherited the right to buy a small stake in Yahoo! at a price of $2 million. Masa revealed that Hippeau had advised him to invest. He still had to find the money, but in fact he was pondering a much bigger investment. His team's reaction was enthusiastic.[7]

The following day, Masa flew to San Jose to meet with Yang and Filo at their tiny, cramped office on Pioneer Way in Mountain View, a few miles from the Stanford campus. Moritz, also present, remembers Filo's area being littered with Rollerblades, CD cases, soda cans, and a blue-plaid polyester blanket. Masa appeared oblivious of the organized chaos: he was focused on the deal. When Yang suggested moving to a local French or Chinese restaurant, Masa said he was happy ordering pizza.

"It was probably the first and last pizza Masa ate," says Yang, knowing his taste for the most expensive sushi served at his home or office in Tokyo.[8]

After a few minutes listening to Yang's pitch, Masa jumped in. "I really love Yahoo!," he said, "I really want to invest in Yahoo! I really want to own a lot of the company."

"Well," replied Moritz, "we're not selling a lot of the company."[9]

Masa switched tack. He was "the gateway to Japan," the natural partner for Yahoo! It all sounded plausible, but Moritz had a bigger concern. If Yahoo! took SoftBank money, Sequoia's stake in Yahoo! would be diluted. Masa turned to Filo and Yang. What did they think their business was worth? The founders hesitated. Maybe $40 million, said Yang, aware that this figure was way above the $3 million value Sequoia had calculated a few months ago.

Masa never skipped a beat.

"It's a deal," he said, beaming.

Much to Moritz's chagrin, Masa had gate-crashed the party and secured a minority stake in one of Silicon Valley's hottest start-ups.

Oh shit, Yang said to himself, I should have come in higher.[10]

Three months later, Masa invited Filo, Yang, and Moritz to a second meeting. The venue was the Pebble Beach Pro-Am tournament, a gala event set up by Bing Crosby where professional golfers square off against amateurs on one of America's most picturesque courses to raise money for charity. The rain was pelting down so hard that the tournament was called off. Masa spent all day on the sodden golf course, his toes pink with cold, but this time he was flush with cash. He said he wanted to put $100 million into Yahoo, raising the implied valuation more than sevenfold inside three months. In return he demanded one-third of the company, in addition to his current 7 percent holding. An awkward silence ensued.[11]

A venture investment of $100 million would rewrite the Silicon Valley playbook. Top-flight venture capital firms at that time typically managed funds of around $250 million. No one had made a wager of that size on a single start-up in return for a minority shareholding. True, Masa's check was cashable, no small thing when Yahoo! was still burning money. On the other hand, Yahoo! was working with Goldman Sachs and Sequoia to take the company public. Even with his audacious offer, Masa's implied valuation of Yahoo! was at the lower end of the $300–$400 million the founders hoped to raise through an IPO.

Yang played for time. "We don't need that kind of money."

Masa replied: "Jerry, everyone needs $100m."[12]

Yahoo! needed millions to invest to establish itself as a top-class consumer brand, Masa argued. When Yang and Filo continued to stall, he turned to Gary Rieschel, SoftBank's new venture capital recruit, and asked him to name Yahoo!'s top competitors.

Rieschel: Well, there's Lycos, Excite, and AltaVista.

Masa: Which is the strongest competitor to Yahoo!?

Rieschel: Excite.

"Well," said Masa, with a touch of menace, "if I don't invest in Yahoo!, I will invest in Excite and I will kill you."

The room fell silent.

Don Valentine, the battle-hardened Sequoia founder whom Moritz had brought along as extra muscle, took Yang aside: "He might just be crazy enough to give the money to someone else," said Valentine. "If I were you, I would take it."[13]

Yang mulled the offer before returning to the room. Okay, he said, Yahoo! would take Masa's money. But they would also go ahead with the IPO to become a public company. As everyone sat down to do the paperwork for the $100 million investment, Masa slipped in a last-minute demand.

"If you want the money, you have to set up Yahoo! Japan. If not, it is a deal-breaker."

Yang was skeptical. Yahoo! had only fifty people, and scaling up in Japan would be a huge commitment. No problem, said Masa. He would provide the $2 million start-up costs and the engineers to build the directory for Japanese consumers online. SoftBank would hold 60 percent of the equity in Yahoo! Japan, with Eric Hippeau joining the board.

Yang folded. The parties shook hands.

Moritz, who two decades later would accuse Masa of distorting the entire start-up entrepreneurial ecosystem in Silicon Valley, remains rueful about his Yahoo! experience to this day. "Shame on us. We blinked."[14]

The date for launching Yahoo! Japan was set for April 1, an acutely tight deadline. SoftBank still had to develop a search engine in the Japanese language and list all the relevant consumer sites, starting with market leaders in real estate, cars, personal computers, food, travel, and finance. To do this, they had to create a Japanese equivalent of the "hot list," a list of thirty thousand or so categories for making searchable the countless websites in cyberspace. Originally, the US Yahoo! team was supposed to translate their hot list into Japanese, but by mid-February the data dump had still not arrived. Finally, the Japan team was told: "Sorry, we can't do it. Good luck!" The Japanese team had to start from scratch.

Takumi Kageyama, editor in chief of *Unix User*, was just the type to be entrusted with the task. A calm man with a meticulous approach to words and data, he worked all hours and came up with fifteen thousand names. He was helped by Taizo, Masa's youngest brother, who was fifteen years his junior and at the time a third-year undergraduate at the Tokyo University School of Economics. Taizo and his friends plastered ads all over the campus to find students who could surf the web, find relevant websites, and then divide them into categories. To meet Masa's April 1 deadline, they needed to hire around a hundred students a day. They just about made it.[15]

On April 12, 1996, Yahoo! US went public. The shares closed at two and a half times what Masa had paid for them. With his 41 percent stake in the company, he had made an instant paper profit of $150 million. It was a breathtaking coup that set people chattering in Silicon Valley. A new tech investor with deep pockets had arrived in town, all the way from Tokyo.

For Masa's part, he'd muscled his way into a high-stakes negotiation over a share in one of the hottest tech start-ups in the US. He had an appreciating asset that he could leverage to make other bets on internet start-ups. Most important of all, he'd parlayed his stake into a partnership in his home country, where internet usage was taking off. In a matter of years, Yahoo! Japan would prove a fabulous consumer business with a strong brand and profits to match.

From then on, Masa was in the business of trying to repeat the Yahoo! formula: find a cutting-edge internet business in the US, then import the idea to Japan on his terms. The process would gradually be expanded into a cycle that fed SoftBank's growth: attract leading foreign partners into joint ventures; own majority control of those ventures; eventually take the units public; use the proceeds to do more such deals. It was a push-me, pull-you approach: cultivating US tech executives while playing on Japanese fears of falling behind the West.

A torrent of deals followed. Masa guided E-Trade, E-Loan Inc., Morningstar Inc., and many others into Japan, almost always taking majority stakes in the Japanese units and often putting SoftBank executives in charge. As its network of companies grew, so did SoftBank's market value and power, to the point where it would come to be valued at more than $100 billion.

But that was all to come. In the summer of 1996, SoftBank was still experiencing growth pains. Sales had tripled in two years, but debt had ballooned almost tenfold, supported by a flood of corporate bond issues. This was fine as long as investors bought SoftBank's growth story. By the summer of 1996, according to Jordan Levy, SoftBank was on the edge. "Masa needed $300 million of [annual] free cash flow."[16]

To solve SoftBank's cash squeeze and repair its balance sheet, Masa needed to find a company with low debt, solid free cash flow, and high growth prospects, preferably in the tech sector. The target was Kingston Technologies, a manufacturer of computer memory boards based in Fountain Valley outside Los Angeles. The company's cofounders were

Chinese immigrants, David Sun and John Tu, one born in Chongqing in mainland China, the other in Taiwan.

Back in 1982, they had founded and sold a computer hardware company, each earning about $1 million, only to see their savings virtually wiped out in the 1987 Black Monday stock market crash. Their new business, Kingston Technologies, made memory boards for major PC manufacturers and older computers to boost performance. With newer software and operating systems requiring increasing amounts of memory to function efficiently, Kingston soon turned into a star performer.

Like Masa, both Sun and Tu were notoriously private. Sun's passion was golf. He regularly rose at 5 a.m. to play a round on the local links. Tu loved buying classic cars, though he always left his keys on the desk so employees could take a spin in the new roadster.[17] But unlike Masa, who gorged on debt, Sun and Tu never took out a bank loan. They ran a family business that plowed profits back to finance future growth and allocated 5 percent of profits every quarter to their staff. When buyers came knocking, the answer was a polite but firm no.

In the summer of 1996, Kingston was looking for a Japanese distributor. John Tu was given Masa's name. He flew to Tokyo to meet the Soft-Bank boss, who took him out for an expensive raw fish meal. He found the extravagance mildly shocking, and he didn't much care for the sushi either. Next day, he had a bigger surprise: Masa said he was coming to California to personally inspect Kingston Technologies' facilities.

"But we only want a distribution deal," Tu protested in vain.

Masa camped out at the Four Seasons hotel in Beverly Hills, Los Angeles. Next day, he arrived in a chauffeur-driven car at Kingston's factory in Fountain Valley. He was wearing a suit and tie and was accompanied by Ron Fisher. Straightaway, he told Sun and Tu he wanted to buy their company. The offer was $1.5 billion for 80 percent of the company. The Kingston cofounders had no intention of selling, but Masa was adamant. Tu thought his Japanese visitor was crazy.[18] Sun agreed. There was no way Kingston was worth that kind of money.

Masa turned up early next morning, dressed casually, California-style, in sweater and chinos. Again, he repeated his offer; again, he was turned down. On the third day, he came back, and this time Kingston's cofounders accepted, mindful they could hand over a chunk of the proceeds to their staff. A baffled Tu asked Masa why he didn't seem to care about overpaying for a company he barely knew. Masa shrugged.

"When I see the water in the swimming pool, I just jump," he said.

Sun and Tu were still left wondering why Masa was in such a hurry. Later they heard he needed to consolidate Kingston's cash flow to shore up SoftBank's stretched balance sheet. Gary Rieschel remains adamant that the acquisition made no strategic sense. "Kingston was a hardware play that was no way going to produce the returns," he says. "Masa fucked up."[19]

Under the deal, a cash-strapped Masa secured a seven-year payment schedule, where only half would be paid up front and the rest in installments. For their part, Sun and Tu insisted on full management autonomy, retaining a 20 percent stake in the company, with any percentage of future profits added on to the payment installments. Masa and Ron Fisher appeared satisfied, but when the SoftBank finance people in Tokyo ran the numbers, they reckoned the total cost of the Kingston acquisition with earn-outs for the two founders over seven years could potentially rise to $4 billion (according to a subsequent account provided by SoftBank whistleblowers). The total purchase price risked rising to a multiple of seventy times earnings—enough to bankrupt SoftBank.

"You can take the responsibility for running SoftBank into the ground," SoftBank's CFO Kitao told Fisher.[20] Kitao's fears grew when he discovered that Kingston was in the business of making semiconductor memory boards. Prices had fallen 75 percent in the previous twelve months. This was a cyclical business, and SoftBank had offered top dollar well after the market had turned. He demanded Masa insist on a renegotiation of terms. Sun and Tu obliged.

Under the deal announced on August 15, SoftBank modified the earn-out clauses and acquired an 80 percent stake in Kingston for $1.5 billion, to be paid in four installments. These would be financed by $875 million in bank debt, half of which would be retired quickly through the issuance of new SoftBank shares. As *The Wall Street Journal* pointed out, Soft-Bank was one of the few Japanese companies to leverage its own share price to expand its business.[21]

Masa was furious: "That kind of talk really ticks me off. What we've got here isn't a self-created bubble."

On August 26, 1996, Nikkei Business pinpointed the company's financial strains: SoftBank's spending on acquisitions since 1995 was ¥500 billion ($5 billion), and it had a total interest-bearing debt of ¥389.2 billion ($3.89 billion), despite the fact that its consolidated revenue was only ¥171.1 billion ($1.71 billion).[22] Moreover, Kingston Technologies' net assets were valued at only $186 million compared to a sale price of $1.5 billion. This gap implied either a superhuman belief in Kingston's ability to grow or that Masa had hugely overpaid.

SoftBank's credit rating—the key to raising funds in the bond market to finance acquisitions—depended on retaining investor confidence. Facing a storm of criticism, SoftBank grudgingly announced a moratorium of one to two years on further acquisitions. That turned out to be a prudent decision. Several months later, Masa called John Tu and informed him he could not meet a $300 million installment required under the terms of sale. Could Tu fly to Tokyo? By nature averse to confrontation, Tu suggested that David Sun take his place.

Once in Tokyo, Sun was informed by Masa there was no way he could come up with the money he owed. Sun shrugged and said SoftBank had overpaid in the first instance and so he would forgive the debt. When Sun informed his cofounder, Tu replied: "Okay, but before you give away $300 million again, please call me."[23]

Nearly three years later, on July 15, 1999, Masa finally acknowledged his colossal mistake. SoftBank sold its stake in Kingston back to the cofounders for $450 million, less than one-third of what he had originally paid. Yet no one appeared to notice. Internet valuations were going through the roof. The value of SoftBank's 40 percent stake in Yahoo! dwarfed the sums lost in Kingston.

Masa rode his luck. He never cared about profits. Growth was all that mattered. David Sun and John Tu counted themselves lucky, too. Flush with cash, the two cofounders handed over $100 million to their employees. Theirs was a fairy-tale ending.

11

MURDOCH

O n the evening of June 11, 1996, Rupert Murdoch made a Hollywood-style entrance into Japan's TV market. As the champagne flowed and ice fountains showered sparks, clips of Bruce Willis's action movie *Die Hard* appeared on giant screens inside Tokyo's five-star Park Hyatt hotel.

Like Willis's character, the lone New York cop who rescues his estranged wife and hostages from terrorists in the Nakatomi building in Los Angeles, Murdoch had just engineered the seemingly impossible. In the space of six months, the native Australian had secured the first-ever license for a foreigner to operate in one of the world's most tightly regulated broadcasting markets. Soon Star TV, his Hong Kong–based satellite TV service, would be beaming movies, soap operas, and sports, either dubbed or with Japanese subtitles.

Murdoch, then sixty-five, was an irresistible force, blessed with phenomenal energy, his mind constantly churning. The globe-trotting media mogul was feared and loathed by the British establishment. The feeling was entirely mutual. In the 1980s, he had broken Fleet Street's print unions and saved the UK newspaper industry. In the early 1990s, he turned his sights on the BBC.[1]

Murdoch lined up BSkyB, his own TV broadcaster, to deliver programming via satellite to dishes installed on the top of homes rather than via terrestrial broadcasting like the BBC. The project involved huge capital spending and marketing that brought News Corporation, Murdoch's parent company, close to bankruptcy in 1992. Five years later, after a corporate restructuring, BSkyB was the acclaimed world leader in satellite TV broadcasting.

Murdoch's dream was to launch a "cosmic armada," a fleet of high-powered satellites broadcasting to three billion consumers in Australia, America, Europe, and Asia. He owed the regulatory breakthrough in Japan to John McBride, a fluent native speaker who worked in government relations for Murdoch's Ansett Airlines in Tokyo. Having obtained a license for the first direct flight from Sydney to Osaka, McBride asked his Ansett boss for a reward in the shape of a fifteen-minute meeting with Murdoch.

Tall, ambitious, and gregarious, McBride had originally come to Tokyo to study classical Japanese literature. Still only thirty-one, his favorite pastime was schmoozing in the gym or in Tokyo's bars, where he picked up gossip from diplomats, bureaucrats, and journalists. The most valuable tip came from a Japanese contact who revealed the authorities were considering opening the broadcasting market, fearing that Japan was falling behind in telecommunications technology.

Despite knowing nothing about television, McBride asked Murdoch to give him six months to see if he could secure a license for a foreign operator to broadcast. Murdoch agreed on the spot, promising an initial $12 million to plot a feasibility study and a six-month training course in television for McBride in Hong Kong. Murdoch's was a characteristically instinctive decision in an age when not every investment had to go through management consultants or a News Corporation committee. "Rupert sensed a chink in the market and backed me," McBride recalled. "Those were cowboy days."[2]

In the summer of 1996, Japan was in the middle of a TV revolution. Having come down in favor of deregulation, every Japanese broadcaster, media company, and trading house clambered to grab a share of the new market for satellite TV, whose multichannels promised programs for niche audiences with premium advertising rates attached.

From his perch at SoftBank, Masa was eager to join the digital TV revolution, building on his software and magazine publishing business. Terrestrial television was a saturated, heavily regulated market dominated by incumbents, including NHK, the state broadcaster. Satellite TV offered an opening, but when Masa tried to squeeze in as a partner to DirecTV, the digital satellite operator serving the US, he was snubbed. Murdoch's arrival in Japan offered a second chance.

When McBride sounded him out as the keynote speaker for the Star TV launch party, Masa accepted with enthusiasm. The first step was an informal dinner with Murdoch and his then-wife Anna with Masa and Masami at Kicho, a five-star restaurant, at $1,500 a head. That evening, Murdoch enthused about his first serious trip to Japan. Rising at 4 a.m., he and Anna had jumped into the back seat of McBride's Honda and stopped off at Tokyo's Tsukiji fish market. When one of the burly fishmongers pulled down a tuna for slicing, Rupert was almost skewered by a flying fishhook. The other highlight for the Aussie couple was joining the "morning zombies" doing their 6 a.m. stretching exercises in the city's parks.

Masa quickly sensed this was the moment to make his pitch. He recounted his life story: rising from modest origins in rural Japan. He highlighted the pocket speech translator, which he claimed he had sold to Sharp for $1 million. "I should have charged a higher price," he said, only half joking.[3] Then he shifted his theme to the transformational power of the internet, where Murdoch was still something of an ingenue.

Masa's joie de vivre and his technology stargazing left a lasting impression. Despite their twenty-six-year age gap, Masa and Murdoch had much in common. Both were "bet the company gamblers," though Masa acted on pure instinct, whereas Murdoch liked to assess the risks more thoroughly. Only when the Aussie tycoon was satisfied would he put all his chips on the table.[4]

Like Masa, Murdoch was restless and fidgety, seemingly lacking in concentration. Unlike Masa, his mind erred on the side of whatever would titillate his audiences rather than the arcane world of microchips. He regularly called editors early in the morning or late at night to listen to the latest gossip from inside the Vatican, Downing Street, or Hollywood. Politics was good; politics with sex even better.

When it came to the Japanese TV market, both men needed each other. Murdoch had money and knew broadcasting. Masa knew about communications technology, but as usual he was short of cash. That summer, he faced another crunch, exacerbated by a steep decline in SoftBank's share price caused largely by the cost of the Kingston Technologies' acquisition, which was unnerving investors and creditors. He needed a showstopper deal.

At the Star TV launch, on June 11, 1996, Masa delivered a pitch-perfect speech in front of a VIP crowd at the Park Hyatt. News Corporation was a great innovator, and Rupert Murdoch's arrival signaled a vote of confidence in Japan as an international marketplace. As the party wound to a close, Masa approached McBride, by now in charge of the Star TV venture in Japan. Could he arrange a private meeting with Murdoch in his hotel room? McBride was well versed in Japanese corporate etiquette, so this request looked like an ambush waiting to happen. He sounded out his boss.

Still in high spirits after the party, Murdoch agreed to see Masa, who by this time had wangled an invitation for his sidekick, Yoshitaka Kitao, SoftBank's monosyllabic chief financial officer. When McBride offered the Japanese visitors a cocktail, both men refused, citing health reasons. (Masa was still worried about his hepatitis B, while Kitao had long suffered from high blood pressure.[5]) At this point, Murdoch signaled to McBride to leave the room.

Over the next hour, the ambush unfolded. Masa sprang on Murdoch the idea of buying a stake in the Obunsha media group, thereby acquiring the TV Asahi shares they owned. Thanks to Kitao's Nomura connections, SoftBank had exclusive negotiating rights, he said.

Murdoch was wide-eyed: "You have exclusivity in negotiations? You work quickly! When do the negotiations have to be wrapped up?"

"At least for the month of June, we have the first right of negotiation."

Murdoch smiled. "Excellent. I'll get in on this."

Masa: "Can you let me handle most of the price negotiations?"

Murdoch: "Okay, it's in your hands."[6]

The following morning, when Murdoch informed McBride of his late-night deal, the latter was appalled. The Asahi-Obunsha deal was not just a distraction, it risked sabotaging Star TV's entire strategy in Japan. McBride was so outspoken that News Corp executives present were shocked. No one talked to the boss like that.

Murdoch was sympathetic to McBride's argument but remained unpersuaded. He'd given his word to Masa. And he intended to keep it. The notion that a gentleman's word was his bond might seem quaintly chivalrous and hardly consistent with Murdoch's track record as a ruthless tycoon whose legacy was later blemished irreparably by the phone-hacking scandal in the UK. But Rupert Murdoch was always capable of the honorable gesture, even if he kept it well under wraps.[7]

More than thirty years later, McBride reflected on Masa's midnight coup. The Japanese went "right in for the kill." He deployed rational argument, just like an American, singling out the Japan Broadcasting Corporation (NHK) as the public broadcaster ripe for being disrupted. "Rupert bought it, seeing the deal as a replica of BSkyB's challenge to the BBC."[8]

When news broke of the News Corp–SoftBank TV alliance, the media storm lasted for weeks. One of Murdoch's aides calculated that it earned News Corp around $70 million of free publicity, but TV Asahi's conservative critics in the press accused the company of selling a priceless media asset to foreigners. Several compared Murdoch's appearance to the arrival of Commodore Matthew Perry's Black Ships (*kurofune*) in 1853, which brought an end to Japan's centuries-long isolation and heralded a period of turbulent modernization.

Most Japanese still viewed the Black Ships episode with profound ambivalence. Commodore Perry's arrival precipitated the end of the feudalistic Tokugawa period, a watershed in the modern history of Japan. The restoration of Emperor Meiji's authority followed, along with a wholehearted embrace of things Western: steam power, machines, photography, and electric power. But the Black Ships episode also symbolized an enfeebled nation humiliated by an alien invader. The conclusion was uncomfortable: real change occurred in Japan only when prompted by outside forces.

The Black Ships analogy allowed the Japanese media to cast Murdoch as a foreign "baddie." But Masa was singled out too. He found himself the target of death threats and warnings that his two daughters might be kidnapped. McBride had a bodyguard stationed outside his office, though he calculated that Japanese nationalists were too dumb to locate an English-named office in Tokyo.[9]

In the early days, the Masa-Murdoch relationship was ginger-peachy. Rupert was thrilled to be stirring things up in staid Japan—he loved taking on "the establishment" anywhere in the world. Murdoch liked Masa, seeing him as a younger version of himself, though his eyes glazed over when the SoftBank boss invited him to his house in Roppongi and showed off his artificial golf course.[10]

Soon after the deal closed, Masa made a grand tour of BSkyB's operation in the UK, including a trip to inspect the broadcaster's state-of-the-art call center in Livingston, Scotland. An awkward moment later occurred at News Corporation's Culver City headquarters in Los Angeles. Murdoch said McBride should be CEO of JapanSkyBroadcasting (JSkyB). Masa, hypersensitive to status, countered that JSkyB had to be an equal joint venture. He should be CEO, and McBride would be deputy CEO—*fukushacho* in Japanese.

"I will make it a cash cow for you," Masa told Murdoch, repeating the Americanism several times. Rupert relented, but the incident left a sour taste. Some News Corp executives remained skeptical about their boss's foray into Japan. Masa doubled down, insisting that News Corp join SoftBank in putting $200 million into JSkyB. This "face" mattered to Masa at the time. SoftBank's share price was drifting downward, and cash-flow pressures were unrelenting. When News Corp committed, it was a big vote of confidence.

On the technical side, Masa demonstrated an impressive grasp of detail, reciting how the satellites in outer space had to be positioned at precise angles to reach households in Japan, the most saturated satellite market in the world. In JSkyB's case, the company had to build dishes that pointed at both 124 and 128 degrees east, and had a 110-degree-east focus as well. It was a bravura performance.

Masa understood how to piggyback on the Murdoch name, which opened doors to blue-chip Japanese manufacturers like Sony and Sharp. Less visible were the obstacles to Star TV put in place by the five national broadcasters seeking to protect their monopolies. Each lobbied the Ministry of Posts and Telecommunications, blocking Murdoch's efforts to put foreign nationals on the board of his new broadcasting company. The Japanese establishment was fighting back.

Murdoch himself was starting to have doubts about Japan. There were just too many regulatory hoops to jump through. Besides, he was no longer persuaded that Asahi TV was the best cultural fit for News Corp. "It was way too liberal," says McBride, "almost communist."

In May 1997, without informing Masa, Murdoch turned to two new partners: Fuji TV, the major terrestrial broadcaster, and Sony, which manufactured the set boxes but was pushing for a seat at the JSkyB table.[11] Under the new deal, Fuji and Sony would each take a 25 percent stake in JSkyB in return for acquiring News Corp's stake in Asahi TV. It fell to McBride to break the news to Masa that Rupert had switched plans and opened the door to two established Japanese giants.

"He was full of cold fury. He felt we had a friendship and said we should not have presented him with a fait accompli," says McBride. "I said I was sorry but thought it was the best way forward."

Although Masa had an equal 25 percent share in JSkyB, he'd been diluted and therefore had lost face. He also had to explain to investors why his alliance with Rupert Murdoch had been ditched in favor of a Japanese alternative. His mood darkened when he had to negotiate with Nobuyuki Idei, the haughty CEO of Sony. Idei never bothered hiding he was good friends with Murdoch. He treated Masa with mild contempt, viewing him as a dangerous maverick.

This dismissive view of Masayoshi Son was widely shared in the Japanese establishment. Even though SoftBank's boss on paper was one of the richest men in Japan, he was obviously different from the generation of postwar business leaders who had rebuilt the country from the ground up. Many were deeply committed to ethics and culture. They were Confucian capitalists, viewing their chosen profession in almost spiritual terms. These industrial titans published books not just on how to achieve business success but also on the philosophy of life. Kazuo Inamori, who built a ceramics and telecoms powerhouse, later became a Buddhist monk who wrote a bestseller called *A Compass to Fulfillment*. The legendary Toshio Doko, known as "Mr. Turbines," who ran Ishikawajima-Harima Heavy Industries and Toshiba, led a notably frugal existence, eating cold soba noodles for lunch every day.[12]

By contrast, Masa was a gambling man who loved the finest sushi and wine, who lived life on the edge, always with one eye on the next deal. Although he often drew on Japanese history, as if to emphasize his patriotic credentials, everyone in the Japanese business establishment knew he was an ethnic Korean. In their minds, he was airbrushed out of existence.[13]

Masa's revenge was to upstage Sony by going into the set-top business himself. He found an alternative, far cheaper supplier in Taiwan: Acer, the hardware and advanced electronics company based in Taipei. Idei was irritated but accepted, reluctantly, that Masa was at least pushing out thousands of set-top boxes. In a typical Masa marketing flourish, the boxes were given away free by dozens of pretty Japanese saleswomen standing outside railway stations across Japan in return for customers signing up to a long-term contract with the Star TV service.

Murdoch now had another target in his sights. Sony had a Hollywood film studio (Columbia Tristar Pictures) and a giant music business. Murdoch had a newspaper, a TV empire, and a film studio (20th Century Fox).

Like Murdoch, Idei was "old media." He was desperate to revive Sony's dream of getting into TV in Japan. In that sense, he was a more natural partner than Masa, who felt increasingly marginalized. Meanwhile, the balance of corporate power was changing within Japan itself.

In the race to hook up Japan's fifty million households to multichannel broadcasting, JSkyB was still the laggard. In August 1997, McBride, pushed by Sony and Fuji, agreed to partner with PerfecTV, a consortium led by the four leading Japanese trading houses, the giant conglomerates that built their fortunes importing metals, textiles, food, and other goods. By the mid-1990s, they expanded into providing seed capital for new ventures in an effort to counteract low margins in their traditional business, a little like private equity without the debt and the exit.

Masa, sensing that consolidation made more sense than slugging it out in a loss-making venture, agreed to the deal. Nine months later, the Japanese parties concluded a merger, forming Sky PerfecTV, which pulled off an IPO in October 2000. The business was valued at around $6 billion, and Soft-Bank sold a quarter of their stake for $132 million, a decent return on the initial $87 million investment but one diminished by heavy capital spending required for marketing and programming.[14] SoftBank sold their remaining stake in March 2002 for $88 million, so they netted $133 million.[15]

Murdoch's shareholding in SkyPerfecTV was diluted to 11 percent. He sold out to finance his son James's ambition to launch Star TV in India. Rather than sticking to his satellite TV formula, Murdoch switched to Fox TV cable channels, led by Fox News, the edgy conservative brand launched in the US in August 1996. Restless and frustrated with Japan's regulatory shenanigans, he developed a new enthusiasm: China.

Suddenly Murdoch's visits to Asia no longer included a stopover in Japan. Instead, he flew directly to Hong Kong. There his eyes fell upon a pretty (and pushy) young translator and junior Star TV executive whom he insisted on bringing on his business trips to the mainland. Her name was Wendi Deng, a former Star TV intern thirty-eight years his junior. They would later marry and have two children, Grace and Chloe.

Murdoch retained a friendly relationship with Masa, but the satellite TV joint venture which began with a bang in the Park Hyatt hotel ended in a fizzle. Murdoch became a little more wary, especially after his experience during the dot-com bubble. Masa persuaded him to invest jointly in a $100 million fund called eVentures specializing in the UK, Australia, New Zealand, and India. Most of the money went up in smoke. After that, Rupert was no longer quite so available on the phone.

In hindsight, the Masa-Murdoch episode revealed a deeper truth about modern media. Murdoch was so focused on content that he failed to fully appreciate digital delivery of that very same content. He was still old media, a newspaper man at heart. For all his boyish enthusiasm and occasional missteps, Masa represented the new economy. He'd seen the digital future—and it worked.

12

WHISTLEBLOWERS

On August 1, 1997, nine days before his fortieth birthday, Masa's world fell apart. Everything he'd said and done was cast into doubt after the publication of a book titled *Whistle Blown: SoftBank's Crooked Management*. The book set out allegations of hidden losses and share-price manipulation, which shattered SoftBank's image as a dynamic business occupying a unique place in Japan. People were ready to believe that because Masa's company was so different, something must be deeply wrong. In the three months after the book's publication, SoftBank's stock lost one-third of its value, forcing Masa as a major shareholder to absorb hundreds of millions of paper losses.

The whistleblowers were a group of current and former SoftBank employees, hiding behind the pseudonym Kōichi Yoshida.[1] Whatever their motives, they appeared to know a great deal about the inner workings of SoftBank. Caught in the crosshairs were a small number of private companies that sat outside SoftBank itself, which Masa had set up. One of them, called MAC, was the legal entity through which Masa held his 43.3 percent stake in SoftBank—a perfectly innocent arrangement for a company founder. However, collectively, these private companies also undertook activities that blurred the line between Masa's personal interests and those of SoftBank, thereby carrying the risk of misleading investors in SoftBank. According to the whistleblowers, they financed speculation by Masa himself, paid under-the-table salaries to newly hired executives, took bets on currency markets, and hid losses and debt.

In the US, such activities are known as related-party transactions and off-balance-sheet dealings. Almost all corporate scandals involve such vehicles, and as a result they are often illegal or, when they are legal, have long been frowned upon and subject to tight disclosure and governance rules. In Japan at that time, disclosure and governance standards were weak. When the allegations about Masa's private dealings came out, they provoked an uproar. Along with his finance director Kitao, Masa sued the independent publisher, which went by the appropriately provocative name Yell, and its board member Tsutomu Watanabe. Demanding ¥400 million ($4 million) in damages and a public apology, Masa fiercely denied wrongdoing and lashed out against critics:

"People who say I'm trying to cover things up in a black box or whatever must be people who don't understand how economics works," he complained. "Some say it was to prop up SoftBank's share price. Well, those are temporary effects, and if anything there were a lot of cons for personally absorbing all that risk."[2]

For all his protestations of innocence at the time, the next two decades of Masa's career would involve a constant parade of new corporate structures that blurred the line between his interests and those of outside investors, were open to manipulation, and made his firm's performance and indebtedness too opaque to assess accurately. While he saw himself as a technology innovator transforming society, in many ways he was a financial engineer reshuffling assets and liabilities—not that he would ever admit it. More than twenty years after the Kōichi Yoshida whistleblower episode, Masa offered a similar defense when challenged about his own high-risk trades in US technology stocks, alongside SoftBank's. In both instances, he refused to admit there might be some conflict between his personal interests and the company's. Because he had "skin in the game" as SoftBank's founder and major shareholder, he believed his interests were aligned with the company's. Back in August 1997, the whistleblower begged to differ.

"He [Masa] thinks he can do anything"—a view shared thirty years on by Jordan Levy, the gruff American telemarketer-turned-venture-capitalist bought out by SoftBank. While an admirer of Masa's creativity and drive, Levy's verdict on his management style remains unchanged. "Masa did what he liked. Nobody stood up to him."[3]

Whistleblowers in Japan were about as rare as ranch dressing or root beer. In a country where respect for hierarchy remained sacrosanct, workers calling out their bosses enjoyed few protections under the law. But the mood was changing. The collapse of the bubble economy had exposed the underbelly of Japanese society, a succession of corporate scandals, louche conduct, and any manner of dodgy dealings by banks still sitting on billions of dollars of real estate losses. Even mighty Nomura Securities had seen its CEO forced to resign after the firm admitted shelling out $100 million to compensate favored customers for stock market losses.

In SoftBank's case, the whistleblower affair reflected cultural tensions within the company itself. Masa wanted to create the greatest start-up ever seen in Japan. He disdained the "salaryman culture," where employees were given lifetime job security in return for ninety-hour working weeks, respect for seniority, and undying loyalty to the company. Under Masa, SoftBank's culture was half–can-do American, half–Japanese ninja warrior: agile, dynamic, and unpredictable.

The whistleblowers found Masa's showmanship distasteful, but they reserved their sharpest criticism for the "Nomura Seven," the imported investment banking dealmakers led by Kitao.[4] Wearing belts, braces, and flashy gold watches, these Japanese moneymen bossed the workplace. Two decades later Masa hired a cadre of former Deutsche Bank executives with similar mercenary instincts. All the Nomura Seven cared about was SoftBank's share price, a key component in the company's US-style "stock incentive program," which Masa never failed to promote when foreign visitors visited SoftBank's headquarters in Tokyo.

By now, SoftBank had grown into a substantial business employing a thousand people. Aside from the original software distribution and magazine business, it could count its US acquisitions (Phoenix Technology, Comdex, Ziff, and Kingston). Yahoo! Japan was rapidly scaling up, and Kitao's finance division was expanding, largely to keep pace with the company's borrowing needs, foreign-exchange exposure, and relationships with the Japanese banks.

SoftBank's employee stock incentive program operated a two-tier system where everybody was nominally equal, but some executives were more equal than others. After the Ziff acquisition, top US-based executives received SoftBank shares directly through another of Masa's private companies, called MIC.[5] In Japan, some 123 high-ranking SoftBank employees were paid bonuses in SoftBank shares, again in deals intermediated by MIC. But the offer came with a condition: employees were loaned money to buy the shares at a slight discount, to be paid back in yearly installments. The idea was that they would sell a tenth of their shares every year to pay back the loan with interest and hopefully come away with a profit.[6]

Masa's goal was laudable. He wanted to incentivize Japanese employees to increase SoftBank's share price. As a major shareholder, that would benefit him as well as others. But the structure was questionable. MIC was Masa's private company but also a SoftBank shareholder. The transactions involved were "off balance sheet," and therefore largely hidden from the view of outside investors in SoftBank itself, meaning its financial statements did not give a complete and fair view. And employees were having to go into debt to take part in the scheme, imposing a high level of risk on them.[7]

In the event, SoftBank's stock price declined in the short term, leaving the Japanese employees in the red as the value of their debts exceeded the value of their shares. The losses generated widespread discontent among the workforce, and the stock incentive plan was later abandoned. MIC went into voluntary liquidation at the Tokyo District Court on August 10, 1998, with outstanding liabilities amounting to ¥10.7 billion ($107 million).[8] In the event, the employees' repayment due date was extended, SoftBank's share price recovered, and the loans were liquidated at fair market value and the employees therefore shielded from losses, SoftBank Group says.[9]

SoftBank's stock incentive program was very much part of the modern management practices which Masa trumpeted as evidence that SoftBank was a cut above the mainstream Japanese company. Daily internal statements, paperless meetings, performance evaluation by a thousand metrics— all these were supposed proof that SoftBank inhabited a world apart from the stuffed shirts lined up inside the boardrooms of Japan Inc.

The whistleblowers said SoftBank's claim that it used a thousand metrics was a mirage.[10] Managers used twenty different ways to measure performance but then multiplied the individual metrics by the number of company teams. This produced the desired target of one thousand. Two decades later, Masa used the same sleight of hand when he bragged to two American video game executives that SoftBank monitored "an hourly profit and loss account [P&L]." It all sounded plausible until Brian Kelly, cohead of Activision Blizzard, set him straight.

"Forget the Ps [profits]," said Kelly, "they're all Ls [losses]."[11]

Masa claimed paperless meetings were routine and every employee had three computers. SoftBank sounded more like the trading floor of a Wall Street investment bank than a media company. In fact, ordinary workers operated one PC only, while managers or executives had two on their desks. If anyone inside SoftBank had three computers, it was Masayoshi Son.

Masa was an incorrigible self-promoter. Most of the time it was harmless stuff. SoftBank was a young company in a young industry in a country where progress in corporate culture was glacial at best. He was trying to create something new and lasting, and he didn't have a lot of time.

"Everybody is saying, 'Well, SoftBank may be moving "too fast" or it is "too wild" or whatever, "too childish" or a "non-Japanese company."' That total image may have scared some people," he complained after the initial whistleblowing allegations.[12]

Warming to his theme, he insisted that SoftBank's financial position was healthy and he wasn't going anywhere. "I'm still young. I just turned forty. So five years, ten years—I can just prove it over time. I don't have to prove it in six months or twelve months. . . . Our industry is young. That's the key."

In the circumstances, when pure tech companies were thin on the ground and Japan's economy was mired in a banking crisis, Masa's plea for greater understanding was reasonable. But SoftBank's turbocharged growth, whereby the company leveraged itself by loading debt upon debt, raised awkward questions about whether the level of borrowing was sustainable.

After going public in 1994, SoftBank over the next three years spent $4.7 billion, including investments in more than fifty US technology startups, many of them loss-making internet-related companies in Silicon Valley. Profitable US acquisitions like Ziff's publishing business gave Soft-Bank extra borrowing power, which fueled the next growth burst. Masa either was a great judge of potential, or he was spinning plates.

The Ziff acquisition was a case study in leverage and the use of Masa's private companies to mask financial reality. The sum paid—$2.1 billion—was more than double SoftBank's own revenues. SoftBank itself paid $1.8 billion and took most of the Ziff assets. However, the outstanding $300 million was paid for by MAC, which assumed Ziff's loss-making businesses such as ZDNet. The overall effect was to transfer debts and operating losses out of SoftBank, whose balance sheet and income statement looked correspondingly better to external investors as a result.

If you looked only at SoftBank's figures, the Ziff deal's internal-rate-of-return (IRR) appeared better than it was. (IRR was Masa's favored metric for success and represents the annualized return an investment makes, or is forecast to make. On Wall Street, IRR metrics used in private equity deals are widely acknowledged to be easy to manipulate and often misleading.) In the short term, this boosted SoftBank's share price and Masa's paper wealth.

It was financial engineering typical of Masa and Kitao. Yet aside from giving outside investors in SoftBank an incomplete picture, it carried other dangers. The debts and losses that sat outside SoftBank, in the private companies owned by Masa, meant he might become liable for them. A tricky moment might come if these loss-making businesses were ultimately brought inside SoftBank. If their performance improved and they became profitable before they were sold to SoftBank, he might stand to gain. But if they remained unprofitable, who ultimately was going to bear the costs and debts?

The "warehousing" of loss-making acquisitions and debts within private companies like MAC made it hard to gain a true picture of SoftBank's financial health. By 1997, it was preparing to shift from Japan's over-the-counter stock market, typically used by young or small firms, to the main board of the Tokyo Stock Exchange, one of the world's largest and most actively traded bourses. Disclosure rules and corporate governance rules on the TSE, while not comparable to New York or London, were far tighter than the ones Masa had been operating under.

"MAC is a company 99%-owned by myself as an individual," the SoftBank boss said defensively in a newspaper interview. "So instead of thinking of MAC as a totally separate black box, unknown, a weird company, think of it as just myself, because that's what it is. MAC, namely myself, has helped SoftBank to grow. That's true. It is the same thing as I myself helped SoftBank grow. There's nothing wrong about that."[13]

A full disclosure of Masa's private firms would have revealed that he funded their adventures in part by borrowing. But to get banks and others to lend to these private firms, which had no substantial business of their own, he had to agree to secure the loans against collateral: his own

SoftBank shares. But if SoftBank's shares fell, lowering the value of that collateral, panicky banks might demand that the loans be repaid, destabilizing the entire corporate structure.

A key part of the ultimate return that SoftBank made from the Ziff publishing deal had nothing to do with its operational business: instead the currency market moved in SoftBank's favor. In 1995, Masa was desperate to take advantage of record-low interest rates and the strong yen against the US dollar. Ron Fisher, Masa's trusted American lieutenant, later explained that currency moves rescued what might otherwise have been "a mediocre investment" in Ziff.[14]

One prominent London hedge fund manager estimated that the fall in the yen and the later Ziff sale in dollars a mere five years later produced a substantial profit for Masa. "That was the start of his serious personal wealth," he claims.[15]

As an investor, Masa often operated on little more than a whim. Nothing demonstrated this better than his stranger-than-fiction venture with a Hollywood star in Deadwood, South Dakota. Best known for the murder of Wild Bill Hickok, the gunslinger shot in the back while playing poker, the town of Deadwood turned up more than a century later in Kevin Costner's Oscar-winning *Dances with Wolves*. The movie featured a Civil War hero and frontiersman who befriends a Lakota Sioux warrior and immerses himself in Native American culture. Set against the spectacular landscape of the Black Hills, with dialogue spoken in Lakota with English subtitles, *Dances with Wolves* soon became a box office phenomenon, grossing more than $400 million worldwide.

Having directed and played the starring role as Lieutenant John J. Dunbar, Costner decided Deadwood was the place to make an even bigger fortune. He and his elder brother Don opened the Midnight Star casino on Main Street. The gambling den was the first stage of a $100 million luxury resort that Costner named the Dunbar, in a nod to his own movie character. A local writer later described the resort as "a five-star monument to kitsch."[16]

The Costner brothers wanted to acquire 630 acres of federal land next to their $100 million casino in an area known as Slaughterhouse Gulch, part of the Black Hills National Forest. The land was earmarked for a golf course, a reservoir, hiking trails, and a steam train linking the resort to

Rapid City, fifty miles away. In return, the Costners would buy 585 acres in nearby Spearfish Canyon and donate it to the US Forest Service.

The proposed land swap soon turned into a nightmare. Once feted as the champion of Native American culture, Costner found himself accused of desecrating sacred Native American territory. By 1996, amid court wrangles and Lakota sit-ins, the Hollywood movie star's real estate venture was in deep trouble. He needed a friendly source of money, someone with a speculative bent. Exactly how he stumbled across Masa remains unclear; but on March 26, 1996, Masa's private firm, MAC, signed off on a $10 million low-interest loan to the Hollywood star under the title "casino in the desert."

The loan to Kevin Costner can be explained away as Masa's personal business. Masa was also using MAC to lend to himself. On August 7, 1997, four days before Masa's fortieth birthday, an employee emailed him anonymously in English, asking about a ¥1 billion ($10 million) loan from MAC to Masa. Masa, sounding like Captain Renault in *Casablanca*, said he was shocked, shocked that anyone could possibly doubt his motives and sincerity.

"I don't understand what is wrong about it," Masa wrote, admitting that the loan was around the end of 1996 or early 1997. "MAC is 100% owned by myself. I can make a loan to myself without any problem legally. . . . I can disclose about [sic] the loan to myself from MAC at any time. I can disclose anything about MAC anytime." He continued: "If you say you care about SB, that is good. SB is my life. I love SB at least 1,000 times more than anybody."

Not everyone was convinced. "They send us lots of favorable material," said Satoshi Nagura, a New Japan Securities analyst, "but as for unfavorable information they keep quiet."[17]

On November 10, 1997, SoftBank presented its interim results to around 160 business analysts in Tokyo. Masa took more than two hours to answer their questions, many of them tough and heated. It was a virtuoso performance. Gone was the bombast. Even though he hated being held to account in public, he sensed it was time to demonstrate some humility. When the session ended, applause echoed throughout the hall.[18]

Less than three weeks later, on November 27, SoftBank shares hit bottom at ¥1,670. This was the lowest since SoftBank made its debut on the over-the-counter market at ¥1,050 on July 22, 1994. But in the following weeks, the shares rallied. That same month, November 1997, Yahoo! Japan made a stunning debut on the JASDAQ over-the-counter market. The initial offering was ¥700,000 a share, but the opening price was ¥2 million. Masa's insistence that his investment in Yahoo! US should be accompanied by the creation of a Yahoo! Japan affiliate was fully vindicated.

On January 26, 1998, less than six months after the whistleblowers threatened to sink his company, SoftBank listed on the Tokyo Stock Exchange. From now on, all institutions managing passive or "index" portfolios tracking the TSE would have to hold SoftBank shares at their index weight. Active managers would have to decide whether to hold the shares and whether to be over- or underweight. Masa had joined Japan's corporate elite.

Eighteen months later, when SoftBank's stock was on a tear, Masa agreed to settle the libel case he and his top executives had brought against Yell Publishing. The editors had to admit there were some inaccuracies in the book (without specifying which) and to express remorse for any reputation harmed and inconvenience caused, though there were no damages paid, no public apology was made by the independent publisher, and each side paid its own legal costs.

The fate of MAC was more instructive. SoftBank absorbed Masa's off-the-books affiliate on December 1, 1998. By then, SoftBank could afford to do so. SoftBank's internet investments, notably its stake in Yahoo!, were worth hundreds of millions of dollars.

Ben Wedmore, an HSBC analyst who followed SoftBank for almost three decades, remained scathing about the whistleblower episode. "This is a story about Japan, investors, investment banks, regulators, and the government. It is also about growth, revenue recognition, not actual profits made. SoftBank has almost always been an asset play where the profit and loss account is virtually irrelevant."[19]

13

....

BUBBLE MAN

Between 1998 and 2000, the world experienced a speculative frenzy similar to the discovery of gold in the Klondike region of Yukon, Canada, a century earlier. The investing professionals and day traders dabbling in the stock market were the latter-day counterparts of the weather-beaten prospectors and wild-eyed greenhorns trekking across the Canadian tundra. But whereas the gold rush involved a finite precious commodity in a precise geographic location, the internet opened a universe of infinite possibility.

Few of the online enterprises competing for investors' attention had any track record or sustainable business model. To dot-com evangelists like Masayoshi Son, the absence of conventional benchmarks was of no consequence. On the contrary, it was part of the allure. The true measure of a stock's value was not the price/earnings ratio; it was the company's price/future sales ratio, since start-ups by definition had no earnings worth speaking of.

Growth *potential* was an article of faith for Masa, who viewed short-term profit and loss as a distraction. He was in good company during the internet boom. Henry Blodget, a little-known, thirtysomething analyst at second-tier CIBC Oppenheimer, achieved guru status with one big call. In 1998, he initiated coverage of loss-making Amazon with a strong buy and a price target of $400. When the stock jumped immediately from $289 to $480, Blodget became head of dot-com research at Merrill Lynch, the Wall Street powerhouse. From that day on, the word was with Henry Blodget.[1]

Another influencer was Mary Meeker, the Morgan Stanley analyst dubbed the Queen of the Internet. She declared it was time to be "recklessly rational," whatever that meant. Morgan Stanley was courting investment banking business so aggressively that few could recall a Meeker "sell" recommendation, but she still had a point. What counted was not so much direction but timing: *when* to buy and *when* to sell—a big test for a techno-optimist like Masa. As the dot-com bubble inflated, the risks of being caught holding a vastly overvalued asset grew ever higher. It all depended on finding "a greater fool" as a buyer, and Masa at times risked looking like the greatest fool on the block.

In late 1995, around the time Masa was sizing up his investment in Yahoo!, SoftBank opened a makeshift investment office in San Jose, California. At that time, the stock market vibes were very different. Venture capital wasn't a household name, and the importance of the internet was not immediately obvious.[2] Masa's first move was to lure Gary Rieschel to join his US scouting operation, followed by Brad Feld, an MIT-trained angel investor.

SoftBank Technology Ventures spent $230 million on fifty-six investments in the first twelve months; then it ran out of money. The next year was devoted to raising a $300 million fund in which SoftBank took a 13 percent stake. In 1998, everything ramped up. Rieschel and Feld set up a $600 million fund with SoftBank taking a 25 percent stake; a third $600 million fund followed, with SoftBank upping its stake to 50 percent. Both men found the SoftBank founder charming and engaging. He was a good listener, a born entrepreneur who had a real feel for consumer psychology.[3]

"We would get phone calls at eleven in the night, with Masa saying he had just met some tech entrepreneur and we should invest fifty million," Rieschel remembers. "We would say: 'Okay, but what is the business? Where are the figures?' Sometimes we would undo the deals before the investment was made, but usually we would go along."

Ron Fisher, SoftBank's top executive in the US, sat in on all the calls. Sometimes, as Rieschel observed, Masa needed protection from his own worst instincts. Twenty-five years on, Fisher was more generous about his boss. "The biggest discussion between me and Masa was not whether we should invest in those companies, but the size of the investment."[4]

Masa was always doubling down, never quitting. The bigger the sums, the better—because that way lay outsize returns. The man's risk appetite knew no bounds. Rieschel marveled at Fisher's patience. "If there is such a thing as a South African Jew who is a saint, that is Ron." Yet even as those around him were stunned by Masa's crazy spending, there was—at least in the SoftBank boss's mind—some method in the madness.

His mantra was to make SoftBank number one "in eyeball traffic, finance, e-commerce, and content." He had no interest in managing or owning a single dominant force like Amazon.com. His goal was to invest in top players in dozens of niches, locking up 20 and 30 percent equity stakes at a time. Rather than control, he sought influence. Masa called his online empire an internet *zaibatsu*—a reference to the pre–Second World War clusters of companies which dominated the Japanese economy. They were all part of an enormous extended family headed by the parent firm, in this case SoftBank. The advantages of the arrangement were scale and purported synergy.

Among his most high-profile US investments was E-Trade, an online stock-trading service competing against Ameritrade and Charles Schwab, the market leader. Based in Menlo Park, California, E-Trade was rapidly burning cash on advertising needed to build a brand and win customers. The business needed someone with a fat checkbook to bankroll losses. When E-Trade founder Christos Cotsakos announced he needed $400 million, Masa dispatched the funds after a single phone call. In return he demanded a minimum 20 percent of the equity. Cotsakos, a garrulous Greek American, likened Masa to an internet messiah.

General Atlantic, the New York–based private equity firm which held a substantial minority shareholding, initially welcomed the cash-rich newcomer from Japan. "Masa was early on the later VC model of driving growth even if it meant losing money in the short term," says Bill Ford, now the billionaire chairman and CEO of General Atlantic. "If we had been more cautious and incremental, Ameritrade and Schwab would have run over us."[5]

In E-Trade board meetings, Masa exuded confidence but was inclined to be preachy. "He had an audacity which was captivating. He seemed oblivious of the fact that we were the largest shareholder," said Ford. "He was like, 'I have the keys to the future.' He was very serious about changing the world."

When SoftBank sold most of its E-Trade shares four years later, Masa ended up losing $62 million. SoftBank's US operation took the loss, while the parent company's stake in the joint venture E-Trade Japan was later folded into the main part of SoftBank Group's business. All in all, E-Trade turned out to be an indifferent financial investment, but Masa wasn't bothered. He was looking at a long-term presence in the internet "ecosystem," the value of which went beyond sheer numbers.

Big on vision, Masa usually left details to underlings. One day, Mike Moritz, by now a VC veteran, invited Masa to a meeting in a warehouse in San Francisco Bay to meet the founder of Webvan, the online grocer and precursor to DoorDash and Uber Eats. Masa turned up late in a flashy limousine, wearing his usual casual jacket and sneakers. After a brief conversation with Webvan boss George Shaheen, he pledged to invest $125 million. The money arrived just before the company went public.

When Webvan's stock later tanked, Moritz, who was on the Webvan board, lost money. But Masa lost a lot more. That gave some consolation to the Welshman, who was still smarting after being bested during the Yahoo! negotiations.[6]

In full flow, Masa was hard to follow, let alone stop. He stood out in the tech community, not because he was a nerd but because he was an extrovert.[7] Reflecting upon that frantic period, Masa said his logic was: everything is cheap right now, whatever the price. Even though the market ended up overheating and crashing and burning, his initial instinct was still right. "If you look back now, everything *was* still cheap."[8]

Masa had his own ideas about value, but everything depended on how investors rated SoftBank. In Japan, it was still something of an enigma, a media-tech publishing company run by an ethnic Korean with a weird name. In the US, it was relatively unknown among institutional investors, though some retail investors[9] saw SoftBank as a cheaper alternative to US high-tech stocks and made decent money accordingly.

Everything changed on February 16, 1999, when Masa sold 1.5 percent of SoftBank's stake in Yahoo, raising $410 million. Masa needed to access cash to offset SoftBank Group's negative operating income. Investors saw only the good news: the Yahoo! shareholding was far more important than the core profitability of SoftBank's business. Yahoo! was the hottest internet stock, a byword for a world rapidly online. The Yahoo! stake could be used to raise cash or, more obviously, as collateral for obtaining loans from Japanese and international banks. In short, Yahoo! was Masa's ultimate insurance policy.

Compared to the frenetic approach to investing in the US, Masa appeared to have had a plan to make real money in the post-bubble economy in Japan. He was a breath of fresh air in a country gripped by a sense of inertia, a passive helplessness in the face of what seemed to be intractable structural problems.[10]

In the 1990s, Japan had eight prime ministers as the political system wrestled over whether to bail out the banks. Since bankers were widely held to be responsible for the collapse of the bubble and its consequences, a rescue would have amounted to political suicide. But doing nothing wasn't an answer either: it spelled political gridlock and a paralyzed financial sector, the lifeblood of the economic system.

Despite various commissions and independent studies recommending mergers, takeovers, and liquidations, all were ignored by successive governments. Some interpreted this behavior as inherent in the Japanese character: ignoring a problem in the hope it would go away, or waiting until the inevitable crisis, which then gives a rationale for acting. At the time, the prominent British economist Andrew Smithers summed up the dilemma: "Without action, crisis; without crisis, no action." In another sense, many Japanese felt that the "lost decade" was a just payment for the excesses of the bubble. This sense of penitence was reinforced by the catastrophic Kobe earthquake in 1995.

Yet the "lost decade" is a superficial trope which fails to capture the full story of Japan during this period. The 1990s were not lost, nor did the depressive consequences of the bubble bursting last only a decade (it took nearly twenty years and a global financial crisis before the banking sector was fully restructured). In truth, outside the financial sector, life went on. The doorman at the department store maintained his friendly greeting and polite bow. Even as unemployment rose, there was no sign of popular unrest. Manufacturing innovation continued, Japanese companies hugely increased their offshoring, and the long-awaited modernization of central Tokyo took off. Throughout this period, Masayoshi Son was steadily growing into his role as an agent of change.

Masa was offering something very different. SoftBank didn't make anything. It was an investment vehicle as well as a services company with the internet at its center. He sold cheap goods online, luring customers with the Yahoo! Japan brand, which served as the portal to a plethora of e-commerce sites: currency sales (Forexbank), insurance (InsWeb), an auto retailer (CarPoint Japan), a neighborhood directory company (GeoCities Japan), a mutual fund information provider (Morningstar Japan), a stock-broker (E-Trade), and a toy store (eToys Japan).

SoftBank played its familiar role of middleman, selling services to Japa-nese households which had trillions of yen in low-yielding savings accounts and were looking for places to put their money. By one estimate, Masa owned 70 percent of Japan's internet economy. "Microsoft, Intel and Cisco are all makers of digital technologies," the analyst Mahendra Negri explained. "SoftBank has always been a service firm, and, with the internet, services have become the center of the technology industry."[11]

In its insurgent role, SoftBank enjoyed tacit support from within the Japanese government. Bureaucrats remained wary of Masa's "shoot from the lip" criticisms of excessive caution and slow decision-making, but an influential minority were counting on e-commerce and business-to-business transactions to lower Japan's bloated price structure and spur a productivity surge, along the lines of the internet's impact in the US. Masa's skill was to navigate between these two worlds, the new economy and the old bureaucracy.[12]

In June 1999, Masa revealed another element in his disruption strat-egy: a joint venture with Nasdaq, the then-junior stock exchange in New York that specialized in tech companies. SoftBank planned to set up a pipeline for hot start-ups, including its own joint ventures such as Morn-ingstar Japan, E-Trade Japan, as well as SoftBank Investment Corp, which ran venture capital funds. The potential conflicts of interest were hiding in plain sight. With its majority stake in Nasdaq Japan, SoftBank was bound to give preferential treatment to allies and friends. Its gravita-tional pull raised the potential value of internet companies preparing to go public; its privileged position as a shareholder also promised to boost the actual value of its own publicly traded stock.

Masa appeared oblivious to the reputational risks. Indeed, he dou-bled down by buying stock in a major Japanese bank, with a view to launching a takeover. The financial institution in question was Nippon Credit Bank, known as "the politicians' bank" because of its connec-tions with Tokyo power brokers.[13] Along with other leading Japanese banks, NCB had made bad bets during the real estate bubble, forcing the government to take it under its wing.

Why Masa had his eyes on NCB, later rebranded Aozora, was not exactly clear. Some analysts believed it was part of a bigger plan linking internet stocks, e-trading, and Nasdaq Japan with ready-made financing; a form of horizontal integration aimed at making SoftBank the dominant IPO player.[14] Others believed Masa was simply following fashion. As Japan's financial crisis began to ease, outsiders, particularly American private equity firms, were looking to make a fast buck. They figured that the Japanese government had taken on most of the bad loans, and there was plenty of scope for a turnaround which would end with a handsome payday. Masa came tagging along behind.

One day, Thierry Porte, a Morgan Stanley banker handling the Aozora sale, spotted Masa in the five-star Hotel Okura in Tokyo. SoftBank's boss shouted: "I want to buy your bank." The tin-eared bravura prompted Porte to warn him it wasn't a great idea to be yelling market-sensitive information in a hotel lobby.

Masa's banking plan triggered strong opposition at the top of SoftBank. Kitao complained that Masa's plan was riddled with conflicts of interest. All SoftBank's affiliated start-ups would list on Nasdaq Japan, while the SoftBank-affiliated Aozora would no doubt finance these companies before and after they went public. The reputational risk was serious, Kitao warned. "The public might suspect group companies being involved in manipulation with one another. As an investment, you may make money, but what you want to do is a digital information revolution. Don't lose focus by getting involved in all sorts of things."[15]

Kitao was "a motherfucker, tough as nails," in the words of Jordan Levy, the gritty New Yorker who was part of SoftBank's team in the US. But Masa still felt powerful enough to ignore him. Tensions rose as Kitao, already driven mad by the flood of US internet investments, told his boss that valuations had reached "insane" levels. It was time to sell.

Masa refused to budge: "Kita-yan," he admonished, "you are selling too soon." This was a constant refrain from the SoftBank boss, whose instincts as an investor were far superior to his skills as a trader.

In June 1999, Lehman Brothers raised its twelve-month target price for SoftBank to a gravity-defying ¥400,000 ($4,000), 2.7 times its current value. This would have made Japan's media-tech conglomerate one of the most valuable companies in the world. All told, Masa had invested $1.7 billion in more than one hundred internet companies. Out of that total, SoftBank had sunk $906 million into eight companies that had gone public, an investment worth $14.1 billion at the time. Yahoo! at its peak was worth $125 billion. Stocks like Cisco and Qualcomm were star performers because they formed the backbone of the internet. E-trade and WebFirst also proved durable bets. But others like Kozmo.com, More.com, Shopping.com, SportsBrain, and Webvan were like comets in the night sky.

During this frenetic period, old friends and business partners like Jordan Levy detected a change in Masa's behavior. He mixed with the likes of Bill Gates, GE's Jack Welch, and Oracle's Larry Ellison on the golf links and was no longer available for a slap-up dinner. "He had outgrown us," Levy recalled.[16]

That same month, June 1999, shareholders voted to make SoftBank a pure holding company, turning the parent company into a giant internet investment fund. SoftBank was now at the center of a web of related companies, enjoying far more flexibility to raise capital and shuffle assets. Meanwhile, investors could gain exposure to many SoftBank affiliates with the purchase of one stock. SoftBank was cheap to buy relative to the paper value of its portfolio, while its exposure to Yahoo! and other US tech stocks on a tear offered excellent returns during the dot-com bubble.

The precise moment when everyone including Masa lost their heads in the bubble economy is open to question. Some place the date around mid-1999, when Masa started hanging out at the Fairmont Hotel in San Jose, renting a penthouse suite with a long carpet and a fish tank full of koi.

For Jordan Levy, the moment of maximum madness came in November 1999, when SoftBank created a new $1.2 billion venture fund called SoftBank Capital Partners. This was a solo fund, without the cushion of outsider funding. The business was in Mountain View, California, with four hundred thousand square feet of office space. Levy, Masa, Rieschel, Fisher, and others put in their own money, alongside SoftBank itself.

Over the next twelve months, more than 90 percent of the $1.2 billion was invested—at the peak of the market. At the end of 1999, the question was not whether the bubble would burst, but when. Masa seemed unfazed. When asked how well he slept at night, he replied simply: "I sleep very well." Later, in a conversation with Ron Fisher, he elaborated on his investing philosophy: "There are things you can control and things you cannot."

Levy, Rieschel, and others marveled at Masa's limitless attitude to risk. Their stomachs churned as stocks shot higher and the sums of money at risk grew ever greater. Masa saw things differently. If you are born in a slum with nothing, losing everything is relative. You just go back to square one. Then, like the Korean slum dwellers in Tosu, you build back up.

14
....

THE CRASH

The meeting that changed Masa's life took place at the wedding cake–styled Fuhua Mansion building in Beijing at 4:30 p.m. on October 31, 1999. It lasted barely six minutes.[1]

Jack Ma was among several Chinese entrepreneurs invited to a series of "speed-dating" sessions arranged by SoftBank's new venture capital fund in China. An elfin figure, several inches smaller than Masa, Ma stood out because he spoke the best English, having worked as a teacher and tour guide. He described his business as an electronic Yellow Pages matching buyers and sellers. Its name was Alibaba.

It was an odd choice for a Chinese company, but Ma liked the allusion to the *Arabian Nights*, where a simple woodcutter speaks the words "Open Sesame" and a cave opens to reveal a glittering fortune. Back in the real world, Alibaba's online business was barely six months old. The company's only revenues were a few meager sponsorship deals on a clunky website, but it was pulling in more than a thousand new registered users a day, an explosive rate of growth in a mass market.

Masa understood the commercial opportunity immediately. He was also drawn to the hungry look in Ma's eye, the "animal smell" of a fellow underdog. He offered Alibaba's founder $40 million on the spot, in return for 49 percent of the equity. Ma turned down the opening bid, but said he would consider $20 million: "Alibaba is just a baby, and a baby does not need this amount of cash."[2]

It took guts—or epic foolishness—to turn down Masayoshi Son. By 1999, he was a minor celebrity in China, admired by an emerging class of private sector entrepreneurs aware of his early investment in Yahoo!

and the success of Yahoo! Japan. Because of his position on the Cisco board, he knew that router sales had begun to take off. Internet usage was about to explode. With tens of millions of prospective customers desperate for a digital connection, Masa was on the hunt for an online presence in mainland China.[3]

Chauncey Shey, the bespectacled US-educated president of SoftBank China Venture Capital, was not convinced by Ma. Nor were other partners, including Masa's old Berkeley chum Hong Lu. Alibaba's founder had turned up thinking SoftBank was pitching to him and not vice versa, and he appeared unprepared. He couldn't even say when his business would become profitable—not that Masa was worried. In his eyes, growth was all that mattered.

Masa ended up overruling all his colleagues. He dismissed objections that Ma was no engineer, no great product guy, just a young man with a vision. That last objection was the one he found most irritating. Masa saw something of himself in Jack Ma, with his unbridled ambition. Masa was set on forging an enduring partnership, one which would make him the richest man in Japan and Ma one of the wealthiest in the world.

A few weeks after the Beijing encounter, Jack Ma contacted his partner Joe Tsai, a Taiwanese-born investor and Yale Law School graduate who was his right-hand man. "You have got to go to Tokyo because this guy called Masa wants to put a lot of money into us." Tsai retorted that Alibaba had $5 million from Goldman Sachs and did not need any more money. Ma stared at him and said: "If it's Masa, you gotta make the trip."[4]

Ma and Tsai arrived at SoftBank headquarters and were ushered into the boardroom with a long table, where Masa sat with around ten of his top team alongside. Only the boss spoke, and this time he was curt. His initial offer stood: $40 million for 49 percent of the company. The two Alibaba executives looked at each other in disbelief. This was eight times the Goldman money, for almost half the company. Alibaba would have, in effect, a controlling shareholder who was not even the founder.

"That's not going to happen," said Tsai, breaching protocol. He proceeded to spin a tale about having a "board" which would not accept SoftBank's terms. Masa pulled out a giant pocket calculator and came up with a revised offer: $20 million for 40 percent of the company. No, came the reply. The Japanese came back again. And again. And again.

Eventually, the two sides settled on a deal: $20 million for a 30 percent equity stake, valuing a business with minimal revenues and no profits at more than $60 million. It was an inspired bet that Alibaba would be the first Chinese internet company to become a global brand. Despite the fact that Masa was still a relative newcomer to the Chinese market, Alibaba turned out to be the most important investment in his entire career.

At the end of the twentieth century, China was the last frontier in the global economy, a vast market of more than one billion consumers but still weighed down by the dead hand of bureaucracy. The Communist Party was nevertheless keenly aware of the need for change. It was time to stir the country's animal spirits, long suppressed during Chairman Mao's reign of terror. In early 1992, Deng Xiaoping, paramount leader, embarked on his southern tour, promoting economic development and reform at the expense of ideology. "It doesn't matter if the cat is black or white," Deng famously said, "as long as it catches mice."

In those days, there was no internet access in China. People had to register their fax machines with the local government. Foreign residents routinely had their mail opened before delivery. Anyone picking up a copy of *The Economist* in Beijing saw controversial articles—say about the Falun Gong cult or maps of the India-China border in the Himalayas— cut out by censors using scissors.[5]

"The system was so rigid," Masa remembered. "To sneak through the back door and start your own business behind the backs of state-owned enterprises was almost criminal."

SoftBank's boss made his first visit to China in 1995. He could feel the energy, but the country was unmistakably backward. "They weren't dumb people, they were smart people. They were just struggling because they didn't have the tools," he recalled.[6] "But once you gave them civilization, the potential was huge because of the population. And they were eager for change."[7]

Fortunately, Masa had Hong Lu available to navigate the system. By now Lu had sold their original video software business in California and used the cash in 1991 to set up a telecoms equipment manufacturer in China. Unitech Telecom was based in Hangzhou, on China's east coast.[8] Unitech Telecom was largely a hardware play. Soon it merged with Starcom Networks, a profitable local software company. The new company, UTStarcom, specialized in "the last mile solution"—the technical term for relieving speed bottlenecks in communications networks caused by limited bandwidth. With its antiquated telecoms system, China badly lagged behind the West. But high-speed broadband would soon transform the consumer experience, and UTStarcom was determined to be there at the start.

In those early days of the internet, Chinese entrepreneurs assumed foreigners knew best when it came to management and technology. Westerners, usually Americans, were paid multiples of the local Chinese workforce. After the dot-com bubble burst, the tables turned. Chinese business leaders like Jack Ma recognized that foreigners did not have a monopoly on wisdom. In fact, the Chinese knew their domestic market better than anyone, as they never ceased to remind Western visitors in later years.

After Masa's first visit, Lu urged his old friend to invest in UTStarcom and in China more generally. "See, what did I tell you? You can't formulate a proper corporate strategy for the twenty-first century without considering China," Lu said. "If you don't invest, our company will be bigger than yours."

"Wow," replied Masa, "you still talk very big."[9]

Hong Lu proposed that Masa make a $30 million investment in return for a 30 percent stake in the new UTStarcom. At the time, the company was barely making $10 million in revenue. Masa didn't even blink at the 10x valuation. "He never negotiated on the terms," says Lu. "He just said okay."[10]

Masa was making a calculated bet on China's future, confident in the belief that the internet was coming and tens of millions of consumers would soon be flocking online. Where fainter hearts sensed danger in the Wild West telecoms market in China, Masa spotted long-term opportunity. He wasn't bothered about valuations, recognizing that these could change in the blink of an eye. Nevertheless, he wasn't a soft touch. When UTStarcom recorded a loss in 1999 and delayed plans to go public by a year, Masa, who'd been counting on a big payday, exploded.

"You are too nice a guy, Hong Lu," he chided his old friend. Lu countered that Masa had lost even more money on his ill-advised investment in Kingston Technologies. The two partners then had a good laugh. In those days, Masa didn't always take himself too seriously.

A quarter of a century later, Lu described Masa as always overconfident, too reliant on instinct rather than input from his team. He also came across as curiously detached, acting like an alien who'd landed on earth with sackfuls of cash and a plan to take over the world. "He is like out of space. He does not think the way normal people think," said Lu. "In those days, he would start meetings after midnight. People were suffering and he thought it was okay."[11]

Masa told everyone he could "smell the money" in China. He put together a "three-hundred-year Vision" for SoftBank, laid out on a five-meterlong "scroll" composed of A4 sheets stuck together. The scroll contained investment targets for SoftBank's expansion into China, a master plan which Masa would study lovingly every day.[12]

The pursuit of longevity or immortality enjoys a distinguished tradition in both China and Japan. Confucian, Daoist, and Taoist thought emphasize the ideal of personal harmony through the fusion of body and spirit to achieve selflessness and virtue. From an early age, Masa liked to cloak his hard-driving, high-risk approach to business in a broader vision centered on the pursuit of human happiness through the application of technology. Around this time, he began writing and rethinking SoftBank's business plan according to where technology was heading. "I'm probably on version one thousand of my vision or something," he said in October 2023. "Even today."[13]

Yet there was a paradox about Masa's character. Alongside the can-do Californian spirit and the Confucian vision were defects in emotional intelligence which Lu had noticed at Berkeley and which continued to let him down. One day, Chauncey Shey organized a dinner with the Chinese premier Zhu Rongji, the second-most-powerful man in China. A modernizer who negotiated the terms of China's entry into the World Trade Organization, Zhu had set up a technology advisory group to help him better understand the implications of the internet revolution.

Masa turned up late, leaving Zhu seething. When Masa finally arrived, Zhu just watched him, saying nothing but leaving the rest of the dinner table in no doubt that this was a personal insult. It would not be forgotten lightly.

"Masa made an assumption about China as a [easy] market and he was wrong," says Gary Rieschel. "The Chinese leadership were totally different characters than the Americans. He [later] found it much harder to negotiate deals."[14]

In February 2000, when Alibaba and SoftBank closed their deal, Jack Ma's start-up held $25 million in the bank. SoftBank owned around 30 percent of the equity. Alibaba's value rose to a peak of $210 billion in late 2020 as it became the dominant player in e-commerce in China, delivering an astronomical return for SoftBank. Yet Alibaba was both a financial blessing and a psychological curse. Masa spent the next twenty years in search of another Alibaba, desperate to prove to the rest of the world—and perhaps himself—that his investment was no fluke.

In the last week of January, after his star appearance at the annual World Economic Forum in Davos, Masa's net worth was going up by $6 billion a week. Doubts about the sustainability of SoftBank's growth were lost in dot-com euphoria. At the Velfarre disco event mentioned in the prologue, Masa revealed that he had chartered a plane from Davos at a cost of $280,000 (¥30 million), triggering wild applause. In addition to the Nasdaq Japan venture, he announced a $1.5 billion SoftBank Internet Technology Fund, describing it as the largest ever in Japan.

Over in California, Rieschel and his team raised $1 billion from institutional shareholders for yet another new US venture fund, with SoftBank pledging a further $2 billion. But when Masa arrived at the Fairmont hotel in San Jose, he was the bearer of bad news.

"I don't have the money," he said disarmingly.

Rieschel was taken aback. Having talked big numbers and closed a deal with top US financial institutions, his team was staring at humiliation. Over a frenetic weekend, they agreed with Masa to scale back the fund to a still ambitious $1.8 billion. "We fixed it," recalls Rieschel, "but I asked myself, 'What is going on?'"[15]

The answer was that the traditional five- to seven-year venture capital cycle was over. In the beginning, everyone, including Masa, had been buying, and the valuations had kept rising through each round of funding. But at the end of the cycle, when the stock market bubble burst, investors like Masa were holding overvalued assets which could not be IPO'd at acceptable prices. So VC investors like Masa were left without investment returns and with mounting debt. This is precisely what happened in March 2000.

At first, it wasn't entirely clear how bad the sell-off would be. A downward leg was followed by a mild recovery followed by another jagged slide. The slump was creating a snowball effect, where investors lost confidence in high-tech stocks in general and in SoftBank's entire internet portfolio, including its star performer Yahoo! Japan.

On the evening of March 24, Masa proposed issuing ¥300 billion ($3 billion) worth of shares at market value to shore up SoftBank's balance sheet and secure its investment plans. The share placement was one of the biggest ever in Japan. Masa was gambling that through sheer force of will, he could shift investor sentiment.

A fierce debate took place inside the SoftBank board. Mindful that SoftBank stock might fall further, Masa argued this was the right moment to recapitalize the business. Other board directors, led by Kitao, said it was too risky. Who knew when the bottom of the market might come? A motion supporting a share sale was put to a vote, only to be rejected. It was a rare rebuke of Masa's authority, the most serious in his career to date.

More than twenty years later, Masa remained philosophical about the dot-com crash. Markets recovered, just as they recovered after the tech correction in 2022–23. "In the short term, they [the board] were more right. In the long term, I was more right. But the company always has limited amounts of cash, so I had to listen. I had to compromise."

SoftBank instead turned to asset sales to raise cash. On March 29, it sold ¥28.5 billion ($285 million) of SoftBank Technology shares. This was followed by a 3–1 share split—a move designed to appeal to Japanese retail investors by lowering the price per share. Overall, however, the sums matched debt maturing only within the coming twelve months. The money fell way short of Masa's expectations.

The point of no return arrived in the week ending—appositely—on Friday, April 13, when the Nasdaq composite index finished 25 percent down from the high reached just over a month before. "The biggest bull market in Nasdaq history has given way to the fastest bear market ever," wrote Floyd Norris on the front page of The New York Times.

SoftBank's stock was falling further and faster than most. By the middle of April 2000, its share price had tumbled by more than half, to ¥94,000. Press sentiment in Japan, never entirely convinced by SoftBank's growth story, turned sharply against Masa. The Asahi Weekly magazine published an article on May 5, 2000, about the stock market crash titled: "Collapse of the Dotcom Bubble, Looming Crisis for the Son Empire."[16] A few days later, the *Asahi Shimbun* newspaper wrote about a "Hunt for the Class A War Criminal"—a lurid comparison between Masa's activities and the atrocities of the Imperial Army during the Second World War.[17]

SoftBank, the *Asahi* critics said, was gunning for the highest-possible market valuation by investing in companies and taking them public with booming valuations. By implication, Masa was responsible for the bubble and the stock market crash. SoftBank had no "real" businesses. It did not make things like cars or consumer electronics. In the eyes of critics, it was a pumped-up fraud.

On May 27, 2000, the worst fears were confirmed when SoftBank reported losses before taking into account asset sales of ¥51 billion ($500 million) for the year ending March 2000. This "ordinary income" was the metric most closely watched by the market because it gave the most accurate reflection of how SoftBank's actual business was performing.

As SoftBank shares continued to sink, Masa desperately tried to shore up working capital. With Kitao increasingly disaffected, he hired Kazuhiko Kasai, an experienced, low-key executive and former vice president of Fuji Bank, to bolster the finance team. In October, "Kaz" negotiated credit lines totaling $1.5 billion with ten Japanese financial institutions, giving SoftBank breathing room.

In the US, one of the first casualties of the crash was SoftBank's latest venture fund. Gary Rieschel had his own money in the venture fund, and he held SoftBank stock. He lost a sum "in the nine figures" (at least $100 million), a figure still too painful to discuss more than twenty years later. Pressed for a more precise figure, the most he was willing to reveal was, "three numbers disappeared."

On December 27, Masa gave an interview to the hostile *Asahi Shimbun*, in a bid to reassure investors. "This is a period of transition that any growing industry experiences. But in the long term, the price of internet stocks will rise again. Everyone recognizes the growth potential of the internet but stock prices do not reflect this." He added: "We have just stumbled. We may have to reflect, but precisely right now on the dip, this is the second chance to buy."[17]

That was a stretch, even for optimists like Masa. SoftBank shares continued to fall, bottoming out at ¥2,980 on January 11, 2001. At that point, SoftBank was worth less than ¥1 trillion ($10 billion)—less than one-twentieth of its value eleven months earlier. Masa's own paper worth was around $3.2 billion, making him one of history's biggest ever losers.

He'd lost more than a vast chunk of his personal fortune. His reputation was shot. The man of the future looked like a man whose time had come and gone.

PART 3

THE OPERATOR

15

BROADBAND REVOLUTION

A t the turn of the millennium, Japan was a country in search of a savior. The banking crisis remained unresolved, the post-bubble economy stuck in a period of prolonged deflation. A succession of corruption scandals involving corporate Japan and members of the ruling conservative Liberal Democratic Party (LDP) contributed to a pervasive sense of gloom.

Amid political stasis, the public mood began to shift. The crisis demanded a new face and a fresh approach. The man who stepped forward was unlike anything the country had ever seen, a fiftysomething LDP politician with wavy gray hair and telegenic looks whose nickname was "Lionheart." Junichiro Koizumi was far removed from the anonymous men in dark suits who came and went as LDP leaders during the 1990s. He was a neoliberal who promised to purge "the forces of resistance" within the party. His campaign centerpiece was a plan to privatize Japan Post, then theoretically the most valuable company in the world, thanks to its role as a safe box for Japanese household savings and life insurance premiums.

Like Masa, Koizumi was a maverick. But whereas Masa was an ethnic Korean and an outsider, Koizumi, for all his revolutionary talk, was a blue-blooded insider who believed in incremental change. His father was LDP royalty, and his first wedding was attended by 2,400 people and featured a giant wedding cake in the shape of the Japanese Diet building. Where Koizumi and Masa found common ground was in their determination to shake Japan out of its torpor and restore economic vitality through competition. From 2001, Koizumi went on to serve five years in office as Japanese prime minister, enjoying record popularity in his first year and a thumping reelection.

It was perhaps no accident that Koizumi's arrival on the political scene coincided with Masa's reinvention as a convention-busting entrepreneur. After his spectacular losses in the dot-com crash, Masa remained sanguine. In one sense, nothing had changed. His worldview, centered on the information technology revolution as the driving force in society, remained constant. He just needed to pursue a new project that would validate that worldview, assuming—and it was a big assumption—he could find the money.

In the early weeks of 2001, Masa went missing. Nobody at the head office saw the boss; appointments were canceled, clients told to come back another time. Only a handful of SoftBank executives knew Masa was about to bet the company on a plan to bring high-speed internet access to Japan, the most ambitious venture to date in SoftBank's two-decade history.

Masa's vanishing act coincided with a change in Japan's telecoms regulations ("The IT Basic Law") providing for more competition in the domestic market. But operating a broadband business, and later a mobile phone network, meant declaring war on the dominant national telecoms carrier and former state monopoly (NTT). It required huge up-front investment, with $1 billion annual losses projected over several years. Yet SoftBank was virtually broke, its share price had fallen by 98 percent, and its market capitalization had shrunk from $200 billion to $2 billion. When people told him he was crazy taking on NTT, one of the biggest and most valuable companies in the world, he had a typically cheeky riposte.[1]

"Well, that makes me excited. If I fight with the small guy I feel it's an unfair fight, but if I pick a guy who is the toughest, the biggest, then I can be serious. It's a fair fight. People looked at me and were lost for words. 'You are truly crazy.'"

Masa never entertained failure. He'd outlined his plans for broadband two years earlier at a cocktail reception at the British embassy, where he met Sir Peter Bonfield, then chief executive of BT. Masa said he intended to force NTT to sell internet access wholesale to SoftBank, whereupon he would cut retail prices for the consumer by 50 percent. Bonfield knew Japan well, having previously worked for Fujitsu, the electronics giant. He thought Masa's game plan was a recipe for losing money.

Two decades later, Bonfield admitted he missed the larger point: Masa had grasped the new economics of the digital revolution far earlier than rivals. By now Masa's mantra was familiar: customers and market share mattered more than cash flow and profitability. "The value was dollars per customer," Bonfield said. "He was right, and we were wrong. And he did the same thing with mobile a few years later."[2]

Masa looked beyond Japan's economic stagnation to grasp that there was a huge opportunity as the country adopted 3G technology mobile phones ahead of the rest of the world. By 2000, millions of Japanese were using their handsets to communicate by email and text message. The difficulty was that SoftBank was short of cash, and Masa was a laughing-stock after the dot-com debacle.

At the height of the internet boom, SoftBank and its various corporate entities at one time controlled or had stakes in more than 350 individual companies. Its online empire included selling books, food delivery, medical advice, used cars, every service imaginable. But all the websites in the world were worth nothing without "connectivity." Masa needed enough customers willing and able to pay for the goods and services available online, and this meant having access to the internet. SoftBank's move into broadband was therefore not so much a giant leap of faith, it was a rational business decision and an economic imperative.

There were many challenges for SoftBank's broadband revolution, starting with the fact that Japanese consumers were relative newcomers to spending time on the internet. Unlike Americans, who operated an "always on" approach with a fixed monthly price for internet access, Japan operated a dial-up, pay-as-you-go system with a large telephone bill at the end of the month. The whole business was a quaint anachronism, a recipe for suppressing demand. To succeed, Masa had to create a *new* market with a new brand. He chose Yahoo! BB, building on his highly profitable Yahoo! Japan.

Financing a new broadband network required a fire sale of SoftBank assets, including the prized Ziff computer publishing empire bought just five years earlier, a sale of its stake in UTStarcom, the China internet venture, the disposal of the holding in Aozora Bank, as well as selling down more of his stake in Yahoo! in the US—a task assigned to Ron Fisher.

The disposal of assets was necessary but not sufficient to raise cash. Masa needed continued access to the financial markets. In the run-up to the dot-com bust, SoftBank had pulled off a remarkable balancing act. Billions of yen were raised through corporate bonds and billions of yen spent on internet-related acquisitions, without scaring off investors or the main Japanese banks. But after the dot-com crash, SoftBank was hemorrhaging cash, and its credit rating was slipping. Maintaining market confidence was a precondition for Yahoo! BB's success; it was also a matter of corporate life and death for SoftBank itself.

Thomas Edison once declared that vision without execution is hallucination. Masa's dream was a mass market of Japanese consumers plugged seamlessly into high-speed internet, each paying monthly bills for Yahoo! BB and SoftBank's plethora of online services. Execution was another matter. Masa needed Japanese engineers and managers to turn his dream into commercial reality.

SoftBank had to deal with NTT, which controlled Japan's telecoms infrastructure: the telegraph poles, base stations, the conduit or "colocation" services. Alongside Japan Railways and Japan Tobacco, NTT embodied Japan Inc. Privatized in 1985, the behemoth still enjoyed close ties with its former overlords in the ministries. Its executive ranks were packed with graduates from the elite universities of Tokyo, Keio, and Waseda. Aloof, risk-averse, and wedded to hierarchy, they inhabited an utterly different world from Masa, the college graduate from California with the oddball Korean-Japanese name.

Masa wanted Yahoo! BB to be cheaper, faster, and more effective in delivering data and images than rivals. At this stage, however, he was plainly not on top of the technical detail. On several occasions, work had to stop so he could be "educated" by his own software engineers. Masa found a kindred spirit in his new technology officer, a proverbial "mad scientist" by the name of Takashi Tsutsui. Originally a medical doctor and later a university lecturer, Tsutsui's obsession with computers went back to his childhood in Osaka. He joined SoftBank in 2000, a mercurial character whose impatience rivaled Masa's. In Masa's eyes, that made him the ideal man for the job. When SoftBank's engineers protested that the geeky new recruit was a misfit, Masa scolded them for failing to think big enough. Tsutsui was a "genius," he declared, "a legend in software development circles." If the engineers and coders had a problem, they should clear their desks. A number did.[3]

Back in 1999, Masa tried to circumvent NTT's dominant position by using a fiber-optic network controlled by Tepco, the electricity and power company. This took the form of a joint venture with Microsoft called Speed-Net. But the technology did not work, and the business model was suspect.[4] Two years later, Masa settled for ADSL (asymmetric digital subscriber line). On the plus side, ADSL used existing telephone networks, and it was cheaper. SoftBank soon augmented its ADSL expertise by purchasing a pioneering telecoms start-up, Tokyo Metallic, which had run out of money. The problem with ADSL was twofold: it relied on NTT to provide access to the local network, and it was slower than fiber-optic broadband, the next big thing in telecoms. In sum, ADSL risked being viewed as an interim solution, not the industrial standard.

From his perch at Morgan Stanley in New York, Masa's financial adviser Jeff Sine politely pointed out these flaws to his Japanese client. Masa exploded.

"You have lost your passion," he told Sine.

"I never had the passion," Sine replied, "and you can't lose something you never had."[5]

On June 19, 2001, SoftBank unveiled one of the most disruptive moves in the history of corporate Japan, announcing that Yahoo! broadband's access would be at least half the price of its rivals. This was the so-called Yahoo! price shock. As a gambit, it too was straight out of Rupert Murdoch's playbook: a bold price cut aimed at pursuing market share regardless of losing money.

"We didn't approve of the move," says Dr. Sachio Semmoto, then chief executive of broadband start-up rival E-Access, whose business model relied on existing market prices, "but thanks to Son, the market expanded three or four times."[6]

Masa set a target of one million new Yahoo! BB subscribers by the end of the year. The cost of acquisition was roughly around $300 a month, taking into account SoftBank's later offer of free modems and free usage for two months. In a repeat of his satellite TV sales tactics, he instructed attractive young salesmen and -women, known as the Parasol Units, to mount pop-up stalls outside railway stations promoting the offer. The gimmick paid off, with one drawback.

Masa's aggressive broadband promotion triggered a surge in demand that SoftBank struggled to meet. Yahoo! BB customers complained that they had no internet connection. Many canceled. Masa accused NTT of sabotage and lodged a formal complaint at the Ministry of Communications, on the grounds that the operator was deliberately delaying hooking up half a million SoftBank customers to its own network in the Tokyo metropolitan area.[7]

Masa fulminated, by telephone and in person. Nothing happened, but nothing much did happen inside the labyrinthine Japanese bureaucracy when it came to dealing with complaints. Officials were usually hand in glove with their opposite numbers at NTT. Many hoped to find a comfortable perch as an adviser or consultant to the telecoms giant once they retired from the ministry. They didn't care much for this troublesome outsider, of whom they knew little. Finally, Masa declared he'd had enough.

Without warning, SoftBank's boss turned up in front of the same staid bureaucrat he'd been talking to and asked for a lighter. When asked why, he replied that he intended to close down Yahoo! BB, come back to the ministry building, douse it in kerosene, and burn it to the ground.

"Our customers can't wait anymore. As a businessman, I would rather die than tell them to fill in any more forms and send them for approval at NTT's broadband department. If things carry on like this, my business is over."[8]

The trembling bureaucrat promised to look into the matter. Sure enough, a few days later Masa received a call from the ministry explaining there had been a misunderstanding and that NTT East's dark (unused) fiber was available. Over the years, Masa's "suicide mission" grew more florid in the retelling. Americans loved the image of the mad little Japanese guy threatening to torch the establishment. One Wall Street boss said Masa's story left an indelible mark: it was so at odds with the Japanese he had come to know but never really understood.

Word soon spread in Japan about Masa's act of defiance in the face of an indifferent or obstructive state. Some likened Masa to the *dokegata* (clown or trickster) in medieval Kabuki theater who cheers up the local populace with unexpected acts, stories, and comic turns. In modern terminology, the word "jester" has been devalued, but in an earlier age, the jester, as in *King Lear*'s fool, enjoyed license to do and say what the court or the establishment could not or would not say. To a degree, this explains why Masa, the quintessential outsider, was tolerated in Japan, both by the government and the powers that be in business.

"The trickster is not a negative character in Japan," explained Takashi Nawa, a longtime McKinsey executive and student of Japanese business culture. "His bold, counterintuitive actions can reveal the hidden essence of ourselves."[9]

During the broadband war, Masa was working eighteen-hour days, seven days a week, to appease the hundreds, if not thousands, of customers still waiting for their broadband connection. He traveled up, down, and across the Japanese archipelago, asking no less of his SoftBank colleagues. Yasuyuki Imai, current director and chairman of SoftBank's mobile phone business in Japan, was in charge of speeding up construction of the broadband network. Masa, often dressed casually in his favorite Argyle sweater, visited him every day at 2 a.m. for an update, setting out what he expected to be completed by the morning. For the next eighteen months, Imai came to work each Monday with enough clothes to last a week and went home only on Sundays.

SoftBank's problem was that cash flow was continuing to deteriorate as a result of the tens of millions invested in broadband, even as net profits rose after asset sales in Japan and in the US. There, Ron Fisher worked long into the night plotting disposals, which included a dribble of Yahoo! shares, a stake in E-Trade, and a (still) valuable stake in Cisco Systems. The last was a case study in creativity.

When John Chambers, Cisco's boss, balked at floating Cisco Systems Japan, Masa used his leverage as a major shareholder to extract a high price for being bought out. First he persuaded Chambers to acquire about 1 percent of SoftBank stock for $100 million; then he encouraged Cisco to coinvest in a $1.05 billion venture fund to invest in internet businesses in the Asia-Pacific region, to be managed by SoftBank. He extracted a further $275 million for Cisco buying back SoftBank's share of Cisco Systems Japan. By the end, Chambers was left wondering whether he had anything left in his wallet.

When these cash-raising exercises failed to reassure the market, Masa said critics simply did not understand his company. "People say SoftBank does not have adequate cash flow. But we question the idea that you only make cash flow by selling products," he told analysts. "Selling products and listing companies both produce cash flow. We have superb cash flow."

Masa later described this period as the toughest battle of his life. He likened his struggle with NTT to the "warring states" period in fifteenth- and sixteenth-century Japan. SoftBank was like the Choshu, Satsuma, and Tosa clans, which were not particularly strong, were short of money, and enjoyed scant support among vested interests. Yet the force was with SoftBank, just as it was with the clans. "What we did have was state-of-the-art," he said, "meaning we were taking on swords and armor with guns."[10]

Japan's business community watched the broadband war unfold with awe and ambivalence. They admired Masa's boldness in taking on the closed telecoms market, but they suspected that he might himself have contributed to speculative excess. A popular Japanese book at the time, *Net Bubble*,[11] argued that SoftBank had artificially inflated internet stocks, first with speculative investments and later dressing up companies for flotation on Nasdaq Japan, which had proved a multimillion-dollar flop.

Masa turned to a new board member, Tadashi Yanai, boss of Fast Retailing (Uniqlo), for support. Yanai understood consumer psychology and how to build a nationwide brand with razor-thin margins. These were the skills Masa needed to succeed with his high-risk broadband venture. Yanai first contacted Masa in 1994 after reading *Accidental Empires*, Robert X. Cringely's book on Silicon Valley and the rise of the personal computer revolution. Seven years senior to Masa, he knew little about computers, but he sensed that the future was digital. One day, he invited the SoftBank boss to appear in a Uniqlo advertisement for his new clothes range. When Masa declined, Yanai arranged a meeting in person.[12]

The two men became the friendliest of rivals. Both were golf fanatics; both were two of Japan's "three big mouths"; both later vied over who was the richest man in Japan.[13] Yanai liked to label himself Masa's Big Brother, mainly because his company went public one week before SoftBank. Fast Retailing's stock code number was registered 9983, one digit ahead of SoftBank, which registered 9984, a fact that Yanai never failed to mention to interviewers.

Yanai joined the SoftBank board because he thought that if a prominent self-made man like Masa was seen to fail, the whole start-up culture in Japan would go down with him. He saw himself as the grown-up in the room. He became increasingly skeptical and vocal about the management of SoftBank during his eighteen years on the board. Masa's impulsive and erratic behavior irritated him. On one occasion, the Uniqlo boss reprimanded Masa for dressing up in an Elvis Presley costume, which he considered inappropriate behavior for a top CEO in Japan. "Son always wants to be center stage," he reflected. "It's like he wants to be in a Hollywood movie which always has a happy ending."[14]

In October 2001, SoftBank reported a loss of $550 million in its consolidated interim report, ratcheting up pressure to reduce the $4 billion of interest-bearing debt on its books. In response, SoftBank sold more Yahoo! shares, together with E-Trade and CNET, two of its more successful US internet investments. More bad news came when an analyst questioned whether E-Trade Japan was truly an online broker—only 15 percent of its business was done via the internet, the rest through call centers. There was less to SoftBank's digital image than met the eye, it appeared. In November, the ratings agency R&I downgraded SoftBank bonds.

The pressure was unrelenting, but Masa never flinched in his bid to reach one million broadband customers by the end of the year. When colleagues raised doubts, he simply called for patience. On the eve of Christmas, the market finally caught up with him. Jerry Yang, Yahoo! cofounder, remembers his CEO Terry Semel walking into his office in Mountain View, California. "I have bad news, Masa has to sell his [SoftBank's] stake in Yahoo! because of a margin call."

A margin call meant that Masa would have to deposit further cash or securities to cover unrealized losses on stock he had provided as collateral for a loan from a bank or broker. Regarding the disposal of the Yahoo! stake, SoftBank today insists there was "no financing that would have required a margin call on SoftBank Group itself," adding that Masa himself did not own Yahoo! stock. The sale was merely a fundraising exercise. In this case, however, the funds required amounted to several hundred million dollars—on short notice. "He was in distress," Jerry Yang maintains. "He had to dump his Yahoo! stake."[15]

The sale of a 3 percent equity stake was material, enough to scare other Yahoo! investors fearful that dumping so much stock would further depress the share price. Seeking a friendly buyer, Yang turned to Edward Whitacre, chairman of SBC, formerly BellSouth and the forerunner of the reconstituted AT&T, then based in San Antonio, Texas. SBC subsequently bought seventeen million Yahoo! shares from SoftBank America Inc. for $300 million, reducing SoftBank's stake in Yahoo! US from 20 to 17 percent. "It was a fire sale," says Yang.[16]

Slowly, the smoke cleared. Within a year of its broadband launch, Soft-Bank had spent close to $870 million building out its giant gigabit Ethernet "backbone" network that linked up Japan, while leasing copper wire from NTT to connect up the last mile to individual homes. Yahoo! BB provided internet access to Japanese residential customers at twelve megabits per second—eight times faster than Americans were used to—for about $21 a month. Every day, as many as seven thousand new subscribers fired up their plug-and-play DSL modems. From modest, unpromising origins, cut-price Yahoo! BB was the world's fastest-growing broadband service.[17]

Apart from its superfast internet access, Yahoo! BB offered a new voice-over-IP feature that used the internet for telephone calls, rather than traditional transmission technology. Calls from Tokyo to New York were less than three cents a minute, an impressive reduction in the sky-high costs previously levied by NTT. In the near future, Masa promised, VoIP calls would be virtually free, a mortal threat to NTT's fixed-line business. Yahoo! BB's next step would be video-on-demand services pumping TV and Hollywood movies into every Japanese living room, said Masa. All these fancy promises depended, of course, on the studio moguls playing along, a fact that he conveniently glossed over.

A profile in *Wired* magazine, titled "Fat Pipe Dream," summed up the skepticism about Masa's "crazy" gamble on broadband. "To Son, crazy is a slightly warped outlook that sparks innovation. Of course, there's the other kind of crazy—as in Napoleon assuming the Russian winter wouldn't be so cold. Give Son's dealmaking record a scan, and he starts to look more like he's marching into Moscow in mid-September."[18]

Masa, however, was betting on first-mover advantage. "In this industry, the first mover, the pioneer, very often gets a big success," he said, rattling off his list of American favorites, AOL, Cisco, Dell, Intel, and

Microsoft. "These companies did not necessarily have big capital to begin with, but they had the vision and the passion."

By the end of March 2002, SoftBank's interest-bearing debt had fallen over the previous two quarters from $4 billion to just below $3 billion, but net income had dropped from $292 million (March 2001) to a $669 million loss (March 2002). NTT, Japan Telecom, KDDI, and other rivals were rolling out low-cost DSL/VoIP services. Borrowing from Masa's playbook, NTT offered consumers three months of service, plus price breaks on new PCs. And it was trying to hike fees for firms seeking to piggyback on its infrastructure or interconnect their calls with NTT customers, thus threatening SoftBank with a hefty retroactive bill.

Once again, Masa needed to find the cash flow to shore up SoftBank's balance sheet. Kitao—who in 1999 had moved to SoftBank Investment (SBI), an asset management subsidiary of the newly formed SoftBank Group holding company—smelled blood. SoftBank's deteriorating credit rating threatened the standing of SBI, he warned. If Masa wished to sell SoftBank's 26 percent stake to maintain its independence, Goldman Sachs was ready to step in as a friendly buyer. "This is our last resort," said Kitao, who knew this was his chance to run his own show.

Masa had no alternative but to agree. In truth, both men had outgrown each other. In SoftBank's first phase as a public company, the ex-Nomura man was an ideal foil. He brilliantly exploited the government's gradual liberalization of financial services ("The Slow Bang") to shift the balance of power between borrower and lender in the domestic bond market, allowing Masa to raise huge sums to finance his growth plans. Toward the end of his tenure, Kitao bridled under Masa's maverick leadership, but at the end of 2001, the two men parted on good terms.

"Kita-yan," Masa told his ex-CFO, "I want to have dinner with you once a month and consult with you."

Masa could afford to be magnanimous. He had a new financial engineer—Kasai-san. And so SoftBank and SBI went their separate ways, the former selling its stake in 2006 and growing into a global media conglomerate, the latter developing into a top Japanese financial services business engaged in banking, insurance, and venture capital.

In January 2003, Masa appeared at the World Economic Forum in Davos. Once he had strutted onstage as Japan's Bill Gates. Now he was a fallen idol, excluded from the conference's official list of "top business leaders" in attendance. Nevertheless, SoftBank's boss turned up and shook every hand that mattered. He even secured a meeting with Steve Schwarzman, the private equity billionaire and cofounder of Blackstone. The two men met in a dowdy Swiss restaurant with a modest menu and "crap seats."

Schwarzman was curious to see what had happened to Japan's onetime wunderkind. He left with the impression of someone convinced he had done nothing wrong, believing he would eventually be proved right.

"I used to be the richest guy in the world. I lost 99 percent of my money," Masa said, "but I am coming back."[19]

16

GOLDEN GOOSE

In late sixteenth-century Japan, a samurai by the name of Musashi Miya-moto developed a new fighting technique using two swords simultaneously, which was known as *Niten-Ichi-ryu*. Masa, the self-styled samurai, also rel-ished dual combat. He was still losing money but making gains in market share against the dominant player, NTT. Meanwhile, he was increasingly drawn to China, where Alibaba's Jack Ma was battling to be the number-one e-commerce company, a contest in which SoftBank had a direct interest.

Toward the end of 2002, Ma paid a visit to Tokyo, unaccountably failing to make his usual courtesy call at SoftBank, still Alibaba's largest shareholder. Despite his financial woes, Masa still believed he ranked well above Ma in the corporate pecking order. When he caught wind that Ma was in town, he called the Alibaba boss, who sheepishly admit-ted he was en route to the airport.

"Turn round," said Masa. "I need to talk to you right now."

Ma canceled his flight and made his way to SoftBank headquarters. Far from being irritated, Masa was in a buoyant mood.[1] Yahoo! Japan had just seen off eBay in the Japanese online auction market. eBay's retreat marked a crushing blow to its ambition to serve as a "truly global marketplace," a leading force not just in the US but also in Asia.

"We can do the same thing in China as in Japan," said Masa. Alibaba's boss was thinking along the same lines. eBay had just taken a 33 percent stake in his Chinese rival, EachNet, for a modest $30 million, and Ma recognized the threat left him no choice. Alibaba had to expand beyond business customers and enter the business-to-consumer (B2C) market.

"It was spontaneous combustion [between the two]," according to Joe Tsai, Ma's longtime business partner and later chairman of Alibaba. Back in Beijing, however, some Alibaba executives were vehemently opposed. The business-to-business (B2B) operations were barely cash-flow positive. Launching a credible B2C rival to eBay would involve tens of millions of dollars of marketing costs, guaranteeing up-front losses over many years. With its EachNet investment, eBay had locked up 90 percent of China's e-commerce market. The Americans had the brand name, deep pockets, and a local partner. Who would be stupid enough to take on that might?

There was another snag: buyers and sellers did not transact on the Alibaba website. They simply obtained their information from online product catalogs and then went offline to negotiate. eBay had its payments and logistics worked out so consumers could commit to the purchase online, the so-called closed loop.

Ma argued it was pointless distinguishing between consumer and business users. Small-business and consumer behavior was similar, because one individual usually made decisions for the whole organization. Besides, said Ma, Alibaba had the backing of SoftBank. And SoftBank had just seen off eBay in Japan. His argument carried the day. Soon afterward, the Alibaba team came up with a brand name for their new venture: Taobao, which meant "seeking treasure."

When Taobao was launched on May 10, 2003, visitors to the website had no means of identifying its connection with Alibaba—or SoftBank. Masa and Ma followed Sun Tzu's advice in *The Art of War*: "Let your plans be dark and impenetrable as the night, and when you move, fall like a thunderbolt." On July 10, two months later, lightning from heaven struck. After much internal speculation about the rise of the mysterious online competitor, Alibaba announced that Taobao was indeed part of the family. The news provoked a raucous cheer within the company.[2]

Taobao's corporate arrangements were equally tightly held. Joe Tsai devised a structure whereby SoftBank held 50 percent of Taobao, which was constituted as a joint venture. Alibaba therefore did not have to consolidate Taobao's loss-making operations in its accounts, making its own operating profits and cash flows look healthier. For his part, Masa agreed that SoftBank would take 50 percent of the losses on its balance sheet. He was happy to finance Taobao's start-up costs, ultimately raising his total investment in the Alibaba empire from $20 million to $100 million in 2005.[3]

Masa contributed something more valuable than dollars. His insights into consumer psychology and the operation of an online marketplace proved indispensable. The challenge was not just how best to generate a critical mass of online traffic; the billion-dollar question was whether to prioritize buyers or sellers. "If you have no products online you don't have buyers," Tsai explained. "The problem then is that sellers won't come to the marketplace."

Masa was adamant that Taobao make listings free for sellers. With an abundant number of products on offer, buyers would flock online. He delivered the Alibaba team a characteristically ambitious metric for success: 10x as many product listings as eBay. Of all the metrics which Taobao measured, this one turned out to be the most valuable. Alibaba colleagues suggested that they insert a clause to that effect in the investor agreement, which gave SoftBank as a fifty-fifty shareholder additional rights relating to performance targets.

Tsai thought this was a step too far. What would happen if they did not hit the target? Would that mean giving up equity? No way! He suggested a personal letter from Jack Ma, avoiding Alibaba letterhead, which pledged that everyone would do their best to meet the 10x target. "The language was not legal, and Masa loved it," Tsai remembered. "He called it the 'Man's pride' letter."[4]

In Masa's mind, and in Japanese business culture in general, trust mattered more than legalese. What counted was the commitment to deliver on a promise because that involved "face." In future years, as the sums involved added many more zeros, the scope for misunderstanding grew, and the lawyers' time would come. But as a rule, Masa preferred Man's pride, the Asian version of an English gentleman's word.[5]

Masa's long-term faith in Alibaba produced fabulous rewards, but not everyone had Masa's patience. Just before SoftBank upped its investment in the Taobao operation, Goldman Sachs chose to exit Alibaba. The Wall Street bank paid $3.3 million for a 33 percent stake in 1999 and sold it for more than seven times that amount five years later. At the time, it looked like a respectable return. Ten years later, when Alibaba completed its IPO, that same stake would have been worth $12.5 billion. Goldman's exit turned out to be one of the most costly lost opportunities ever.

Back in Japan, in the spring of 2004, Masa was still bleeding losses from his broadband operation. Then, quite unexpectedly, a new investment opportunity appeared in the shape of Japan Telecom, the country's number-three telecommunications provider. Japan Telecom had 1.7 million customers, the bulk of whom were corporate. Assuming Masa could raise the finance, it was a neat fit with the individual subscribers who made up more than 95 percent of Yahoo! BB's revenue.[6]

Seven months earlier, in August 2003, Japan Telecom had been acquired by Ripplewood, a US private equity firm headed by Tim Collins, a curmudgeonly Kentuckian of Anglo-Scottish and German heritage. Collins had a short fuse, yelling at his employees in language which invariably left the Japanese confused and the Americans often embarrassed. Temperament aside, Collins was brilliant at spotting undervalued assets. He understood better than most that depressed Japan was the land of opportunity for any businessman with a contrarian bent.

In 2000, Ripplewood teamed up with J. C. Flowers, an ex–Goldman banker, to join a consortium to buy Long-Term Credit Bank, a failed Japanese lender. The Japanese authorities, which had nationalized LTCB in 1998, were delighted to have the bank taken off their hands. Five years later, Collins and Flowers sold the rebranded Shinsei bank for $2.8 billion, making a handsome return.

Foreign investors were also welcome in the Japanese telecoms market. British Telecom and Vodafone found favor because successive governments in Tokyo looked admiringly at the impact of deregulation in the UK. Greater competition produced lower prices for long-distance calls, improved service for consumers, and a willingness to invest heavily in the network.

From their UK base, BT and Vodafone built impressive overseas networks. Between 1999 and 2002, Vodafone engaged in a complicated series of transactions that eventually allowed it to acquire control of Japan Telecom and the promising mobile businesses it controlled. But the purchase proved a disappointment. Vodafone had its eye on so many different international markets that it failed to invest enough time or energy in Japan.

In 2003, Vodafone decided to keep control of the mobile operations but to sell Japan Telecom's fixed-line business to Ripplewood, whereupon Tim Collins hired two top American executives to shake it up in preparation for future sale. His top pick was William Esrey, the former boss of Sprint, the number-three US telecoms carrier. That summer Esrey and his former Sprint COO William LeMay were forced to resign after a controversy over $100 million of taxable stock options and poor financial results. Esrey jumped at the chance for a second act. He negotiated a deal where he would work two weeks a month on Japan Telecom, spending one week a month in Japan, with his wife coming along for the ride. The couple stayed at the Hyatt in Roppongi Hills in Tokyo, where they could leave their clothes. A car and driver completed the package.[7]

Within six months, Esrey's second act was over. Collins, it transpired, had gone to Masa and told him SoftBank's ADSL broadband play was a disaster, his cash flow was terrible, and Yahoo! BB was headed for bankruptcy. Buying Japan Telecom, however, would save the business, giving SoftBank scale and pricing power. Esrey was stunned. ("We did not expect to sell. We were just beginning to build a team.") But he agreed to join negotiations over the sale of Japan Telecom's fixed-line operation, which took place in a room at the five-star Imperial hotel. At the first meeting, Masa spotted that Collins was wearing an expensive watch and declared he would like to buy it on the spot.

Collins: You can't afford it.

Masa: Yes, I can.

Collins: Maybe I will give it to you if we do the deal.

Esrey thought the exchange was childish but revealing: "They were both trying to show one was smarter than the other. Both were big egos talking about themselves with little recognition of the other's interests. Neither was a good listener. It was an unusual negotiation."[8]

Tim Collins had a rule of thumb that "the buy" was more important than "the sell." In layman's terms, this meant that the act of acquiring an asset cheaply was the point at which an investor added value, rather than securing a smart exit. Masa also believed his investor magic came from purchasing rather than selling. The difference was that he always "overpaid," and not just because big money gave him status. He believed that he, uniquely, had the imagination to see a business's long-term growth potential.[9]

Collins took a more short-term view, concentrating on what he and his private equity partners could earn by flipping the asset: a handsome multiple on his original investment. He thought Masa was ready to pay a ridiculous price and was therefore content to sell. The alternative of spending hundreds of millions of dollars building a new business in a cutthroat telecoms market in Japan held few attractions.

By contrast, Masa adopted an approach that, depending on your point of view, demonstrated the patient qualities of Asian business or a cavalier attitude toward returns. In this case, he saw how his acquisition would help build critical mass in the Japanese telecoms market, where fixed line, broadband, and mobile were rapidly converging. He had one goal in mind: making SoftBank the largest internet service provider in Japan.

Where the Japanese buyer and the American seller found common ground was in their haste to conclude a deal. During the second encounter, Esrey remembers how decisive Masa was in his questions and his answers. "It was wham-bam-thank-you-ma'am. How quickly can we get this done?"

The final agreed deal valued Japan Telecom and its fixed-line operation at $3 billion, giving Ripplewood and its coinvestors four times their money in a matter of months. A delighted Collins ended the negotiation with a homily on the need to build a solid team of executives. Masa listened politely, but Esrey saw in his eyes that SoftBank's boss was already contemplating his next move into the mobile internet. Japan Telecom was a pioneer of IP-VPN leased-line networks and Ethernet services to business. Not only did it deliver customer scale, it also gave SoftBank in-house expertise in the technologies of the future.

Having consolidated SoftBank's position in Japan, Masa turned his sights once again to China. Alibaba was still a loss-making private company, but its online auction business Taobao was eating eBay's lunch in China. Sensing the threat, eBay tried to corner the advertising market, buying exclusive ads on the major portals. When that failed to work, the Americans approached Jack Ma and Joe Tsai with a $150 million bid to buy them out.[10] "We were so unsophisticated," says Tsai. "We were stupid enough to counter with a range of $600 million to $900 million."

The Americans walked away: "Let's just be friends and have a nice dinner," one said. In fact, a second eBay approach followed and then another. When Masa heard about the overtures, he spotted a chance to exploit his position as a major shareholder in both Yahoo! and Alibaba. He made his first move in May 2005 at a three-day gathering of American and Chinese tech entrepreneurs in Pebble Beach, California, best known for its five-star golf courses.

Ahead of a steak and seafood dinner, Alibaba's Ma and Yahoo!'s Yang took a stroll on the windswept links. After ten minutes the cold was too much for Ma, but there was enough time for a basic meeting of minds. Ma declared he wanted to enter the search business, while Yang signaled he might be open to funding the high-cost venture in return for Alibaba equity.

From Yang's point of view, the drawback was entering another loss-making business when Yahoo! was under mounting pressure in the US. Back in 1995, Yahoo! was everyone's glamour stock. Ten years on, the new cool thing was Google, with its superior search engine and advertising model. In China, Yahoo!'s dream of turning into a truly global media company had collided with the Great Wall of state control. The Chinese Communist Party was set against foreigners controlling or owning internet operators in the domestic market. Yahoo's choice of local partner was questionable too: an internet wild man, Zhou Hongyi, whose trademark was an AK-47 accompanied by bullet-riddled sheets from target practice in his office.

After a round of golf, the serious three-way negotiations between the Americans, Chinese, and Japanese players began at the Inn at Spanish Bay, next to the golf course. The mood was a world apart from the friendly exchange between the parties two years before. "The Yahoo! deal was four pages and a handshake," says Yang. "This time we were lawyered up to the wazoo."[11]

A fortnight later, "Project Pebble" took another step forward. Jerry Yang met with Jack Ma and Joe Tsai on the sidelines of the Fortune Global Forum, hosted that year in Beijing. Masa was absent, a casualty of one more dip in the seesaw Sino-Japanese relationship, triggered improbably by a soccer match. Things had gone wrong after Japan's 3–1 victory over China in the China-hosted Asian Cup prompted Chinese spectators to burn the Japanese flag, rock the Japanese team bus, and assault an embassy vehicle belonging to a Japanese minister. In April 2005, just ahead of the conference, violent anti-Japanese riots erupted in Beijing and Shanghai in response to the Japanese Ministry of Education's approval of a new history textbook that the Chinese viewed as a Tokyo government–backed attempt to whitewash the past. Beijing was also irked by Japan's efforts to gain a permanent seat on the United Nations Security Council. Only two visas were granted for the Fortune conference. Masa's name failed to make the list.[12]

At this point, everything was still to play for. Alibaba was being courted by eBay, though CEO Meg Whitman's attitude was more condescending than her company's precarious position in China warranted. Meanwhile, Yang had not entirely given up on finding a more suitable partner for Yahoo! China. In the background was Masa playing banker, consolidator, negotiator—and kingmaker.

From day one, Masa was adamant that Jack Ma stay the course, pursuing growth and market share, not profitability. He knew that both eBay and Yahoo! wanted to invest in Alibaba, and that provided the leverage to play one off against the other. And he had the broad outlines of an agreement in his head, a deal that created "The Golden Triangle" between Alibaba, SoftBank, and Yahoo!, with the Americans relegated to the sidelines. And so it played out.

The deal involved several dazzling pirouettes of the kind Masa loved. Jerry Yang agreed that Yahoo! would invest $1 billion in Alibaba shares and hand over Yahoo! China to it, so that the American internet operator ended up with a 40 percent economic interest in Jack Ma's e-empire. Soft-Bank, meanwhile, in effect allowed its stake in Taobao to be folded into Alibaba in return for money and shares. At the end of these head-spinning financial maneuvers, SoftBank got $360 million in cash and, after investing some of these proceeds, a 30 percent economic stake in Alibaba.

"Masa made out like a bandit while retaining his stake in Alibaba," says Joe Tsai, looking back on the landmark deal with a touch of admiration. Jerry Yang's verdict on a three-way conference call at the end of the deal was half impressed, half rueful. He told Masa: "I feel like your ATM machine."

Yet the deal was not totally one-sided. Yahoo! had a 40 percent stake in Alibaba, while Ma and Tsai had full control of Taobao, their homegrown golden goose. The two men had even bolder ambitions for Alibaba, including an online payments business named Alipay. Masa grasped Jack Ma's level of ambition, and he sensed he had made a brilliant long-term bet on the future.

For the moment, Alibaba and the Chinese government were relatively relaxed about the presence of two major foreign shareholders, one from the

US and the other from Japan. As Alibaba's value increased exponentially, in tandem with the growth in mass internet usage in China, politics intervened. But so did personal pride. Ma and Tsai wanted the credit and the financial rewards for building a global business.

In 2005, it could still be argued that SoftBank made Alibaba. Ten years later, the two firms' relative status had flipped. By then, Alibaba had emerged as China's most important and dynamic company, a star of the global business scene worth some $200 billion. As Jerry Yang says, "In many ways, Alibaba made SoftBank."[13]

17

MOBILE MAN

As a student of history, Masa liked to remind colleagues that all empires were built on infrastructure. The Romans built roads, the British created railways and underwater cables, and the Americans developed electricity, highways, and telecommunications. Each rose to become the most powerful civilization in the world. Where, he asked himself, was Japan?[1]

Japan once thought it was destined to become the number-one global economic power. But the dynamism of the postwar period, marked by the promotion of science, the mastery of advanced technology and managerial techniques, and the pursuit of value-added manufacturing, had petered out. In Masa's mind, SoftBank was the catalyst for desperately needed change. The means to the end was world-class digital infrastructure, based on a faster, cheaper, and more advanced internet service than rivals, on a par with its up-and-coming neighbor South Korea.

Masa's dream had long been to connect a mobile phone operator to his Yahoo! broadband service. That way, Japanese consumers could access data, images, and messages all on one digital device. Other tech visionaries like Apple's Steve Jobs were thinking along the same lines. But the smartphone was still several years away, and Masa still had to obtain a mobile phone license in Japan, the most tightly regulated market in the world. After waiting for months for the Ministry of Posts and Telecommunications to act, his patience once again snapped.

In mid-October 2004, Masa held a press conference at Tokyo's Okura hotel and announced he was suing the government. It was a rare public intervention in a country where companies generally avoided the courts and the number of lawyers per head of population was far lower than in the US. But Masa argued that the ministry's refusal to release spare wireless spectrum left him no option.

"The people of this country need free competition," said Masa, flanked by two American antitrust lawyers, one acting for Microsoft, the other advising the Bush administration in Washington.[2] The message to the Japanese government was unambiguous: SoftBank was willing to mobilize every asset, including foreigners, in its bid to disrupt the domestic mobile phone market.

In April 2005, SoftBank won its mobile license. But Masa failed to obtain the desired 800MHz "platinum band" that allowed for nationwide coverage. He was obliged to accept the new 1.7GHz bandwidth, which, though faster, carried less range. This created a dilemma: either Masa compromised on his goal of a national mobile phone network, or he sacrificed quality for reach.

Time was pressing. In eighteen months, under government moves to liberalize the telecoms market, mobile users would be able to switch networks while retaining their original phone number. One possible consequence of "portability" was a stampede of customers to the two powerful incumbents NTT Docomo and KDDI.[3] The biggest loser would be Vodafone, which, having sold its fixed-line business in Japan, was clinging to its dream of turning around its subscale business in the country. SoftBank would be left at the starting gate.

Around this time, Masa met Bill Morrow, the gregarious American head of Vodafone Japan, at a corporate dinner in Tokyo. Morrow was barely a few months in the top job, but knowing his business was in a vulnerable strategic position, he let slip it might be up for sale. If SoftBank was interested, they should explore talks with Vodafone, the UK-based parent company.[4]

After Morrow's overture, Masa executed a 180-degree pivot. Rather than building a business from scratch, he resolved to acquire an existing operator. When he mentioned Vodafone Japan, his team was aghast. Though it still had fifteen million customers, the business was best known for its poor connection rate, lackluster brand, and second-rate management. Vodafone Japan was a neglected outpost in a global empire assembled over the previous decade by its voraciously acquisitive British parent, one of the biggest mobile phone operators in the world.

During the dot-com years, when every operator was desperate to secure wireless spectrum, Vodafone splashed out hundreds of billions of dollars. Nothing was too big to buy. The most lustrous prize was Germany's Mannesmann, bought in 2000 for $190 billion, then the largest merger in history. Although it had sold its fixed-line business to Ripplewood (which quickly flipped it to Masa), it was still making a huge bet on mobile in Japan. The trouble was, nobody seemed to be able to do much with this business.

On a visit to Tokyo, Vittorio Colao, then in charge of southern Europe, remembers enduring a Bain & Co. presentation on the Japanese consumer which summed up his company's failings. Most of Vodafone's global team were present that day: Bill Morrow, accompanied by a Portuguese executive, a Spaniard flown in from Australia, and two Italians, a Sicilian called Fabrizio, and Colao himself, a tall, super-fit cycling fanatic. Around 3 p.m., as everyone was collapsing with jet lag, the Sicilian leaned over to Colao.

"Vittorio, we are fucked: look around, not a single Japanese in the room," he whispered. "We have to relaunch the Japanese consumer offer, and half of us are almost asleep!"[5]

On Christmas Eve 2005, Masa called Arun Sarin, Vodafone's Indian-born CEO, who was on vacation in Hawaii. Sarin knew Masa from their time on the board of Cisco Systems in California. He considered Masa very un-Japanese, a hyperconfident guy who threw a lot of stuff at the wall. Some of it stuck. Masa asked if they could arrange a meeting in London early in the New Year. Suspecting something was afoot, Sarin agreed to talk.

When Masa arrived at Vodafone's London office on Park Lane, near the Hilton hotel, he was accompanied by a scruffy Deutsche Bank trader by the name of Rajeev Misra. The first thing Sarin noticed was that Rajeev was chewing betel nut, a stimulant beloved of Indian auto-rickshaw drivers, with saliva coming out of the corner of his mouth. It was an inauspicious start for the man who would play a central role in the Vodafone Japan acquisition and later become Masa's financial magician at SoftBank.

Born in Jamshedpur, the Indian city named after the founder of Tata Group, for whom his father worked at the time, Misra was trained as a mathematician and physicist, first at the prestigious Indian Institute of Technology in Delhi and later at the University of Pennsylvania. For a while he helped design satellites at the Los Alamos facility in New Mexico, where scientists developed the first nuclear bomb. It was the height of the Cold War as Ronald Reagan talked up his Star Wars program, the space-based defense against nuclear attack. Some believed Reagan's dream was science fiction; others suspected it was a brilliant bluff. The Indian kept his thoughts to himself.

Misra had no desire to spend his life among theoretical physicists; he wanted money. After a brief spell writing code at Microsoft in Seattle, he moved to Wall Street, first to Merrill Lynch and later to Deutsche Bank, where he was an early recruit in Edson Mitchell's drive to make Deutsche a global force in investment banking. Rajeev specialized in interest-rate swaps and derivatives, the complex financial instruments used to hedge risk. His expertise was in structured credit. Rather than making straightforward loans, he designed bespoke deals that sliced and diced risk and collateral, often with the unspoken aim of maximizing the amount of overall leverage that investors would tolerate. This became a critical feature of SoftBank's future global expansion.

Rajeev Misra soon rose to become head of global credit at Deutsche Bank. He first met Masa on a visit to Tokyo in 2002, when SoftBank was on the road to recovery after the dot-com bust. Masa's compulsive personal borrowing, secured against his SoftBank stake, had raised accusations of recklessness and conflicts of interest. Nonetheless, his habit continued, and Misra arranged loans between $300–$400 million to finance Masa's personal spending and investments, accepting his one-third stake in SoftBank as collateral. Though Masa's wealth had shrunk, he still had a taste for fine art, French wine, and real estate, and he paid for his own travel and entertainment as well as dabbling in stocks and shares. The personal spending would later amount to tens of millions of dollars a year.

Misra and Masa cemented their relationship in 2005 on a four-day trip to India when Misra introduced the SoftBank boss to telecom billionaires Anil Ambani and Sunil Bharti Mittal. Years later, on a private jet en route to Tokyo, where he was due to meet Masa, Misra recalled: "He kept saying linear TV was dead and the world was moving to TV on demand via a desktop computer. He was five years ahead of his time."[6]

Soon after the India trip, Masa called Misra and asked him to come to Japan to talk about a top secret acquisition. The Deutsche banker politely declined, saying his wife was about to give birth to their third child. Masa ignored the rebuff and said he wanted to pay $20 billion for Vodafone Japan. Misra replied that he was crazy. SoftBank was not worth much more than $10 billion, he was losing $1 billion a year on Yahoo! BB, he had no serious relationship with international banks, and his only easily sellable asset was Yahoo! Japan.

"Find me the money," said Masa.

That was how they both ended up at Vodafone's offices in London. The meeting soon turned frosty. Masa was borderline arrogant. He boasted to Sarin that he was the owner of Japan Telecom, a Japanese native, and he knew a lot better than the British company how to take full advantage of the telecoms business.

"I see myself doing things in Japan which you as a foreigner can't."[7]

Sarin replied that Vodafone Japan was not for sale. He had a great business, he was investing in 3G, and he had really good handsets—a dig at clunky rival products in Japan. Masa repeated that *gaijins* (foreigners) would never succeed long term in Japan. Then, without tabling a formal offer, he said he was "good for $15 billion"—an unexpected move that required Misra to come up with the funding.[8]

Sarin again declined. He left his visitors with a parting shot: "If you [Masa] ever come back, bring Anshu Jain [head of Deutsche Bank's global investment banking operation]."

When news of the Masa-Sarin encounter reached the Deutsche Bank hierarchy, all hell broke loose. Why was Misra supporting Masa's crazy plan to buy a clapped-out telecoms company in Japan that was bound to be killed by NTT? Any commitment to a corporate loan above $1 billion had to go before the bank's investment committee—or else it was a sackable offense. His immediate boss, Anshu Jain, was appalled: "Who is this guy Masayoshi Son anyway?"[9]

Like Misra, Jain attended Delhi Public School, an institution beloved of elite Indians, but that was about all the two had in common. While Misra loved playing the antiestablishment bad boy, padding around the office in bare feet, a cigarette in hand, Jain had Brahmin written all over his clean-shaven face. He was charming, handsome, and impeccably turned out. His only fault was finishing off other people's sentences, usually with the words "Tell me something I don't know" or, even more irritating, "Okay, so let me tell you how this goes. . . ."

Anshu Jain was known at Deutsche as "the father of fixed income," better known as bond trading. After Edson Mitchell died in a plane crash just before Christmas 2000, leaving a gaping hole in Deutsche's senior management ranks, Jain took over as head of global markets and turned the debt-trading business into a powerhouse. Misra was one of Jain's "Band of Brothers," a mathematical wizard who could calculate risk down to the last decimal point. This would soon earn the Deutsche trader and his oddball team of speculators tens of millions when he oversaw a $13 billion bet against subprime mortgages ahead of the global financial crisis, a story immortalized in Michael Lewis's book *The Big Short*.

In the second meeting in London, Jain sweet-talked Sarin, saying the SoftBank-Vodafone tie-up was "a win-win for all parties." The British company, he reminded him, would get cash that it could return to shareholders. Masa then jumped in, raising his bid to $16 billion. The move caught Sarin by surprise. He had expected the offer to go up by small increments.

"I really, really want to buy this asset," said Masa, hustling as usual.

Sarin said he was still not interested but agreed to take the cash-and-shares offer to the Vodafone board. As Jain and Masa looked at each other knowingly, Sarin issued a final warning: "This number is not going to clear the market."

Masa returned with a third offer, valued at $17 billion and sweetened by $12 billion in cash. This was an attractive offer, but Sarin was still nervous as the rest of the proceeds came in the form of loan-like instruments issued by SoftBank. Any exposure to SoftBank was a risk. After all, its stock had fallen by 98 percent during the dot-com crash. What might happen next time round? In the event, Sarin had no need to worry. When the terms of the final deal were unveiled on March 17, 2006, the market welcomed the bid, marking up Vodafone shares by 7 percent. Investors liked the cash and were less focused on the risk of being exposed to SoftBank. They seemingly turned a blind eye to the fact that a debt-ridden Japanese business was attempting to buy a target company *almost twice its size*, while the deal itself amounted to the largest leveraged buyout ever done in Asia.

The Vodafone Japan deal has first to be judged in the context of the economic cycle. In 2006, talk was cheap, and credit was even cheaper. This was the Year of the Deal, when companies went on a global shopping spree, running up a bill reaching more than $4 trillion, the equivalent to spending $500 million or so every hour.[10]

In the case of SoftBank-Vodafone Japan, being able to persuade financial markets that the heavily indebted Japanese conglomerate could repay the billions borrowed to fund the deal was critical. The financial wizardry was the work of two men: Rajeev Misra and Kazuhiko Kasai. To get the deal done, SoftBank needed at least a BBB rating from the credit rating agencies, saying it was risky but not suicidally so. This in turn would support a high-yield bond to provide most of the financing. Since SoftBank had only a BB rating, the two men put together a team of credit experts to persuade ratings agencies like Moody's and Standard & Poor's that there was less risk of default than feared.

"The key was to look at the whole of SoftBank's business and construct a scheme where all cash flow went to the bondholders ahead of any dividend payout," says a banker involved. "And there were lots of debt covenants to give reassurance to the banks and get a better credit rating. And we had outrageous cash-flow projections for the new [Vodafone] business."

In addition to this novel financing method, known as "whole company securitization," SoftBank agreed to pay a whopping ¥60 billion ($600 million) break fee if the transaction did not go through. This turned convention on its head. Normally it is the *seller*, not the buyer, who offers to pay a break fee. SoftBank used the device to reassure the Vodafone board that might otherwise have been tempted by rival US private equity bidders Cerberus and Providence Capital Partners circling the company. The clincher came when SoftBank promised to repay interest and principal on the billions involved on a pre-agreed schedule. With the BBB credit rating, everyone was ready to sign up to the deal.

Masa was always borrowing money, but the Vodafone Japan deal was in a different league. Some close to him believe this was the moment Masa got hooked on leverage. "He borrowed a shit ton of money from Deutsche Bank," says a longtime associate. "It's like a drug. When you enjoy the benefits of leverage with all this upside, you can't get off it."[11]

Masa never forgot the debt he owed Misra and Deutsche Bank. Ecstatic at landing his prize, he played down criticism that he'd overpaid. True, he took big, bold risks. But he insisted, somewhat alarmingly, that he would never countenance anything that would sink SoftBank "in one go."[12]

As a toddler, Masa had grown up surrounded by his family's red pigs. His father had encouraged his unshakable self-confidence, repeatedly calling him a genius. Pigs could climb trees, Mitsunori used to say, citing the old Japanese adage. Having acquired a third-rate mobile phone business and faced with brutal competition from NTT Docomo and KDDI, Masa was about to find out whether pigs really could climb up trees or indeed fly across the skies.

With the acquisition of Vodafone Japan, Masa completed his transformation from investor to operator. The business had fifteen million fickle customers. Masa immediately inflated these numbers by adding Yahoo! BB subscribers (five million) and those signed up to his fixed-line business, now rebranded SoftBank Telecom (six million). Thus fifteen million suddenly turned into twenty-six million customers. In Masa's favorite marketing slogan, SoftBank's customer base amounted to 0.27 hundred million people. "It's not much fun if you're not measuring things in hundreds of millions," he explained.[13]

Turning round the Vodafone brand looked daunting, but not overwhelmingly so. By now, the number of mobile phone subscriptions in Japan had reached the equivalent of 80 percent of the population. The good news was there was still room for growth. The battle for the remaining 20 percent was going to be cutthroat.

To win or retain customers, the phone carriers offered subsidies on handsets to make buying them cheaper, thereby luring people to their networks. The operators bore up to 90 percent of the up-front cost of buying a phone, a sum which they hoped to recoup over time through monthly tariff payments. This practice expanded the market but dented profitability because digital phones were getting "smarter" and therefore more expensive.

There was a second drawback: customers gamed the system, canceling their phone contract after one year, too soon for the operators to be able to recoup the cost of the handset subsidy. To make matters worse, Japanese customers as a rule shunned internet access, preferring to use voice calls, which were much cheaper.

Masa changed Japanese consumer behavior with a marketing masterstroke. First, he bought expensive, flashy handsets from mobile phone manufacturers such as Nokia and Samsung and personally supervised the different colors and features. Then he introduced a new installment plan that obliged customers to pay back the full cost of their handset within twelve to twenty-four months. Anyone who switched over ahead of time had to pay the remaining charge in full.

The beauty of this arrangement was that SoftBank was guaranteed to recoup its initial cost. Then came a clever twist: SoftBank securitized its claim on the debt owed by the customer for the handset. This way, it was able to generate extra financing to cover the heavy costs of establishing a credible rival to NTT Docomo and KDDI. In effect, Masa was generating cash today from promises to pay tomorrow.

Finally, Masa introduced aggressive new pricing known as the Gold Plan, though his initial rollout cut more corners than a Formula One car. After slashing his rivals' offers by more than 25 percent, SoftBank put up big advertising placards claiming customers could enjoy a "zero rate." Yet this tariff applied only to calls between SoftBank customers during certain hours; calls to other carriers involved a rate of ¥21 per thirty seconds. The zero rate didn't apply to business customers either, and it was initially restricted to customers paying by installment.

After complaints from KDDI and NTT, the Japanese Fair Trade Commission stepped in and censured SoftBank.[14] Masa's boast about standing on the side of the consumer rang hollow. But he bounced back, this time with an even bolder pricing plan, the White Plan. He offered a basic tariff of ¥980 a month, with SoftBank users able to make free calls outside prime time without other restrictions. The SoftBank offer was a full quarter of the price of rivals. Japan's telecoms revolution was underway.[15]

Branding was also critical, because Vodafone Japan's image among customers was rock-bottom. Masa partnered with Sasaki Hiroshi, a veteran creative director formerly at Dentsu, the most powerful advertising agency in Japan. They came up with an inspirational answer: a talking Hokkaido-breed white dog as the new face of the SoftBank Mobile brand.[16]

This lovable canine was called "Dad" or "Father" (*Otosan*), the patriarch of the otherwise human Shirato (literally, the White family). No one asked why a white dog was top dog, nor why the Japanese nuclear family talked politics. The point was that family members with a SoftBank phone now enjoyed a further discount, allowing them to talk to each other for free, 24/7. Within days of the launch in June 2007, *Otosan* became the most popular TV ad in Japan. SoftBank Mobile subscriptions soared.

Shoppers also had a new retail experience, with white walls and eager young staff, later supplemented by a talking robot called "Pepper" roving around the showroom. Finally, Masa rebranded the local baseball team in Kyushu that he'd acquired in January 2005. From now on, the Fukuoka Hawks would be known as the Fukuoka SoftBank Hawks.

SoftBank was determined to take down Docomo, but it didn't have enough shops to form a nationwide sales presence and lacked radio stations for its network. Money was tight. Masa went to Ericsson, which provided the mobile phone infrastructure in Japan, and asked for a grace period of several months on fee payments. Carl-Henric Svanberg, the Swedish boss, was taken aback. He feared SoftBank might wriggle out of its bills.

"You could always make an excuse and not pay because of faults in the infrastructure and mobile phone coverage," Svanberg remembered, "but it was a risky maneuver."[17]

There was something about Masa that the Swede finds appealing to this day. The chutzpah, the charm, the man's supreme optimism about the future. Whatever it was, Svanberg ended up giving Masa the benefit of the doubt. His gut instinct turned out to be correct. Masa kept his word and paid up on time, helped by a wonder product from America.

STEVE JOBS TO THE RESCUE

Before the blockbuster Vodafone Japan deal, SoftBank was a loss-making broadband operator with a plodding fixed-line telephone business and a boss hell-bent on growth. The mobile internet was always central to Masa's expansion plans. The missing piece was a break-through consumer product to compete with his archrival, NTT Docomo. The man who supplied the answer was his old friend Steve Jobs.

The relationship between Masa and Jobs was a special one. Both were autocratic mavericks who possessed buckets of self-belief and an uncanny ability to anticipate the future. Both had a deep understanding of aesthetics, technology, and consumer behavior. A visitor to Masa's office in Tokyo once saw fifty different telephone handsets mounted on a wall, allowing him to study each feature before deciding on SoftBank's own product design.[1] Masa loved to quote Jobs's most famous line from Apple's Think Different advertising campaign in 1997: "The people who are crazy enough to think they can change the world are the ones who do."

Masa first encountered Steve Jobs in the mid-1980s at the annual Comdex trade fair in Las Vegas. Sometime in the summer of 1998, they had their first serious conversation under a cherry tree at the Woodside, California, home of Larry Ellison, boss of the Oracle software group and a fellow Japanophile.[2]

Ellison's home was in fact more like a village, a compound of intricately fashioned wooden houses modeled after a Japanese emperor's palace. The twenty-three-acre estate took almost a decade to design and build, including a lake and a waterfall operated by an on-off switch. All the buildings were constructed without nails and had mud-plastered walls, designed to withstand a 7.3 Richter-scale earthquake. In total, Ellison's homage to Japanese culture and history was worth around $70 million.

The talk around the table that day was about crazy internet valuations in the stock market. But Masa and Jobs were more interested in what would happen *after* the dot-com bubble. "I said that I was focused on the internet—and he agreed the internet was the future. Apple's product would have more and more focus as a device connecting to the internet. So we talked a lot about the vision of the internet."[3]

Both men grasped that the internet represented a paradigm shift. Movements in the Nasdaq were one thing; the advent of the networked world, in which Apple played a leading role as innovator and SoftBank the part of investor and operator, was quite another.

The story of Steve Jobs was the myth of the entrepreneur-innovator writ large.[4] Having founded Apple Computer in his parents' garage in 1976, he was forced out in 1985, returned in 1997 to rescue it from bankruptcy, and turned it into one of the world's most valuable companies with a suite of smash-hit products from Mac laptops to the iPod music device. Like Masa, he was paranoid about rivals stealing his ideas. No Apple project was more top secret than the iPhone, the touch-screen smartphone that would sell billions and revolutionize personal communications.

By Masa's account, on a visit to California, sometime in the summer of 2005, he showed Jobs his own sketch of a mobile-enabled iPod that had a large display and used the Apple operating system (OS). The new device, he predicted, would be able to process data and images. Jobs pooh-poohed the idea but could not resist dropping hints about the iPhone.

Jobs: "Masa, don't give me your shitty drawing. I have my own."[5]

Masa: "Well, I don't need to give you my dirty piece of paper, but once you have your product, give it to me for Japan."

Jobs refused to reveal any more detail, but Masa spotted the flicker of a smile on the Apple boss's face. After pressing him further, Masa wangled a follow-up meeting at Jobs's Tudor-style country home in Palo Alto. At that meeting, Masa claims Jobs agreed in principle to give SoftBank exclusive rights to distribute the iPhone in Japan.

"Well, Masa, you are crazy," said Jobs. "We have not talked to anybody, but you came to see me as the first guy. I'll give it to you."

Nothing was written down on paper. There was no discussion of price or volume. Just another gentleman's agreement, based on the assumption that Masa would have the financial wherewithal to build or acquire a mobile phone business. "It was superconfidential. I never saw the [iPhone] product before it arrived in Japan [in 2008]," Masa claims. "Steve never even told me the name."[6]

The iPhone tale has a mythical quality. It assumes Jobs gave his word a full *three* years before Apple launched the iPhone in Japan. Yet that very promise may well have given Masa the confidence to go ahead with his highly leveraged deal to buy Vodafone Japan, knowing that he had a game-changing product in the pipeline. Whatever the precise chronology, Masa pulled off the distribution deal of the century, which enabled him to build a profitable consumer business in Japan, massively enhancing the SoftBank brand.

On March 17, 2006, Masa clinched his $17 billion deal to buy Vodafone Japan. Two weeks later, Jobs flew to Tokyo, where Masa challenged the Apple boss to uphold his end of the deal. "You didn't give me anything in writing, but I made a $17 billion bet based on your word," he said. "You had better feel a tiny bit of responsibility because I didn't even have anything in writing."[7]

Jobs laughed and said: "Masa, you are a crazy guy. We will do what we discussed."

In the spring of 2006 Masa was in an almighty hurry. Mobile phone users in Japan would soon be free to transfer their telephone numbers to rival operators. As noted earlier, unless SoftBank came out with a compelling new offer on price or product, it risked losing hundreds of thousands of customers to Docomo NTT and the number-two operator KDDI.

Steve Jobs was also racing against the clock. Three years earlier, he was diagnosed with a rare form of pancreatic cancer, but he'd delayed opening his body for surgery and the cancer had spread to his liver. From the day of his operation in October 2004, he knew he was living on borrowed time. In public, he insisted to colleagues and investors he was cured. In private, he was more focused than ever, devoting every hour to two secret projects, the iPhone and a new tablet computer called the iPad.[8]

Apple launched its first iPhone, with low-capacity 2G technology, in the US in the summer of 2007. The device was incompatible with the more advanced technologies being used in Japan. For that reason, Japanese telecoms giants saw Apple more as a designer and manufacturer of personal computers and music players. They couldn't imagine the Americans producing a game-changing new consumer product in their space. By contrast, Masa grasped that Steve Jobs was about to become the disruptor-in-chief as faster technologies became ascendant not just in Japan but around the world.

In November 2007, the boss of AT&T, distributor of Apple's 2G iPhone in the US, gave the game away. Speaking at the Churchill Club, a business event in Silicon Valley, Randall Stephenson let slip that Apple's next iPhone would be 3G compatible. From then on, even as more than two million American consumers enjoyed a groundbreaking experience on a brilliant screen with a flick of their finger, the industry was abuzz with rumors of Apple's next-generation product.

Within weeks, Docomo NTT's CEO Masao Nakamura held talks with Jobs at Apple's Cupertino headquarters, followed by Masa himself. This suggests that the exclusive iPhone distribution deal may not have been as watertight as Masa thought, though he later claimed that he was in regular touch with Jobs, exchanging ideas on features for the new iPhone. "I created all the characters, the emoticons that went in the iPhone. I gave him many ideas."[9]

Jobs offered Masa some advice that he might have taken on board in later years. "Masa, doing one thing right is super tough. And two people can do 99 percent the same thing, but 1 percent makes a huge difference. I don't want to get distracted. I would rather focus on doing one thing right."[10]

Both Masa and Docomo were desperate to get their hands on the new 3G-enabled product that was tri-band, operating on multiple networks and therefore capable of being rolled out all over the world. Docomo's mobile phones operated on a 2GHz network in Japan's cities. Once in the countryside, where mobile phone towers were less prevalent, mobile users would flip to a more reliable "platinum band" 800MHz service. There was one drawback: NTT's dual-band network had to be tested thoroughly to ensure the switchover worked smoothly. The risk of a delayed iPhone rollout was therefore serious.

Because risk-averse Japanese regulators favored incumbents, SoftBank had to settle for the inferior 2.1GHz spectrum, whose advantage was that it was single-band, nationwide, and therefore did not require a switchover.[11]

Technology mattered, but personal chemistry counted even more. "There was a deep connection between Masa and Steve Jobs," says Ron Fisher, SoftBank's man in the US, who attended several meetings between the two men. "Jobs understood that when you are trying to change consumer behavior in a place like Japan, you need a maverick."[12]

On June 4, 2008, Masa announced that SoftBank would sell the iPhone, confirming he had beaten Docomo to the punch. The following month, Soft-Bank began distribution in Japan. By September 2011, when SoftBank lost its exclusivity over the iPhone, its market share had grown to 23 percent, up from 17 percent at the point when the mobile business was acquired from Vodafone.[13] Steve Jobs's decision to stake all on SoftBank was vindicated, but the success also pointed to Masa's ability to scale up rapidly, overcoming a maze of logistical, regulatory, and marketing obstacles.

Yet at this moment of triumph, when SoftBank's fortunes were touching new heights, the world's financial markets started to creak. The first sign of trouble came in March 2008. Bear Stearns, the scrappy New York investment bank, collapsed. Bear had doubled down on mortgage-backed securities, sophisticated debt instruments linked to the US housing market which offered higher risk but also higher returns than government bonds.

From Fed chairman Alan Greenspan down, many believed that US house prices could only go up. When confidence faltered in 2008, leveraged investors like Bear were left exposed. Over the summer, market sentiment soured further. Suddenly the value of all the supposedly supersafe securities was in doubt, especially those linked directly to the riskier subprime housing market or collateralized debt obligations (CDOs), which pooled a radioactive soup of different debts into a single tradable instrument. Along with hundreds of other active investors, SoftBank fell victim to a market meltdown.

What became an existential crisis for Masa and SoftBank began with a seemingly innocuous decision. Yoshimitsu Goto, a senior member of SoftBank's finance team, put ¥75 billion ($750 million) of cash into a trust recommended by Goldman Sachs. Goto's strategy was to use the expected proceeds to redeem three debenture bonds earlier than their maturity date in 2010. This would have helped SoftBank's cash flow at a time of heavy spending on mobile but also reassured markets still nervous about the company's high debt levels.

Goldman marketed the trust as a solid investment with better-than-average returns. The CDOs had a triple-A rating and offered an attractive yield. However, the contract came with a caveat. The trust had 160 entities, but if any eight of them defaulted, SoftBank would lose all the ¥75 billion ($750 million) invested.

On September 15, 2008, Lehman Brothers, one of the top Wall Street investment banks, collapsed. Financial markets went into a tailspin. In Tokyo, rumors spread about SoftBank's exposure to CDOs and other synthetic products. "Our share price went to hell, and I had my personal debt," Masa remembered. "I didn't sell SoftBank stock to build my house or buy my jet or whatever. I helped many of the group companies. . . . My debt became bigger than the asset value of SoftBank [shares] I owned, so I was personally broke."[14]

In November, he pledged 45 percent of his SoftBank stock as collateral, at the time worth around $2 billion. This implies his personal borrowing was several times that sum. In the following weeks, he was forced to sell down his shareholding in SoftBank from around 35 percent to 17 percent. "I lost almost all my worldly assets," he later confessed.[15] Another longtime SoftBank colleague confirms: "He was pretty well wiped out."[16]

Aside from managing his personal borrowings, Masa had to find a way to calm market jitters about SoftBank's viability. On October 17, having watched SoftBank's share price halve since early August, he called two senior financial executives into his office and asked what they thought of announcing SoftBank's quarterly results one week ahead of time, shifting from November 5 to October 29. On the CDO exposure, Masa wavered, arguing that the losses had yet to materialize, and premature disclosure could panic investors.

However, in a rare display of independent thinking, SoftBank's head accountant, Kazuko Kimiwada, insisted on full disclosure. "If there's any negative news, you flip out," she told Masa. "My job is not to surrender to that [impulse]. I have pride as a professional in my job."[17]

Masa relented. Not only did he agree to disclose the CDO exposure, he also pledged further debt reduction and, unusually, provided extensive earnings projections. The ultimate effect was to stabilize market sentiment, helping SoftBank's share price recover. But it was a close-run thing.

Goto, who went on to be SoftBank's chief financial officer, was mortified by his misjudgment in investing in CDOs with Goldman Sachs. He asked for an appointment with Kasai, where he presented his boss with his letter of resignation. When he saw it, Kasai shouted at Goto: "You fool! If you have time to write that, spend it instead thinking up a way to get through this!"[18]

After the hara-kiri resignation that wasn't, the follow-up meeting with Goldman representatives went less smoothly. SoftBank executives pointed out that they had been promised excellent returns on their investment. The Goldman posse said to a man that nothing was written down on paper. Ah yes, said Goto, but you *said* as much. The Goldman standoff highlighted a sharp cultural divide. In the US, a legal obligation was something that appeared in written form. In Japan, everything came down to trust. Goldman had violated that trust. Masa froze out the Wall Street bank for several years thereafter.[19]

In the weeks after the Lehman collapse, everyone at SoftBank remained on edge. Even Masa, who'd famously claimed he'd lost little sleep during the dot-com collapse, seemed unusually twitchy. The standoff over the timing of SoftBank's earnings announcement was a reminder of the burden of being a public company. Masa complained to colleagues that it was tedious explaining to analysts and journalists why SoftBank's shares went up and down like a yo-yo.

For a brief period, as the value of his company continued to plummet, Masa toyed with a radical option: taking SoftBank private. That would avoid public scrutiny (and accountability), and it would give SoftBank a grace period when it could repair its finances away from the public eye. But mounting a leveraged buyout of a company SoftBank's size would require raising several billion dollars in debt financing at a time when financial markets were deeply stressed.

"Sure, I can do that for you," said Kasai, "but won't you be settling for a smaller vision? I thought SoftBank was going to spread its wings and soar high."

Kasai carried the day. He was lower-key than his punchy predecessor Kitao. Be straight with the banks, he once advised a junior colleague. If you're straight with them, they will work with you. We don't want a repeat of the 1990s in Japan when all the bad stuff was hidden.[20] Kasai was making the case for fair and open dealing between borrower and lender. Masa understood the doctrine of mutually assured destruction, especially later in his career when SoftBank's borrowings and leverage took on even greater proportions.

Kasai, who had five other jobs, including president of the SoftBank Hawks baseball team, played catcher in his high school. He was one of Masa's most trusted executors, one of a small circle of Japanese managers who made sure that his boss's visions were not hallucinations. When he died suddenly from cancer in 2013, aged seventy-six, Masa gave an emotional tribute, calling Kasai "the all-time greatest catcher."[21]

In 2008–09, Kasai was making most of the big calls to calm investor nerves. SoftBank committed to reduce net interest-bearing debt to zero by 2015. Having taken on $23.8 billion (¥2.38 trillion) of debt in June 2006 after the Vodafone deal, SoftBank exposure was still at $20.7 billion at the end of September 2008 after Lehman Brothers collapsed.[22] It was only at the end of March 2009, after SoftBank's first-quarter 2009 earnings, that credit spreads narrowed, and Masa first felt a measure of relief.

Around this time, Masa bumped into Rajeev Misra. He explained that the past few months had taught him a painful lesson, making him a humbler person. "I bear the scars," he said. "I'm paying down SoftBank's debt and paying off my own debts. No more acquisitions."

Misra was minded to believe him, until he heard those last three words.

PART 4

THE EMPIRE BUILDER

19

THIRTY-YEAR VISION

After SoftBank's near-death experience, it was only natural for Masa to take another vow of abstinence on dealmaking. His life followed a recurring pattern. A blizzard of ideas followed by intense enthusiasm and focus, leading to overreach, failure, and repentance—until the whole process started over again. Some friends likened Masa to Sisyphus, the ancient Greek king condemned by the gods to roll a boulder uphill for eternity. There was a certain tragic quality to Masa's endless ups and downs. Forever eyeing the future, he was incapable of dwelling on past or present accomplishments. It was a recipe for perpetual dissatisfaction.[1]

His restless energy derived from an unshakable self-belief. He was a survivor. He had come back from the dead twice in his life, once as a victim of hepatitis B in his mid-twenties and then after the dot-com crash in his early forties. The global financial crisis was, in this sense, no different. Through the missteps and setbacks, he drew comfort from his technocentric view of the world and his faith in human progress. Even if his timing was sometimes off, he was right about the general direction. As he once observed: "One should not follow the times. You need to read them, set things in motion and wait."[2]

In early 2009, thanks to a giant rescue operation to shore up the banking system led by the Federal Reserve and US Treasury, confidence began to return to the world's financial markets. The mood further improved after the Chinese authorities announced a massive stimulus program to help their own economic recovery. The crisis was not over, but the world had moved on from that terrifying week in September 2008 when a meltdown in the financial system appeared imminent.

As SoftBank's share price recovered, Masa sensed an opportunity to loosen the shackles and launch a fresh start. The ideal moment was Soft-Bank's thirty-year anniversary in 2010. Here was a chance to celebrate and to rally employees and investors around a new vision. Longevity resonated in Japan, where companies involved in construction, herbal remedies, hospitality, and sake brewing traced their history back to medieval times. Masa's private talk of SoftBank lasting three hundred years was ready for public consumption. It wasn't Hollywood froth; the vision played consciously to a Japanese audience sensitive to long-term purpose.[3]

The one question Masa conveniently failed to address was what happened to SoftBank after he left the stage. Although he'd talked to friends about living past 120 years of age, maybe even 130, he was after all mortal. When a friend asked him whether he might consider handing over responsibility for running the company to his family, his answer was blunt. "No way," he declared. "I don't have any sons."[4] He was of course overlooking his two daughters.

On the evening of July 2, 2009, Masa held an impromptu dinner at SoftBank's headquarters in Tokyo. The discussion topic was Masa's "Thirty-Year Vision," an event timed to coincide with his company's anniversary the following year. SoftBank's top technical experts were present, along with a special guest: Masa's younger brother Taizo, founder of a mobile gaming company called GungHo.

Among his three brothers, Masa was closest to Taizo, though he often treated him like a scolding father. Taizo, fifteen years younger, was a talented high school student, more academically gifted than his elder brother. But in his teenage years, he was a bit of a playboy, a jazz lover who twice flunked his entry exams into the elite University of Tokyo. Masa called him a "loser" and told him to turn his life around.

Masa then prescribed a rigorous routine: some eighteen hours a day of studies marked out in a color-coded road map showing progress ahead of schedule (green), slippage (red), and progress according to schedule (yellow). When Taizo sought praise from Masa, he received a dressing-down. Masa singled out Taizo's performance in the yellow grid and castigated him for slacking. Everything was about exceeding expectations, he explained. Taizo's swotting eventually earned him a place in the considerably less prestigious Tokyo University of Economics, and he had gone on to become a multimillionaire in his own right, following GungHo's debut as a public company four years earlier.[5]

That night, Masa bossed the conversation, expanding on his theory of paradigm shifts in technology from the microchip to the internet, mobile technology, and artificial intelligence. After he had finished, a few executives chipped in. Then a young unknown, Takayuki Kamaya, thirty-four, a new recruit to the investor relations department who was standing in for his boss, spoke up.[6]

"If I may make a suggestion regarding the Thirty-Year Vision, I think that it would be better if it wasn't just about making more money or increasing market capitalization, but rather about how SoftBank can make a global contribution, how it can become a company that earns the gratitude of people all over the globe."

"What's your name?" Masa demanded.

"Kamaya," the young man replied, sheepishly.

"Where have you been hiding?" said Masa, half joking.

Kasai, SoftBank's finance man, explained that Kamaya had joined Soft-Bank as a mid-career hire, having worked previously at Sanyo, the Japanese consumer electronics company. After the meeting, Masa summoned the head of HR. There was a ban on mid-career hires after the Lehman crash: Why was it ignored? Apology received, Masa admitted that the young man was a good prospect and commandeered him for the CEO's office.

Masa's freewheeling style made SoftBank an exhilarating place to work, especially for young university graduates. In mainstream Japanese companies, the seniority system stifled initiative from below. Masa loved to surround himself with young talent. They were his samurai, loyal almost to a fault. SoftBank was a modern Japanese company, but women rarely made it into Masa's inner circle, apart from the accountant Kimiwada.

A month later, at another office dinner, Masa instructed the group to begin brainstorming about the world in 2040. He instructed Kamaya to focus on technology as an agent of change. Four questions were relevant: What would computer chips look like? What applications and solutions would future chips make possible? How would people's lifestyle change? And finally, what was the business and competitive outlook?

Masa took a close interest in this "Vision" project, spending more than a hundred hours with the team over a month. This was relatively generous, since he considered his time so precious that he divided his diary into five-minute segments. His time management often left Western visitors baffled. One prominent American hire traveled from New York to Tokyo, assuming his new boss would discuss SoftBank's strategy, competitors, and positioning in the US market. Masa showed little interest, and the meeting lasted barely twenty minutes. (The recruit still took the job, though his tenure was short-lived.)[7]

Around this time, Masa was focused on a separate project to build a new home in Tokyo, a spectacular residence which would dwarf his mansion in Roppongi. That property alone was worth ¥7 billion ($70 million), including the price of the land. Among its star features was a $3 million electronic golf range in the basement which simulated conditions on real courses. When Masa pushed a few buttons, the floor tilted, an ocean-scented breeze swept the room, and a light rain fell from the ceiling. Bill Gates, a keen golfer, was impressed when he paid a visit.[8]

Masa's new luxury home in central Tokyo was on a different scale. The planning application featured a building complex four stories high and a basement two floors underground, digging to a depth of twenty-two meters. In London and New York such cavernous spaces were known as "iceberg basements." They housed gyms, playrooms, saunas, swimming pools, wine stores, and, in one instance, a ballroom. They were the stuff of fantasy, affordable only by oligarchs and hedge fund billionaires. In densely populated Tokyo, where most residents lived cheek by jowl, such extravagance defied belief.[9]

The cost, including the purchase of land, was estimated to be north of $85 million (¥8 billion). It covered six square miles of floor space, with five-star amenities such as a bowling alley, a twenty-five-meter swimming pool, and an updated version of the simulated electronic golf course. When local homeowners demanded to know who was moving into the property, the answers were vague, ranging from an anonymous American family to a religious group with deep pockets.[10]

The original planning application dated October 2009 identified the builders as Taisei Corporation, a civil engineering company founded in 1873 and based in the northern half of Tokyo. The other name that stood out was that of Jeffrey A. Sine, the registered CEO of the Japanese development company running the megaproject. The fact that Jeffrey A. Sine was a Wall Street banker whose prized client was Masayoshi Son was not noted.

A few months earlier, Sine had cofounded the Raine Group, a boutique New York investment bank. After a career at Morgan Stanley and UBS, where he counted Rupert Murdoch among his clients, Sine decided he'd had enough of unwieldy investment banks which had almost gone under during the global financial crisis. It was time to go solo.

Sine's other passion was sponsoring plays and musicals on Broadway and London's West End, some of which had won prestigious Tony Awards. Working with Masa also had its moments of drama. He'd spent months in the doghouse after challenging SoftBank's boss on his choice of ADSL in the Yahoo! BB broadband launch. Overall the relationship remained close; so close that Masa asked Sine in 2009 to be the secret front man for his housing project.[11]

"Masa is very good at publicity he wants," said Sine, "but he is very strong on avoiding unwanted publicity. Top of the list is anything to do with his personal life."

In the good times, Masa reveled in his public role as Japan's Bill Gates. But he avoided conspicuous displays of wealth. Stories about an extravagant new home would have sat awkwardly with the public image of a man indifferent to luxury. Official profiles cast him as the man who used a wristwatch until it no longer worked and ate bento packed lunches from the local convenience store. The day after SoftBank's IPO, the most profligate thing he claimed to have done was buy a ¥300,000 golf club set.[12]

Fiercely protective of his own privacy, Masa would sometimes don a pair of dark glasses, turn up his coat collar, and stroll anonymously along the streets of Tokyo. He took his personal security and that of his family seriously. But he also didn't want pesky reporters hanging around his home at midnight waiting for a quote on some story or another. (The practice of doorstepping, known as *yomawari*, was considered de rigueur among Japanese business journalists. Most Japanese CEOs are walled off from the press during the day and shun contact in the evenings when they are socializing in restaurants or bars with clients or senior staff. Hence the midnight doorstepping.)

Back in 2009-10, when rumors spread that Masa was the mysterious owner of the housing development, SoftBank had a standard reply. "We checked with Mr. Son himself," said a spokesman. "This plan has nothing to do either with Mr. Son or our company."[13]

Jeff Sine joked that if Masa didn't behave, he might just keep the luxury property. But as complaints grew about the giant excavation and the incessant drilling, he decided to placate the neighbors. His first stop was a nearby property, the Hatakeyama Memorial Museum of Fine Art, which housed a famous tearoom called Seian.[14]

In Japan, the tea ceremony occupies a venerated place in the country's culture going back to the ninth century. Rooted in Zen philosophy, the process of drinking tea is a means of bringing harmony and inner peace to guests seeking refuge from the outside world. Sine, who had a healthy sense of the absurd, found it comical to compare the spiritual experience of a Japanese tea ceremony with the thunderous drilling in the vicinity.

The meeting between Sine and the two museum owners was equally incongruous. They did not speak a word of English, and Sine had no Japanese. Communicating through an interpreter, the New York banker assured his hosts that his intentions were benign; he just wanted a safe place to live. After paying respect to the traditions of the tea ceremony, Sine made his excuses and left in a hurry.[15]

How much compensation Masa offered to his neighbors for the three-year-long disruption is unclear, but it would surely have reached a tidy sum. Paying out millions was hardly onerous to SoftBank's boss and founder. Despite suffering heavy losses in the global financial crisis, he still held 21 percent of SoftBank stock and could borrow against it. A paper billionaire, he was easily capable of buying a twenty-three-thousand-square-foot plot of land conservatively valued at ¥5.5 billion ($59 million) and erecting a property that could be worth over ¥2.5 billion ($26 million).[16]

A prominent Asian businessman likened the finished development to the fictional Wayne Manor, home of Batman. Upon arrival in Tokyo, he was ferried from his hotel in a blacked-out limousine to an imposing residence, surrounded by tall trees. When the electronic gates swung open, the visitor caught a glimpse of three conjoining houses and an immaculate artificial lawn. Then the car accelerated into a giant basement from which an elevator whisked him skyward into the main house, where Masa stood waiting to greet him, a small balding man with a slightly shy smile wearing a cashmere top and casual trousers.

The guest was struck less by the absence of family mementos than by the proliferation of dog baskets for Masa's favorite teacup poodles. A portion of the house was decorated in the Empire style, the period between 1800 and 1815 when Napoleon modernized France and redrew the map of Europe. Masa, the guest learned, had long had an obsession with Napoleon. The Little Corporal was a fellow outsider, a Corsican of modest origins later crowned emperor of France. Charles de Gaulle declared Napoleon to be a once-in-a-millennium genius, but his brilliance and his capacity for catastrophic errors of judgment could not easily be separated. The same might be said of Masa, the guest reflected.[17]

One of his treasured paintings remains etched in the memory of several other guests. It features Napoleon on horseback, surrounded by his generals. In the background, Moscow is in flames. The year is 1812. Napoleon is about to embark on a humiliating retreat through the winter snow, his army stricken by hunger and disease. The Russians have torched the Kremlin and other parts of the city. One French general stays behind. Masa suggested Carle Vernet's painting highlighted the importance of having loyal lieutenants. Some guests had a different view: the picture encapsulated the perils of overreach, an all-too-familiar character trait in their host.

When Masa led his Thirty-Year Vision brainstorming sessions, he usually began with a piece of advice: start with the conclusion. The destination was key. Another tip was: when you are lost, look further into the distance. "The reason you can't envision it clearly is because you're limiting your field of vision to 30 years," he explained, reminding them of his favorite time frame. "Start bold and think 300 years ahead. Then you can work backwards to what things will be like 30 years from now."[18]

Masa regularly cajoled colleagues to break with the rigid Japanese mindset and give free rein to their imagination. He took inspiration from Japanese history, citing Oda Nobunaga, the first great unifier of Japan, who overthrew the Ashikaga shogunate in 1573. A brilliant samurai warrior, Nobunaga had a superior supply of gunpowder that helped him win the Battle of Nagashino in 1575 and the war. For Masa, the lesson was that technology—in this case, gunpowder—had the power to change history.

Turning to modern methods of communication, Masa instructed Kamaya to consult SoftBank's twenty-thousand-odd employees. He wanted his company's vision to be broadly based, not the top-down work typical of Japan Inc. Kamaya suggested an internal competition where groups of SoftBank employees could pitch their ideas. Initially Masa was skeptical, but then he had a flash of inspiration: SoftBank should canvass people outside the company via Twitter, the embryonic social media and messaging service.

On December 24, 2009, Masa posted his first tweet: "I've decided to start tweeting under my real name [Son Masayoshi] today. It's Christmas Eve, 2009, almost midnight." Five months later, on May 23, 2010, Masa reached out again to the general public: "What is the saddest thing in life?" Ten minutes later, he asked: "I wonder what makes people feel the happiest in life?"

The public's negative answers were skewed toward loneliness, while the positives revolved around family and animals. To mild relief at the top of SoftBank, hardly anyone mentioned money.

On June 24, 2010, Masa stepped onstage in Hall A of the Tokyo International Forum, a giant steel-and-glass convention center capable of holding thousands of guests. Bathed in spotlights, Masa began his presentation. Running to 133 slides, it was characteristically ambitious: "Information Revolution—Happiness for Everyone."[19]

Masa opened with a list of the leading causes of death in the world, accompanied by Japan's rising suicide rates. SoftBank was not motivated by market share or making top-class products, he declared. "We want to increase the number of people being moved by something and increase people's happiness."

His words reprised Kamaya's call for a higher purpose in corporate life, though Masa's worldview was anchored in technology as a force for good. In specific terms, he predicted that the number of transistors in a single chip would exceed the number of cells in a brain by 2018. In one hundred years, human intelligence would be roughly equivalent to a single-cell amoeba compared to computer intelligence. The age of super-robots was fast approaching, with "extra-intelligent computers" coexisting with people and making them happier.

Then came ever zanier predictions about the future. Within three hundred years, chips planted inside or on our bodies would allow humans to communicate with one another via "telepathy." SoftBank could turn into a "telepathy service provider" allowing humans to speak in multiple languages. Who knows, he speculated, people might even start communicating with dogs. (When talking about animals, Masa always referred to dogs. Cats were never mentioned.)

Masa's vision of the future of the human race was like *Star Trek*'s Spock: rational, technology-driven, almost devoid of emotion. In this bloodless world, SoftBank was destined to play a central role, never restricting itself to a single product or service but ready to partner with many different companies in multiple lines of business, a so-called strategic synergy set. Masa had pursued the same course during the internet bubble, when SoftBank invested in several hundred companies, even if none remotely matched the performance of Alibaba and Yahoo!, the standout stars.

Here was the pivotal moment. Masa was shifting from defense to offense. He'd removed the restrictions imposed after the Vodafone Japan acquisition and tightened after the global financial crisis. SoftBank was planning to invest in five thousand companies within the next thirty years, he pledged. These numbers implied that SoftBank could grow six times larger by 2040. When a young assistant later asked where on earth he could find five thousand companies suitable to invest in, Masa responded that salmon spawned two to three thousand eggs at a time. Only one or two would turn into healthy fish making the journey into the sea and back to the river's spawning ground.

There were many ways to read his remarks. This was a story of life where only the fittest survive. Then again, if single companies were to last several hundred years, how did that prospect square with the creative destruction intrinsic to modern capitalism? At the same time, the salmon-spawning analogy spoke to Masa's own investment philosophy, which involved placing bets on every square on the board in search of 10x, 50x, or even 100x returns. To seasoned investors, this made no sense because it implied a wall of money chasing an unattainable prize. In the coming years, Masa's "all or nothing" investing approach would be tested to destruction. If they had read the Thirty-Year Vision speech, no one could say they weren't warned.

Masa's presentation offered an uplifting vision of a future shaped by technology, foreshadowing his embrace of artificial intelligence as the new organizing force in the modern economy. But at the end, he revealed a human side. The man of the future returned to his early life in the Tosu slum, his Korean heritage, and the woman who in effect raised him, his grandmother Lee Wong-jo, who had long since passed away.

"We have here an old woman that we don't see very often. She's a very, very important person to me," said Masa, pointing to a black-and-white photograph on a large screen. "She crossed over to Japan when she was 14. And got married at 14. To a man who was 30-something, my grandfather."[20]

With his parents sitting in the audience, Masa spoke of his childhood when he was forced to hide under a Japanese alias, an experience that became, in his words, an obsession and a neurosis. Wanting to be "normal," he turned against his grandmother. The woman he once loved became an object of hatred.

Masa, his voice quivering, continued his life story. As a teenager, barely sixteen, he made the decision to break with his circumstances, leave Japan, and study in the US. At that point, he asked to accompany his grandmother to Korea. There he watched her hand over patched-up trousers and sweaters to children in the village of his Korean ancestors in Daegu province. "I will never forget her smile that day," Masa said.

Life as a businessman was not about money, status, or reputation, he concluded. It was about making others happy, especially those people who can't give anything in return. Ron Fisher described Masa's decision to unburden himself in public as "truly remarkable," a rare display of emotion out of character in Japanese corporate life.[21]

Three decades after the founding of SoftBank, Masa's Thirty-Year Vision speech was aimed at the investors who had stuck with SoftBank through its peaks and troughs. He had courageously embraced his Korean past and delivered a technocentric vision of SoftBank's future. His catharsis complete, he was ready to reinvent himself again.

20

FUKUSHIMA

At 2:46 p.m., Japan time, the earthquake struck. First came the rumbling tremors, shaking skyscrapers, toppling furniture and sending men, women, and children scrambling for cover. Then came a deafening roar. Waves up to sixty-five feet high raced ashore, tossing cars into the air and carrying blazing buildings into the path of factories, fields, and buckled highways.

The 9.0-magnitude earthquake which hit the northeast coast of Japan on Friday, March 11, 2011, claimed more than twenty thousand lives. Entire coastal towns were wiped off the map. Fixed-line and mobile phone networks collapsed. Business as well as local and central government lay paralyzed. Yet that was only half the story of devastation. By cutting off electricity to the Fukushima nuclear plant, the earthquake set in motion the most serious nuclear accident in postwar Japan. Over the next few days and weeks, the threat of deadly radiation hung in the air.

Sitting in his office at SoftBank headquarters, Masayoshi Son watched the unfolding horror on a live feed on NHK national television. For a while he remained transfixed by the sight of whole towns being swallowed by the tsunami. Then he saw a young girl on the screen. Dressed in a red anorak, she was crying and shouting in the direction of the sea. "Daddy! . . . Mummy! . . ." Masa was momentarily overwhelmed by a sense of powerlessness.[1] "This is a national crisis, the kind that only comes once every thousand years," he said to colleagues. "I have to be the one that goes there." He meant to Fukushima.

The earthquake unleashed feelings that Masa had never experienced and led him to take a series of extraordinary, and sometimes incoherent, actions. Fukushima revealed three fault lines in his story: the tension between his often-benevolent instincts and his vanity; the SoftBank board's struggle to control him; and the limits of his political influence in Japan, which ultimately spurred another leap for global domination. Before the Fukushima disaster Masa's ambition had limits; afterward he became a more rampant and bombastic figure.

The nuclear accident at Fukushima was a national disaster that exposed a failure of crisis management at all levels. Many things were happening at once: a shutdown in electricity supplies to the plant; a meltdown in the reactor cores in three separate units; multiple explosions and fires that threatened to turn the surrounding area into an irradiated wasteland.[2]

A tragicomedy of errors unfolded, with the lead role played by the Tokyo Electric Power Company (Tepco). As owner and operator of the plant, Tepco was the largest electricity supplier in the country, a lumbering giant alongside Japan Tobacco and Japan Railways. Together the trio represented the implacable face of Japan Inc.: autocratic, bureaucratic, and system-built to resist change. For Masa, who occasionally toyed with disrupting Japan's domestic energy market, Tepco was an object of disdain.

Between midafternoon Friday, March 11, and 10 a.m. on Saturday, March 12—the most critical period for handling the accident—neither of Tepco's top managers was present at head office in Tokyo. Company chairman Tsunehisa Katsumata was traveling in China on a business trip, while company president Masataka Shimizu was in Nara, a historical town in the western part of Japan, sightseeing with his wife.[3]

When Shimizu tried to return to headquarters, he found three of the main Japanese transportation arteries—the Chuo motorway, the Tomei motorway, and the Tokaido Shinkansen bullet train—closed. Tepco's president remained stuck in western Japan until midmorning on Saturday. With its top leadership out of action and mobile phone networks down, Tepco was paralyzed.[4]

The day after the accident, Prime Minister Naoto Kan arrived by helicopter to survey the scene. Like most Japanese politicians, Kan was pronuclear, a man best known as the health minister who frankly admitted the government's responsibility for spreading HIV-infected blood in the 1980s. Handsome and vigorous, he suffered a setback after tabloid revelations about an affair with a TV anchor, vigorously denied by both parties. Kan took office in June 2010 as Japan's twenty-ninth postwar prime minister. Nothing in his résumé prepared him for what was to follow.

On March 14, three days after the accident, Tepco indicated that it was considering pulling its workers from the Fukushima plant. Accompanied by five of his closest aides, Kan stormed into Tepco's headquarters at 5:35 a.m. the next day. He told two hundred workers in its operation room that abandoning the reactors and spent pools would unleash a catastrophe, releasing two to three times the contamination discharged at Chernobyl.

Japan's survival was at stake, the prime minister said. If the government failed to contain the disaster, either the US or Russia would be forced to intervene. Tepco was not allowed to accept defeat. The company bore ultimate responsibility for the disaster. The workers in the plant had to put their lives on the line. From then on, the government and Tepco worked in an uneasy harness to cool the reactor cores and contain the radiation threat.

Fukushima exposed willful neglect of earlier warnings about nuclear risk in a country historically prone to earthquakes. The academic and political establishment engaged in a conspiracy of silence, fearful that, if the risks were publicly acknowledged, citizens would demand the plants be shut down and Japan's reliance on nuclear energy be fatally compromised.[5]

On Monday, March 21, ten days after the nuclear accident, Masa, accompanied by his chief of staff and the mayor of Takeo, a city on the other side of Japan, drove in three separate cars to Fukushima, where they were met by Yuhei Sato,[6] governor of the local area. Masa was venturing into a disaster scene unlike anything witnessed in Japan since the end of the Second World War; a hellscape of shattered communities, huddled refugees, and potentially radioactive no-go zones.

What did Masa, the billionaire with an innate streak of techno-optimism, hope to achieve among the chaos and suffering? The immediate problem was SoftBank's mobile phone network; the tsunami had destroyed its base stations, amplifying a dangerous breakdown in communications. "We were a mobile carrier, and we were the weakest of the three and people could not connect to our network," he recalled later.[7] "Many people died as a result. I felt responsible." Masa told the local politicians that he would restore the network and offer free mobile phones to under-eighteens whose parents were missing.

Masa also had a grander plan that he had been working on since the tsunami had struck: a vast evacuation. It involved moving three hundred thousand people from the contaminated coastal area around Fukushima, where radioactive water had leaked. Never one to knowingly undersell an idea, he chose the Japanese word *sokai* for evacuation, a reference to the mass removal of women and children to the countryside from cities targeted by Allied firebombing during the Second World War.

Yet when he sketched out his master plan, Governor Sato balked. The priority was rendering the nuclear power plant safe; the evacuation would have to wait, he declared. Masa erupted with frustration. "It's not the next thing on the list of priorities, it has to be done now," he remonstrated. "Mr. Governor, if you don't do it, who will?"[8]

Masa pointed out that his home state, Saga prefecture, had agreed to take in thirty thousand people. He'd called the governor personally. And he had corralled the mayor of Takeo in Saga to come to Fukushima to deliver a commitment to take in refugees from the disaster zone. Governor Sato was immovable. Baffled, Masa stormed out of the building. The Takeo mayor and his own chief of staff advised him to return to Tokyo. But once he got into his car, Masa insisted they all go to the area's main evacuation site.

The gym serving as a refugee shelter was crammed with people, mostly elderly. Masa, clad in a black puffer jacket, crouched in solidarity with the earthquake victims. Then, one by one, he tried to convince the evacuees to move to Kyushu, hundreds of miles away. In the tight-knit communities of Japan, and certainly in the more remote northeast coastal towns in the vicinity of Fukushima, the idea of displacement to the western island of Kyushu was like moving to another continent. But Masa, displaying a glaring lack of empathy and, as always, convinced of his own logic, repeatedly promised the elderly evacuees the flight fare to Kyushu and a year's maintenance. Not one of them said yes. As he left the gym, Masa turned to his chief of staff and muttered: "How sad."[9]

On his return to Tokyo, Masa convened another meeting of his top team. With no forewarning, he told them that he was going to step down as SoftBank CEO for one year to focus solely on the nuclear disaster. He went on to outline ambitious plans, moving beyond repairing the network and rebuilding a vast nuclear disaster zone. He proposed leading a once-in-a-generation shift into the electricity business, replacing nuclear power with renewable energy.

The rebuff in the disaster zone had been disappointing, humiliating even. But rather than reflect or retreat, it had led him to escalate, proposing an even vaster scheme, one that would place him as the leading protagonist in a national tragedy of historical proportions.

In normal times, SoftBank's top executives dutifully followed Masa's orders. This time, they spoke up. Trying to sound calm and reasonable in the face of their boss's feverish behavior, they made the case that Masa's desire to help was misplaced and the company's interests had to come first. Incensed by the mutiny, Masa started banging the table.

"I'm ready to send all our employees to the disaster sites," he insisted. "I'm going to put all my wealth into this. If you won't allow a year, give me at least three months. I can just leave the rest to [Ken] Miyauchi."

But this time Miyauchi, the ultraloyal COO of SoftBank Mobile, refused to bend to his boss. "Son-san, I can sympathize with that vision, but that's not something one company can do. Surely your responsibility is to your company, to its employees, their families, and its customers."

The discussion went on for more than two hours, growing ever more heated. Finally, Masa called time. "Enough," he said. "I'm going to announce I'm quitting at the next board meeting."[10]

SoftBank executives were shocked by the outburst, at a loss to understand why Masa was so intent on abandoning the company to which he had devoted his adult life and to which he owed his personal fortune. Even more baffling was his lack of focus on Governor Sato's appeal to restore SoftBank's mobile phone network. After all, reestablishing communication lines was a lifeline for the earthquake's victims and a critical measure of national recovery.

Faced with the irresistible force of Masayoshi Son determined to step down as CEO, one of his aides turned to the immovable object of Tadashi Yanai, the Uniqlo boss. Yanai was familiar with Masa's impetuous behavior and his passing fads. He promised he would have a word ahead of the next board meeting. "Don't worry," he told Masa's aide. "There's no CEO who will simply abandon his business. Son-san will never do such a thing."

Yanai's confidence was entirely misplaced. At the next board meeting, Masa preempted the discussion by announcing he intended to step down as CEO. Calling for a decisive response to the national crisis, he unveiled his plan for SoftBank to be the agent of transformation, leading Japan's shift from nuclear energy to alternative renewables such as wind and solar power. "I will step down," he warned. "Please do not try to stop me."

Yanai pushed back, hard. "The reason you are praised by the public is because of what you do as CEO of SoftBank, and that's nothing to do with energy. Energy is a matter of the state."

Still, Masa wouldn't budge, to the amazement not just of the Japanese board members but also outsiders, led by Alibaba's Jack Ma and the two Americans, Ron Fisher and Mark Schwartz, the ex–Goldman Sachs banker. The discussion grew ill tempered. Frustrated, Masa again banged the table, adamant he was leaving.

A fierce debate ensued, which ended in an awkward compromise that showed how SoftBank's board was terrified of losing Masa but equally worried about indulging his impulses too far. In return for withdrawing his resignation plan, Masa won their support for a ¥20 billion investment in electricity generation to help wean Japan off nuclear power.[11] The funds served as the foundation for a future solar energy business within the Soft-Bank Group that would end up owning a number of solar plants in Japan and the US. At the time it was a palliative to Masa, who was still looking for a chance to make a statement about the Fukushima crisis.

After the containment of the Fukushima meltdown and the near implosion of the SoftBank board, Masa persevered with his energy obsession for much of the rest of 2011. The next stage involved the most powerful man in Japan: Prime Minister Kan. In an article titled "A Solar Belt for East Japan," Masa proposed the creation of mega solar plants across the country, and that Japan should become the biggest solar power nation in the world. Kan read the article and arranged a meeting. On May 14, the two men talked for three hours at a restaurant in Akasaka in Tokyo called Kumagawa. Soon afterward, the Kan administration threw its full weight behind the renewable energy bill.[12]

By coincidence, the bill had been due to be put to the Diet on the day of the earthquake. Energy providers would be obliged under its terms to buy renewable energy, a move certain to trigger higher energy prices given the cost of building solar power plants and therefore one that risked being highly unpopular with voters. "I don't even want to see Kan's face here," said disgruntled members of the Diet.[13]

Elsewhere, opposition was beginning to build, partly driven by the pro-nuclear lobby but also by a broader discomfort with Masa's overtly political role. Masa had ignored Yanai's warning that energy was a matter for the state. Instead, he'd gone ahead with meetings with governors and mayors from all over Japan in his personal crusade to convert them to all-out denuclearization.

In late June, after staving off an incipient Cabinet mutiny, Kan abandoned plans to restart nuclear power plants in Japan. It was a momentous decision. Masa was invited to present at a forum on renewable energy held at the office of the prime minister. The following month, he confirmed SoftBank's entry into the energy business, backing up his investment with a reference to fellow media group Google's own investments in the "smart grid," which uses computers to collect data about customer usage and thereby improve energy efficiency. By invoking Google, Masa was deliberately seeking to place SoftBank as a peer in the global tech industry. But the political tides were shifting, and, not for the first time, Masa misread the public mood.[14]

With his approval ratings plummeting in the aftermath of the disaster, Kan suffered a drubbing in the upper house elections in July. Within weeks he and his entire Cabinet resigned. His replacement, Yoshihiko Noda, also of the Democratic Party of Japan, signaled that the new government was ready to reverse course on nuclear power. On November 11, the Keidanren, Japan's powerful business federation, followed up with a report which argued strongly in favor of restarting twelve nuclear power plants. Many detected the hand of Tepco, a Keidanren member.

SoftBank, too, belonged to the organization, but its voice clearly did not count as much. Four days later, Masa attended a meeting with the Keidanren in which he confronted its president, the thick-set, silver-haired Hiromasa Yonekura, a former president of Sumitomo Chemical, a living symbol of Japanese heavy industry. Banging his microphone against the table, Masa declared: "I am absolutely against Keidanren's proposal." No one was listening.[15]

Looking back, the Fukushima disaster brought out the best and worst of Masayoshi Son's character. It showed his capacity for compassion. As an ethnic Korean in Japan, he never felt accepted by the establishment; he remained the outsider. Yet he felt a deep sense of responsibility toward his fellow citizens in those first hours when the mobile network was down and thousands of elderly people were displaced without adequate food or water and no means of communication. Masa was moved by the harrowing pictures of suffering on television and showed great generosity through his donations to the earthquake's orphans and victims. SoftBank contributed ¥1 billion ($10 million), while Masa gave ¥10 billion ($100 million), including all his salary for the year and further pledging his future remuneration as representative of SoftBank Group. As a disruptor who had taken on entrenched interests, he instinctively grasped how the Tepco disaster betrayed the corrupt links between the nuclear industry and its regulators in Japan.

Amid the compassion and righteous anger at the inertia of the state, however, there was also Masa's insatiable ego and habit of inconsistent delivery on promises. He believed the tragedy offered another chance for him to write his name in Japanese history, along with the samurai warriors who had united the country.

Masa's concrete achievements were less than world-historical. Weeks after the disaster SoftBank had yet to fully restore its mobile network: on April 1 he admitted that this failure "pains my heart."[16] Within a year or two Masa's hyperactive focus had turned elsewhere. SB Energy, the renewable-power business set up after Fukushima, gradually expanded, but a decade on still contributed less than 0.5 percent of Japan's electricity generation, and in 2023 it was quietly sold, for a probable price of about $1 billion, a financial and strategic afterthought in the vast portfolio of investments that Masa had assembled. By then Japan's share of electricity from green sources had risen significantly but still lagged behind that of the leading green economies in Europe.

Fukushima did confirm one thing, though. It demonstrated that Masa's burning desire to change the course of human events would not be deterred: not by his own failures, the misgivings of SoftBank's board, or the backlash against him in Japan. Even as the radioactive core of the broken Fukushima reactor still glowed, Masa's relentless gaze was turning to the global stage, and back to America. He was just getting started.

21

SPRINT

In October 2011, Steve Jobs died after an eight-year battle with pancreatic cancer. He was only fifty-six. Masa described his old business partner and friend as a "true genius" with a rare ability to fuse art and technology: "In centuries from now, he [Jobs] will be remembered alongside Leonardo da Vinci."[1]

Masa saw himself as a historical figure too, but, having turned fifty-four, he felt strangely unfulfilled. The Fukushima nuclear disaster left him conscious that life was precious, his time on earth limited. Shortly after Jobs's death, he spoke to his personal banker Jeff Sine. "My ambition is mediocre," he confided.[2]

Sine sensed that Masa had something big in mind. Soon afterward, he discovered that the code name for Masa's master plan was P-100. This was shorthand for SoftBank making $100 billion in EBITDA (earnings before interest, taxes, depreciation, and amortization), a head-spinning eightfold increase on comparable figures in 2011-12. Masa was back on the offensive, determined to make SoftBank a global force in the mobile internet. Knowing he was about to step into a regulatory minefield, Masa recruited to the SoftBank Group board the Indian telecoms billionaire Sunil Bharti Mittal.

Like Masa, Mittal was a cradle-to-grave entrepreneur. Punjabi by origin, he started out making crankshafts for local bicycle manufacturers, later importing small power generators, push-button phones, fax machines, and cordless phones. In 1992, he won eight new mobile phone network licenses from the Indian government to operate in four cities. From there, he built Airtel, a telecoms empire stretching from Africa to Asia.

Mittal knew that Japan was too small a stage for Masa. "The man has balls of steel," he once remarked.[3] At some point, he might plant a foot in India. Joining the SoftBank board in June 2011 offered Mittal a chance to watch Masa close-up. In his first year, he witnessed the brilliant, the average, and the ugly.

Masa was a master of consumer psychology who'd done an outstanding job building the SoftBank Mobile brand in Japan. (The talking dog advertisement was a Mittal favorite.) He'd also mastered mobile technology. One day, he asked Mittal to pick a spot in the world to measure Airtel's broadband speed. Mittal, who used motorcyclists to ride around cities to collect data on speed and reliability, chose Delhi. Masa clicked on his iPad, which gave an instant, precise answer.

Masa's people skills were less impressive. Congenitally impatient, Masa regularly waved aside Japanese executives presenting to the SoftBank board. On one occasion, Mittal watched Masa start scribbling data on the whiteboard while the hapless manager sat cross-legged on the floor. It was a virtuoso performance but no way to run a company.

The same tone deafness featured in SoftBank's plan to buy a controlling stake in Singtel, Singapore's national carrier. The putative seller was Temasek, Singapore's sovereign wealth fund, whose chief executive was Ho Ching, who also happened to be the wife of Prime Minister Lee Hsien Loong. After productive talks, Temasek seemed ready to sell its stake. Suddenly, Masa got cold feet.

Mittal was flabbergasted. So was Jeff Sine in New York. He'd spent two years at Raine Group working on Singtel. No deal meant no payday. Sine was equally taken aback when Masa revealed his new plan: a two-pronged takeover in the US involving Sprint, followed by T-Mobile. In short, the biggest shake-up in the US telecoms market since the breakup of the AT&T monopoly in 1982.

Back in India, Mittal knew his reputation in Singapore was temporarily shot, along with SoftBank's. But sensing Masa had another takeover target in his sights, he arranged a meeting with T-Mobile representatives in Munich. At the last minute, Masa pulled out, saying he was opting to buy Sprint only.

"Don't worry," Masa told him. "We will still do T-Mobile. It's just a different route."

When Mittal expressed reservations at the next SoftBank Group board meeting, Masa brushed him aside. While the two billionaires remained on friendly terms, Mittal felt let down. Masa's willingness to listen, he concluded, depended on whether the answer suited him. He resigned from the SoftBank board two years later.

When Masa announced his plan to buy Sprint in October 2012, he offered to pay $20.1 billion for 70 percent of a dying company. Sprint had been languishing ever since its $35 billion merger with Nextel in 2005. Despite the merger of these two smaller players, an epic round of consolidation had left most of the power in the industry in the hands of two de facto duopolists, AT&T and Verizon. Sprint-Nextel initially tried to maintain two separate networks built with different technology. In the following seven years, the telecoms carrier piled up around $50 billion in losses.

Masa looked beyond the bad numbers. He was borrowing at rock-bottom rates making a bet on scale. Two weeks before the Sprint offer, SoftBank acquired eAccess, a rival Japanese carrier. Overnight, its market share in Japan shot up to second place behind NTT Docomo. In global terms, the new SoftBank-Sprint combination had ninety-six million customers, making it the world's third-largest mobile operator, behind China Mobile and Verizon. "I am a man," Masa said, "and every man wants to be number one, not number two or three."[4]

Crucially, SoftBank's strategy depended on a future merger between third-place Sprint with T-Mobile, the fourth US carrier. Masa assumed he could pull off such a deal and then revive the combined company using the Vodafone Japan playbook, cutting prices, polishing the new brand, and eating Verizon and AT&T's lunch. But Verizon was not Docomo, Sprint was a hodgepodge, and the US was not Japan (which was no bigger in landmass than the state of Montana, as Sine undiplomatically pointed out).[5]

Back in 2011, the Federal Communications Commission had blocked a planned merger between AT&T and fourth-place T-Mobile, with the Obama administration suspicious about attempts to consolidate the market even further. Apart from Washington, municipalities in America had their own say about zoning regulations and the placement of mobile phone towers critical to operating a mobile network.

"Masa was 100 percent right in terms of the operating plan based on the depth of spectrum advantage and the benefits of putting Sprint and

T-Mobile together," recalled Jeff Sine, "but he was 100 percent wrong on the politics."[6]

Despite warnings, Masa pushed for a meeting in December 2013 with the new FCC chair, Tom Wheeler, in Washington. The talks got off on the wrong foot when a story appeared in *The Wall Street Journal* about a proposed Sprint-T-Mobile combination on the eve of the planned meeting. It was a clumsy leak, and Wheeler, an industry veteran and author of several Civil War history books, made his displeasure clear.

"Look, you're wasting your time," he told Masa. "If you decide to go ahead, let me tell you how this plays out. We can just block it."[7]

Masa wasn't listening. He plastered campaign billboards around Washington and stepped up lobbying in Congress. In a speech at the US Chamber of Commerce on March 11, 2014, he compared wireless coverage in the US to air quality in Beijing. American consumers had been browbeaten into accepting a second-rate service. Finally, he claimed he was buying Sprint because he was inspired by his student experience in California.

"It is a debt in my heart that I have to pay back," he said. "This is the best country in the world. I love America."[8]

After his speech, Masa spotted Wheeler in the audience, forcing him to take evasive measures. The sight of the diminutive Japanese chasing the American beanpole was worthy of a Marx Brothers movie, but Masa was fighting a lost cause. An FCC official called SoftBank's boss during one of his regular visits to the US.

"We owe you because you are [via the $20 billion Sprint acquisition] the biggest foreign direct investor in the history of this country, but we are not going to let you do the merger. It's DOA."

Masa was nonplussed.

"What is DOA?" he asked a SoftBank colleague.

"Dead on arrival," came the reply.[9]

In August 2014, Masa took the hint and shelved the Sprint-T-Mobile merger indefinitely. He had miscalculated the politics, but he'd also underestimated T-Mobile, which was run by John Legere, a marketing genius with long, lanky hair who looked like a hippie but fought like an alley cat. Legere was determined to break the dominance of Verizon and AT&T. His concept was to brand T-Mobile as the "Un-Carrier," a customer-conscious insurgent supported by taglines such as "Break up with your crummy carrier and we'll pay for it."

With the advent of the pro-business Trump administration, the scales would eventually tilt back in favor of a merger. But midway through the second term of the Obama administration, Masa's position was desperate. He tried off-loading his stake in Sprint, but no one was interested. Having spent $20 billion, he needed to spend billions more to turn his vision into a reality: he needed an operator.

Standing six foot six inches tall, Marcelo Claure was a grizzled bear of a man whose passions were soccer and making money; lots of money. The son of a UN geologist, he had spent time in Guatemala (his birthplace), Morocco, the Dominican Republic, and Bolivia, his family home. As a student, Claure made his first fortune buying and selling students' frequent-flyer miles while attending Bentley College in Massachusetts. After a spell at the Bolivian Football Federation, he set up his own business called Brightstar distributing new and old mobile phones, including trade-in deals with Apple, AT&T, and Verizon. His formula was deceptively simple: buy cheap, sell expensive.

On a trip to Tokyo, Claure contacted Masa's office and was told the boss was available for a five-minute meeting only. But when he outlined his handset resale concept, Masa grasped it immediately and announced that SoftBank was ready to act as the middleman between Apple and Brightstar.

"You pay me for the used iPhone, and I pay back the customer over the next thirty-six months," said Masa.[10]

Even Claure had to admit it was a genius move. The arrangement delivered up-front money to Masa, and SoftBank would "own" the customer in the future. When Masa pressed the Bolivian for an answer, Claure said he too was in a hurry. In two hours, he was due to board a plane to China.

"Right," said Masa, "this is going to be the fastest contract you have ever signed in your life."

"I just met someone who is crazier than me," Claure later told his lawyer in the US.[11]

Gaining a license as a secondhand phone dealer in Japan turned out to be a lot trickier. Disruption threatened jealously guarded, tightly regulated distribution networks. When SoftBank started business, the police turned up and threatened to shut down the operation. But Masa and Claure together found a loophole in the law. Masa then pitched Claure a second time, offering to buy 80 percent of Brightstar and appoint him to the Sprint board.

Name your price, he said.

Claure balked. Brightstar was the only Hispanic Fortune 100 company. He didn't want to sell. Besides, he thought Sprint was the worst-run company he'd ever experienced. The costs were out of control, he complained.

"Okay, then you can fix it," said Masa.

Claure cashed out of Brightstar, selling for $1.2 billion. He was appointed Sprint CEO on August 5, 2014, the day after the World Cup final in Brazil. Masa had found his operator. In a goodwill gesture, he joined the Claure turnaround project, appointing himself Sprint's new chief technology officer. He also promised to buy the biggest house in Kansas, where Sprint was headquartered. Claure said it was a ridiculous waste of money and suggested Masa buy the house next door, decorated by his wife in the Japanese style. The Bolivian set one condition: his family needed access to the swimming pool. Masa went ahead and bought the neighboring house for several million dollars. But it was still an epic waste of money since he visited the house once and stayed one night only.

When Claure arrived at Sprint headquarters in Overland Park, Kansas, in the heart of America's Midwest, he discovered the company he was about to run was effectively bankrupt. It had around $35 billion debt, with $5-billion-a-year repayments, and there was no prospect of SoftBank injecting fresh funding. Having borrowed heavily to fund the US acquisition, Masa had been served notice by Japanese banks that he couldn't send a dollar more from Tokyo to prop up the business. "You're on your own," Masa said.[12]

In his first week, Claure discovered one essential fact. The key measure of Sprint's health was neither debt nor revenue; what mattered was the application and interpretation of EBITDA. The Bolivian came up with an ingenious solution: rather than give customers free handsets and recognize the cost up front in the firm's profit and loss statement, he would lease all the company's phones to customers. Since Sprint was the ultimate owner of the handsets and the initial outlay was treated as an investment, this had the effect of artificially raising EBITDA. It was an accounting trick. Claure knew it. The banks knew it. But all agreed that desperate times required unorthodox measures, and this was by far the most creative solution on the table.

The second piece of wizardry came courtesy of Ram Sundaram, a Goldman Sachs banker recruited to help the turnaround. Sprint's junk credit rating meant that banks were prepared to lend money only at 11 to

12 percent. He and Claure proposed using Sprint's spare wireless spectrum as collateral and putting it in a special-purpose vehicle (SPV), a device normally used for joint ventures, property deals, or asset securitization. In this case, since the spectrum had no debt, the SPV itself had no debt. Therefore, it could borrow at investment grade at a rate of between 3 and 4 percent, raising $7 billion through the spectrum play alone.

All this required delicate negotiations with the FCC, the banks, and the credit ratings agencies. It also required a mastery of technical detail to which Masa, once focused, proved more than equal. Colleagues marveled at how he could absorb huge amounts of data and information. At the end of weeks of hard bargaining, Sprint raised a total of more than $20 billion at 3.5 percent over seven years, parceled out in $2 billion chunks. In addition to financing crucial spending on marketing and the network, Sprint was able to reduce total debt from $31 billion to around $21 billion.[13]

Not everything came down to accounting wheezes. Claure spent every Friday in a Sprint store, studying customer and employee behavior. He and Masa forced through brutal cost cutting. Instead of summoning usual suspects like McKinsey, they adopted a "zero baseline budget." Sprint had eight hundred lawyers. Why not two hundred? Sprint had one hundred public relations people. Why not ten?

Sprint's quaint Midwest business culture was deeply ingrained. There were name cards in the executive parking garage, and the store sales assistants were obliged to wear dress shoes. Masa led a cultural transformation— with Japanese characteristics. He leased two four-story buildings in Silicon Valley, including a replica of his own executive suite in Tokyo. Ever attentive to detail, he included a fountain in the room where part of the floor was made of tatami, the straw mat traditionally used in Japanese homes.[14]

Masa's Japanese was always formal and respectful, but his English was on another spectrum. He regularly dressed down Sprint executives in public. Internally, these were known as "Masa-cre sessions." Masa thumped the table, waved his arms, and complained about the "loser mentality" at the company. Once he demanded that an advertising campaign be pulled because it was as limp as a rag doll. "Are you stupid?" he yelled.

Claure and Masa also had screaming matches. One of the sore points was the rollout of the wireless network. Masa didn't anticipate how hard it would be to install mobile phone antennas in the US quickly because of local zoning regulations. He wanted to dispense with expensive cell towers by getting permission to put their cell boxes on top of existing local government property. The cheap and cheerful plan worked in Japan, but in the US it was doomed from the outset. Claure later branded the scheme "a total failure." Masa himself confessed that his inability to understand the American regulatory setup was "one of the biggest mistakes of my life."

If there was one bright spot, it was Sprint's earlier acquisition of Clearwire, the US wireless operator with valuable mobile spectrum. Combined with Sprint's own network, the spectrum served as a future platform for high-speed 5G technology. This would prove an indispensable bargaining chip in later merger negotiations with T-Mobile.

Marcelo Claure cut costs, sharpened the brand, and improved customer service. But far from sprinting, he was running to stand still. Masa, too, poured every ounce of energy into the turnaround, working seven days a week, often going on calls from between 10 p.m. and 2 a.m., Tokyo time. The two men talked five or six times a day, each driven by the monumental challenge of mounting a turnaround of Sprint.

"We had a beautiful relationship," said Claure. "I thought I was the gifted child."[15]

He was one of several top foreign hires who assumed they enjoyed a special status, where one day they might even succeed Masa as SoftBank CEO. In fact, Masa's enthusiasms were fleeting, his relationships transactional. Top Japanese executives never made this mistake because they understood that Masa was the boss, and he wasn't going anywhere.

Lower down the ranks, SoftBank insiders joked that Claure was just one of Masa's many brides. Another was Rajeev Misra, to whom Masa remained betrothed after his artful financing of the Vodafone Japan acquisition. But unbeknownst to Claure and Misra, there was a third man in their boss's sights. He was ambitious, driven, and Indian. In every respect, it made for an explosive combination.

22

TWO INDIANS ARE BETTER THAN ONE

In the spring of 2013, Masa was looking for a high-profile hire to realize "SoftBank 2.0," his dream of boosting SoftBank Group's market capitalization to $1 trillion by 2025. His plan to organize a merger between Sprint and T-Mobile was facing regulatory opposition in the US. Compared to the humdrum task of turning round Sprint, the allure of investing in global technology businesses was infinitely more exciting. But to succeed, he needed a star manager.

His search led him to two Indians: his old banker ally Rajeev Misra and Nikesh Arora, the number-four top executive at Google. The new recruits proved to be an explosive combination, raising questions about Masa's judgment as a manager and, by broaching the delicate issue of succession, casting into doubt the stability of SoftBank itself.

Masa first met Arora in 2009 when he paid a visit to Google's HQ in Mountain View. He was looking for an alternative to Yahoo!'s algorithmic search technology, which supplied SoftBank-controlled Yahoo! Japan. Yahoo! was switching to rival Microsoft's Bing as part of cost-cutting measures introduced by Carol Bartz, a computer industry veteran drafted in to save a company in decline. Bartz, who had just taken over from cofounder Jerry Yang, told financial analysts that Yahoo! needed "some friggin' breathing room" so it could "kick some butt." Stripped of the expletives, this meant abandoning proprietary search technology. Sensing that Yahoo! Japan's business model was at risk, Masa approached Google, which he'd used in 2002–05 as the search engine of choice.

Google's CEO, Eric Schmidt, and the two cofounders, Larry Page and Sergey Brin, all said they were too busy to see the visitor from Japan. Masa ended up with Arora, the son of an Indian Air Force officer, with college degrees in India and the US. Arora was fast-talking, physically imposing, and famously dismissive of anyone talking what he considered rubbish. Masa looked past the arrogance; he was drawn to the Indian's energy and his tech smarts. One day, he might even be a successor.

The two men came up with a new partnership whereby Yahoo! Japan paid Google an undisclosed sum for its search technology, allowing it to grab nearly 90 percent of all web searches in Japan. When Masa informed Bartz that Yahoo! Japan was going its own way, she exploded. But as a minority shareholder, there was nothing she could do. Apart from kicking Masa out of her office.

Masa kept in regular touch thereafter. He played golf with Arora and invited him to dinner in Silicon Valley, once or twice at a rented house on Barry Lane while he was renovating his new home in nearby Woodside, a leafy town next to the Stanford University campus. Masa's "starter castle," designed in the neoclassical style and surrounded by trees on a nine-acre estate, was one of the most expensive private residences in California. Masa had acquired the property through a shell corporation—SV Projects LLC—in 2012, paying $117.5 million to the owner, Tully Friedman, a San Francisco Bay–based private equity multimillionaire.[1]

By 2013, his dinner guest cut a frustrated figure. It wasn't the money. He'd pulled in $51 million the previous year. It was the lack of respect, the nagging suspicion that his bosses took him for granted. On one occasion, he recalled, he'd been going over the numbers with Larry Page, the computer genius who cofounded Google. As usual, it was a blowout quarter for digital advertising sales. Google was on its way toward being one of the most valuable companies on the planet, but Page just stared out of the window, lost in his own world.

It dawned on Google's chief revenue officer that Page didn't really give a shit about advertising. He was dreaming about self-driving vehicles, flying cars, even putting a man on Mars. The Next Big Thing. Page, who had taken over from Eric Schmidt as CEO, had little appetite for the mundane business of running the company. He was in fact looking for a successor—and that man was not Nikesh Arora.

By the time Ron Fisher, acting on Masa's instructions, made an approach, Arora had half a foot out of the door. But when the South African delivered the offer, the Indian took one look and said: "Why would I leave Google and take a risk on the basis of that?"[2]

The next meeting took place over dinner at the Four Seasons hotel in Westlake Village, a bedroom community surrounded by hiking and horse trails in the Santa Monica Mountains outside Los Angeles. Masa chose the Onyx restaurant, one of his favorite Japanese eateries. As the wine flowed, he pulled his usual napkin trick, scribbling down an offer. Arora kept adding a zero, and Masa responded by upping the number. Eventually, the napkin was filled with zeros and a plethora of brackets.

It all added up to a guaranteed minimum four-year deal worth $50 million a year, plus a $120 million fee to compensate for the loss of his Google stock options. At $320 million, these were sums beyond the reach of most Silicon Valley executives, let alone any top manager in Japan. And that was before the clincher, when Masa promised Arora access to a company private jet.

"The numbers look okay," said Arora, "but I have to talk to Larry."[3]

The conversation with Larry Page was brief. Google's cofounder had no intention of matching the SoftBank offer. For the first time in his career, Arora discovered he was indeed dispensable.

The SoftBank courtship was not the only intimate affair in Nikesh Arora's life in the summer of 2014. Before he tied the knot with Masa, he married Ayesha Thapar, heiress to a textiles, real estate, and trading empire. The wedding celebrations took place at Borgo Egnazia in Puglia, a five-star resort on the southeast coast of Italy. Hollywood stars led by Brad Pitt, Ashton Kutcher, and Demi Moore were among the guests. Over three days, they mixed with Silicon Valley's richest, led by Page, Brin, Mark Zuckerberg, and Larry Ellison of Oracle, all flying in by private jet.

Masa was also present, though he steered clear of the scratch cricket match on the beach and other booze-filled festivities. One afternoon, he spotted Rajeev Misra. "Ah, Rajeev," said the SoftBank boss, embracing his former partner, "I've not seen you since the Vodafone Japan deal. How about breakfast tomorrow?"[4]

When the two men met at 8 a.m., Masa unveiled his vision to be the world's number-one telecoms company, surpassing China Mobile by market capitalization. He talked about buying BT, merging Sprint and T-Mobile, linking the pipes all around the world, and creating a business worth $100 billion. The code name for the project was P-100 (Project 100), he confided. Afterward, the two men swapped phone numbers. Two weeks later, Misra was in Tokyo. "Come join the family," said Masa, with one of his beguiling smiles. Then, mindful of his blowout negotiations with Arora, he asked: "Are you expensive?"[5]

Misra was always expensive. In the run-up to the Lehman Brothers collapse, when he had overseen the giant short bet against subprime mortgages, he raked in $80 million. Seven years on, life had become a lot more complicated—and a lot less interesting. New regulations curbed the high-risk proprietary trading that had earned the global investment banks billions before the global financial crisis. Right now, Misra was working at Fortress, a US asset management group based in San Francisco. SoftBank sounded exciting—and far more financially rewarding.

Ron Fisher and Nikesh Arora urged Masa not to hire him. The Deutsche man was a debt trader, a master manipulator. Bringing him into SoftBank was a recipe for chaos and infighting, they warned.

Masa refused to budge.

"Two Indians are better than one," he said, with an impish smile.

Misra had in fact thwarted opposition from Arora and Fisher by preemptively resigning from his job at Fortress. He told Masa it was too late for him (and his family) to rescind the decision. Masa was sympathetic and handed him a job title as head of strategic finance. Whatever that meant.

"Will you work for Masa, or will you work for me?" Arora asked him after the Deutsche man shared news of his nebulous job title.

Misra made all the right noises but declined to move his family from London to California or Japan. He preferred being a free agent, decamping for a while in Tokyo, where he had face time with Masa. It was one more sign of how the sockless Indian trader with the slicked-down hair was more skilled than Arora at maneuvering inside large organizations.

In his first six months in 2014–15 as head of SoftBank Internet and Media Inc. (SIMI), an investment subsidiary of the SoftBank Group based in Japan, Arora moved the business away from making a bunch of small bets on early stage companies. He switched to bigger investments in fewer, but more mature, businesses. This was the new conventional wisdom, founded in part on the spectacular debut of Alibaba on the New York Stock Exchange on September 19, 2014. Some fifteen years after its launch, Alibaba had pulled off the most valuable IPO on record, eclipsing Facebook and Google. SoftBank's 32 percent holding was worth almost $70 billion, on paper at least.

The Alibaba IPO gave SoftBank a ton of credibility when lining up investment targets around the world. Arora paid $1 billion for a stake in the Korean e-commerce company Coupang, a big hit. He plowed $250 million into WME-IMG, the American media and sports agency. With his encouragement, Masa took a closer interest in the entertainment industry in general, approaching DreamWorks, the Hollywood animation studio run by former Disney executive Jeffrey Katzenberg.[6]

That putative offer went nowhere, despite successive overtures on Masa's part. Another idea, inspired by Spotify's streaming model, was to use SoftBank money to disrupt the music business. Michael Lynton, then in charge of Sony Entertainment, had two meetings with Masa in Tokyo, once at SoftBank headquarters and once at Sony HQ. On both occasions, Lynton told him that throwing money around was a recipe for mediocrity and waste.

"Listen, Masa, friction is not such a bad thing," said Lynton, "it's part of the creative process."

When Masa asked if he could come back to Lynton at a future date in case he changed his mind, the Sony executive said no.

"Try somebody else," said Lynton.[7]

Thanks to Arora, Masa rekindled his interest in India, investing in businesses like Snapdeal and OYO Rooms, which aspired to be the dominant mid-market hotel franchise in the subcontinent. Arora also pulled off several high-profile Indian hires, including Alok Sama, ex–Morgan Stanley, and Deep Nishar, a former Google and LinkedIn executive. Drawn from the Indian diaspora, these executives were ambitious, highly educated, and money-driven. Many were trained mathematicians, but they applied their engineering skills to finance rather than academia. Over time, their presence, alongside other Indians, particularly those recruited from Misra's Deutsche Bank network, began to change SoftBank's culture, not always for the better.

To some degree, the shift was inevitable as SoftBank evolved from a Japanese technology conglomerate to a global investment group. But it also created dissonance at the top. While Masa continued to talk a high-minded game about technology bringing happiness to society, the expat Indians brought a cutthroat attitude to business, stoking their boss's appetite for dealmaking. Rather than being a builder and operator, as in the days of Yahoo! broadband, SoftBank Mobile and Sprint, he became an investor and trader, with all the extra risk implied.

In the first instance, the arrival of Arora and his merry men spelled the end of the old guard at SoftBank Capital. Levy knew his time was up after he suggested increasing SoftBank's investment in BuzzFeed, a sassy new media venture. The fresh injection of money would have resulted in a $1.8 billion valuation and a 17 percent stake for SoftBank.

"Chickenshit," said Arora, noting that SoftBank's total assets were valued at $180 billion.[8]

Levy understood there was a new boss in town. He had no regrets. He'd spent twenty years with Masa. It had been a wild ride. Still, he had some questions about Arora's long-term job prospects.

"Is this over in under or over eighteen months?" he asked himself, concluding, "No fuckin' way is this going to last eighteen months."[9]

Levy was not alone in assuming Arora's time at SoftBank might be limited. His pay package offended Japanese employees as well as long-time board members like Uniqlo boss Tadashi Yanai, himself a multibillionaire. Arora was "a very smart guy," but his taste for big money showed a lack of respect of Japanese culture, according to Yanai, who by now was questioning Masa's judgment. "Son wanted to transform Japan," he said, "but Japanese culture is very different from Silicon Valley."[10]

Nor did it escape unnoticed that Yoshimitsu Goto, hardworking and highly rated, was forced to step down from the SoftBank board to make way for Arora. Goto had taken one for the team, but many Japanese executives were indignant that an Indian American hotshot was running their company. It was a rare moment of discontent, though as usual they suffered in silence.

Arora took Masa literally—and seriously—when he spoke about succession. Besides, Masa had given him plenty of encouragement. In the summer of 2015, less than a year after coming aboard, he was made "representative director" of SoftBank Group. This title gave him the powers of second signatory, meaning that he could technically sell the company if Masa was incapacitated. This was a big deal, one more clue that he was being lined up as heir apparent.

On his regular trips to Tokyo, Arora was accorded rock star status. An unmarked van with blacked-out windows picked him up at his rented apartment in Roppongi and drove him to Masa's giant mansion in central Tokyo. Sometimes the drivers wore wigs to heighten the sense of watertight security. Upon arrival, Arora was less impressed by the decor (one half Bulgari, the other half Versace, he joked) than the artificial golf course in the basement. A keen golfer himself, he was tickled by the idea of playing any course in the world in all weather conditions. He especially liked Masa's story of playing a round at the exclusive Augusta golf course with multibillionaire Henry Kravis. When Masa shot a little over par, Kravis complained that he must have played the course before. "Not true, Henry," said Masa. "I've only played Augusta in my basement."[11]

Arora was also amused by the sheer extravagance on display. No stranger to spending money himself (his wedding party had stretched beyond Puglia to several more days jiving in Ibiza), he was still taken aback by Masa's obsession with being number one. Everything had to be bigger, nicer, and better. Like Masa's favorite wines from Domaine de la Romanée-Conti (DRC), which he'd first started drinking in the late 1990s. Why, he'd even seen one New York restaurant stay open extra late because it could count on two DRC bottles being served up for Masa and his guests. That was a cool $15-20,000, easily enough to match a single evening sitting.[12]

On August 19, 2015, to celebrate his first anniversary at SoftBank, Arora bought $483 million of SoftBank stock, having borrowed the necessary funds from SoftBank and other banks, putting down one quarter of the sum on his own account. "This involves me taking an enormous risk in my life once again," he said. "However, I am extremely confident about the future of SoftBank Group. I intend to work closely with Mr. Son to make the vision a reality."[13]

During the first twelve to eighteen months, Masa and Arora were inseparable, on the road in India, Indonesia, Korea, Singapore, and London. On a visit to the music baron Len Blavatnik's house in Kensington Palace Gardens (colloquially known as Billionaires' Row), Masa expressed interest in buying Warner Music. It will cost you $10 billion, said Blavatnik, who'd made his own fortune in oil and gas in post-Soviet Russia. Masa suggested $6 billion. "I thought he was more interested in buying property [in my street]," said Blavatnik.[14]

At the annual Allen & Co. media conference in Sun Valley in July 2015, Masa and Arora walked around like a starstruck couple. Attendees saw them huddled together over breakfast or lunch or under the shades at the Duck Pond, where media titans such as Rupert Murdoch, John Malone, and Comcast's Brian Roberts mixed with the next generation of tech moguls to cook up multibillion-dollar deals that reshaped their global industry. Not everyone was convinced that Masa and Arora was a marriage made in heaven. "He falls in and out of love with people. One moment Nikesh [Arora] or Marcelo [Claure] is the greatest person in the world, the next everything has gone cool," recalled one SoftBank insider.

If there was a black cloud on the ex-Googler's horizon, it took the shape of Rajeev Misra. The first sign of trouble came in October 2014, when it became clear that Masa's plan to merge Sprint and T-Mobile to create a new US telecoms giant was never going to get past antitrust regulators. Misra suggested taking SoftBank private.

Pulling off a leveraged management buyout would require raising billions from the banks, with a tight repayment schedule. Arora complained that a buyout would effectively mean a three-year moratorium on spending. His job as SoftBank's chief investment officer would in effect be redundant. The plan was abandoned.

Arora, who'd pondered taking charge of Sprint himself, was unimpressed with financial engineering. He regularly belittled his fellow countryman in front of SoftBank peers, questioning his business acumen. The battle between Arora the bruiser and Misra the schemer was petty and unrelenting. Masa looked on, either incapable of containing the rivalry or operating on the principle of divide and rule.

What happened next is a source of controversy. According to a blow-by-blow account in *The Wall Street Journal*, Misra instigated a dirty-tricks campaign against Arora involving corporate sabotage, computer hacking, and a failed honey trap in Tokyo. He was also accused of paying $500,000 to an Italian businessman to help undermine his rival. To this day, Misra firmly denies all the allegations. As for the $500,000, he insists it covered an oil investment.[15]

The campaign to destroy Nikesh Arora's reputation began with a bogus complaint from largely anonymous international shareholders. They claimed the ex-Googler had received kickbacks from companies SoftBank invested in as the firm poured money into Indian start-ups. These included the e-commerce company Snapdeal.com, the ride-hailing service Ola, and the real estate search portal Housing.com. Separately, Arora, along with two other private equity firms, Apax and TPG, found himself under scrutiny for arranging a non-SoftBank investment in a Greek telecoms company, Wind Hellas. In April, the shareholders of Hellas went public in a letter to the board. They questioned his decision to remain an adviser to a US investment firm, Silver Lake, that could potentially compete with SoftBank on deals. They also criticized his basic competence.

"Mr. Arora's investment strategy appears to be nothing more than throwing a dart at a dartboard," a lawyer representing the investors wrote in the letter. "How many more millions of dollars of shareholder value must be wasted before the board realizes something must be done?"[16]

Amid a steady drip of allegations of misconduct, SoftBank, with Arora's blessing, ordered two independent investigations. Kroll, the corporate espionage company, was instructed to find out who was behind the smears. The second inquiry was led by Shearman & Sterling, the New York law firm. Arora, shuttling back and forth between San Francisco and Tokyo, denied all allegations of impropriety and tried to get on with his job. He was ultimately cleared. But his standing at SoftBank never fully recovered.

One of Arora's first decrees had been to say he would be screening all investment decisions in the future, a decision that caused Masa intense irritation. Ostensibly the Indian American's instruction was intended to avoid "riffraff" ending up on the boss's desk. *But that was the whole point.* Masa did not want his top lieutenant filtering investment pitches. *He* was the guy who looked founders in the eye. *He* made the big investment decisions. That got his juices pumping. That was what he was really good at, going back to his groundbreaking bets on Yahoo! and Alibaba.

"Nikesh wants control of my company. I am too young to step down," he complained to Misra. "You don't want to be CEO. That's why I trust you."

Misra was content to play a waiting game, knowing that Arora, like Marcelo Claure, was misreading Masa. He was in too much of a hurry to consolidate power, too eager to press his case as successor. The final straw came when Masa told close colleagues that he was determined to buy ARM Holdings, the microchip designer based in Cambridge, England. Having coveted the company for more than a decade, Masa was adamant that ARM was central to the next phase of the digital revolution. He wasn't fazed by the $30 billion price tag.

"Over my dead body," said Arora, noting that SoftBank was still paying down billions in debt inherited from the Sprint acquisition. When Masa insisted that ARM was worth $600 billion, Arora challenged his boss to make the numbers stack up. He asked his team in California to do their own independent analysis of ARM's earnings potential.

"We'll see who's right," he said.

Insulting Masa's judgment in front of his peers was suicidal. Those present at SoftBank headquarters that day in Tokyo made a mental note. The Google guy was toast.

On Tuesday, June 21, 2016, Nikesh Arora announced his resignation as president and COO of SoftBank. Twenty-four hours earlier, an internal investigation into the dirty-tricks campaign that cleared him of any wrongdoing had been made public. Masa praised his onetime star hire for his "world-class execution skills" and his contribution to "SoftBank 2.0."

Arora was in a state of shock but agreed to do an interview that saved face on all sides. He said Masa had signaled he would be ready to step aside when he turned sixty, in roughly a year's time. But when he asked Masa, "Are you ready?" the SoftBank boss was evasive, saying his work was not done. Masa also told him that Japanese employees would never accept a foreigner running SoftBank Group, but Arora kept that fact to himself.

Later that night, Arora sent out a torrent of tweets further explaining the reasons for his departure. Masa meanwhile spelled out his position. "I want to cement SoftBank 2.0, develop Sprint to its true potential, and work on a few more crazy ideas. This will require me to be CEO for at least another five to ten years—this is not a time frame for me to keep Nikesh waiting for the top job."

The SoftBank succession plan was no more. The board didn't raise a peep. Nor was it surprised. Seven years later, Uniqlo's Tadashi Yanai remembers his first reaction to news that Masa was considering stepping down in favor of Nikesh Arora.

"Retirement, isn't that a joke?"[17]

23

SMASH AND GRAB

In 2015, the world's top technology investors, including Masayoshi Son, were gushing about digital genetic coding, self-driving cars, next-generation robotics, and something called "the internet of things." This was the fancy term to describe a new high-tech ecosystem where billions of smart devices would talk to each other, transforming every sector of the economy. In this brave new digital age, Masa had long spotted one clear winner: ARM Holdings, based in Cambridge, England.

ARM was one of Britain's most valuable technology companies, but it wasn't a household name like British Telecom, Rolls-Royce, or Vodafone. ARM provided the design for superfast, energy-efficient silicon chips manufactured under license to Apple, Amazon, and Google. By 2016, the company had more than 95 percent market share in mobile phones through five hundred–plus licenses worldwide.

ARM's design prowess put the company at the center of the present and future architecture of the tiny silicon chips that define the modern world. Yet ARM's success grew out of heroic failure. Back in 1978, an Austrian immigrant, Hermann Hauser, launched Acorn Computers. The British-built PC was wildly popular, selling a total of one million a year at its peak, but weak marketing and stiff competition forced Hauser to pivot and take the "totally mad decision" to develop Acorn's own microchip.[1]

The design was based on a simple insight: the fewer the instructions, the faster the performance and the lower the microchip's power consumption.[2] Within months, Hauser's skeletal team had produced a new microprocessor christened ARM, an abbreviation of Acorn RISC machine. The chip had a superior price and performance to its main rival, Intel, and powered the IBM PC for the next fifteen years. In 1989, Apple took a 43 percent stake in ARM at a cost of $1.5 million, later sold for $800 million. Hauser boasted that his company had helped rescue one of the most valuable companies in the world. He was only half joking.

Masa first alighted upon ARM during his acquisition of Vodafone's mobile phone business in Japan. He understood that mobile devices had supplanted the personal computer as the main internet platform. Almost all used ARM chips. When Warren East, ARM's CEO, visited SoftBank's headquarters in Tokyo, he was showered with compliments. ARM was the best in the business. ARM was the future. Masa even bragged he would buy his company one day. East thought it was all "Masa talk." He failed to grasp that when the SoftBank boss paid a compliment, it was never random; it was time to pay attention.[3]

Soon afterward Masa invited East to dinner at the Savoy Grill in London. East brought along his CEO successor Simon Segars, a geeky Essex-born engineer who had developed the microprocessors powering the first generation of mobile phones. Both Brits wondered what was going on. At the end of the meal, none was the wiser. In late June 2016, Segars was packing his bags to go on a family vacation to Jamaica, when the phone rang. Masa was en route to California: Could Segars attend dinner at his hilltop mansion in nearby Woodside? Segars agreed and asked his head of business strategy, Tom Lantzsch, to come along with a pitch on the internet of things.

After a multimillion-dollar makeover, the four-story Woodside villa was designed to entertain, impress, even intimidate guests with its conspicuous display of wealth. That evening, dining under a pergola by an outdoor swimming pool, a bored-looking Masa curtly dismissed his guests' presentation. Shortly afterward, the phone rang in Segars's office in Palo Alto. "I am very excited," Masa said. "I want to meet with your chairman—tomorrow."[4]

Segars said his chairman, Stuart Chambers, was out of contact, sailing his boat in the Mediterranean. Not a problem, said Masa. SoftBank's private jet would fly to the nearest airport in Turkey, and he would land a helicopter on the chairman's boat. Segars chuckled to himself. Chambers's new toy was a fifty-seven-foot, three-cabin sloop—not a three-hundred-foot Russian oligarch's superyacht.

Tracked down at sea, Chambers's response was: "Is this urgent?" He was enjoying a family holiday, and his satellite phone was playing up. Somewhat reluctantly, he agreed to join a working lunch the next day in Marmaris on the Turkish Riviera. Masa flew in from Tokyo, joined by Segars and Alok Sama, who chartered private planes from San Jose and London respectively. It was made-for-movie stuff for Segars, the boy from Basildon. He had never been to Turkey, let alone flown in a private jet.[5]

On Sunday, July 3, Masa arrived with an armed escort at the waterfront Pineapple Restaurant in Marmaris. It made for great theater, but on this occasion the security threat was real. Five days earlier, a suicide bomb and gun attack at Istanbul's main airport had left forty-one dead and more than 240 wounded—a bloody challenge to Turkey's authoritarian president, Recep Tayyip Erdoğan.

Masa apologized to Chambers for disturbing his holiday, presenting him with a bottle of Romanée-Conti La Tâche, his favorite burgundy, with a minimum $6,000 price tag. Chambers hesitated. He suffered from gout and was worried about falling foul of the UK Bribery Act. Masa waved away all protestations.[6]

Lunch unfolded at a dizzying pace. Masa had booked the whole of the second floor of the restaurant, another grand gesture ostensibly justified by the need for privacy. He chuntered on about the internet of things, praised ARM's performance, and finally handed over a one-page letter of intent comprising a premium over its share price, an offer valued at $21.4 billion. Chambers was noncommittal.

"What's the hurry?" the ARM chairman asked.

Masa replied: "I really want to do this deal."

William Rucker was intrigued when he heard about SoftBank's approach for ARM Holdings. The head of Lazard's UK investment banking business was at the peak of his powers, a balding, freckle-faced redhead whose genial exterior masked a competitive streak befitting a member of the Jockey Club. Back in 2006, he had advised Chambers as chairman of Pilkington in its failed defense against Nippon Sheet Glass's £2.2 billion bid. Pilkington was a national name, but it was hardly a national jewel like ARM, a well-run company showing consistent compound growth with £1 billion cash in the bank. But Rucker worried about the company's dependency on semiconductor chips and its heavy investment needs.[7]

Failing to realize that he was dealing with a potential predator, Segars had frankly shared the same concerns with Masa in California. Was ARM too dependent on Apple and Samsung? What would happen when smartphone sales peaked? In industry jargon, this was known as "hitting the air pocket," the moment when growth stalls. Segars was also mistrustful of his shareholders in the City of London, who were inveterate short-termists compared to their US counterparts. "The Americans only talked about the technology, not the earnings. For the British, it was the other way round," confirms one former senior ARM executive.

Shortly before SoftBank's approach, a London fund manager asked Segars why ARM's margins were slightly down. The company was investing, he replied. The fund manager was unconvinced. "When does the investing phase end and the harvesting begin?"

Segars quietly cursed. "In the world of tech, the moment you stop investing you are on the verge of death. There is always something new to invest in."[8]

On Monday, July 4, Rucker convened a meeting at Lazard's headquarters in Stratton Street, Mayfair. Face-to-face with a suntanned Chambers, who'd raced back from Turkey, Rucker was joined by Anthony Gutman of Goldman Sachs and Segars. They quickly concluded there was little chance of ARM remaining independent. A leveraged management buyout would require ARM taking on billions of debt. ARM's cash flow simply couldn't sustain that.

Rucker moved quickly to identify "the killing field," a price range that would demand serious consideration. Based on ARM's discounted future cash flow, exchange-rate movements, and dividends, the bankers landed on a number somewhere above Masa's opening offer. No one objected, and no one called for any serious due diligence on Masa's track record or SoftBank's debt levels. Then they waited for SoftBank's next move.

Masa's financial advisers included Jeff Sine and Alok Sama, both well versed in technology deals. After Arora quit SoftBank, Sama quickly dropped his own reservations about the ARM bid and requested help "to work the system" in London. His choice was Simon Robey, an old Morgan Stanley colleague.

A poker-faced patrician with a rich baritone, Robey was known as the City's "trillion-dollar man." He'd worked on the defense side of blockbuster deals such as Kraft's takeover of Cadbury and the (failed) Pfizer bid for

AstraZeneca, the UK pharma giant. His other passion was opera. Growing up in Cambridge as an adopted child, Robey won a choral scholarship to study English at Magdalen College, Oxford. Like many gifted, money-minded Oxbridge graduates at the time, he jumped to the City of London, joining Lazard and then Morgan Stanley.

After the financial crisis, when Morgan Stanley wobbled, along with other top Wall Street banks, Robey stuck around for a while before striking out on his own. He set up a boutique bank with Simon Warshaw, an heir to the Molton Brown beauty empire. The duo quickly cornered the bids and deals market in London, offering a pukka alternative to the sprawling, conflict-ridden international investment banks.

Robey, who had just received a knighthood in the Queen's Birthday Honours List, turned up for his first meeting in California in a pressed white shirt, tie, and red suspenders. The all-male, casually dressed SoftBank team had a good laugh at the stuffy Englishman. Robey found Masa intensely focused, always in a hurry, and utterly transactional. He warned his Japanese client that only a sky-high unconditional cash offer would carry the day. Masa took note but also took to calling Robey "Sir Suspenders."[9]

Robey's trump card was his close relationship with Sir Jeremy Heywood, the most powerful civil servant in the UK government. In 2004, he had recruited Heywood to Morgan Stanley's UK mergers and acquisitions team. They spent four years in neighboring offices before Heywood returned to Whitehall as Downing Street chief of staff. Four years later, Heywood achieved his lifelong ambition of becoming cabinet secretary, the closest adviser to the prime minister and head of the civil service. Heywood fancied himself as a gray eminence, comfortable in manipulating the strings of power whether Conservatives or Labour held office. In 2010, Prime Minister Gordon Brown left a handwritten note to his successor, David Cameron: "The country is in good hands. Jeremy is running it."[10]

Heywood loved being "in the room" alongside the politicians. He regularly berated colleagues for dealing directly with the prime minister, insisting that as cabinet secretary he was the principal channel. For the most part, Heywood's intellectual brilliance and work ethic served the country well. "Whatever the problem," said a longtime friend, "Jeremy could always see the solution." Heywood's blind spots were his continuing close relationship with Robey and his belief that he was a born dealmaker. There

were advantages in having a hotline between the City and the cabinet secretary, especially in a crisis, but a privileged relationship like that between
Robey and Heywood risked conflicts of interest.[11]

In his first year, Heywood steered government discussions over a
plan to merge the British defense giant BAE Systems with EADS, the
French-German aerospace company. Morgan Stanley was advising BAE
and stood to gain a multimillion-dollar payday if the bid went ahead,
which both Heywood and Robey favored. Heywood was also heavily involved in discussions over Pfizer's bid for AstraZeneca, which happened
to be the first big mandate for Robey Warshaw. When it came to Soft-
Bank's bid, Heywood proved a priceless asset.

The meeting on the seventh floor of Lazard's building was meant to be
the clincher. After four all-cash offers, this was the moment to strike a final
deal. Masa had just flown in from Tokyo, but Chambers held out, saying:
"I don't think it is enough."[12]

Masa was livid, almost as furious as when he turned up in London
a week earlier and his usual suite at the Berkeley was not available. (He
promptly took over a whole floor at the nearby Bulgari hotel in Mayfair
instead.) Having been led to believe his last best offer would be accepted,
he'd lost face. Robey, visibly uncomfortable, said Masa was about to
leave the building. Rucker shrugged. He was confident that SoftBank remained committed to a deal. Staged walkouts were a dime a dozen. Still,
he gave a gentle warning to Chambers: you cannot keep upping the price.
Chastened, Chambers called Masa and invited him to the Lanesborough,
a five-minute walk from the Berkeley hotel. Masa didn't budge and the
two men agreed on a deal.

On Monday, July 18, the ARM board recommended SoftBank's
£24.3 billion ($32 billion) all-cash offer. The SoftBank team could not
quite believe the ARM board had succumbed so quickly. It was "a shocker,"
admitted Sama. Another investment banker involved was blunter: "It was
a smash-and-grab operation."[13]

How was it possible for one of Britain's most valuable technology companies to be bought and sold in less than two weeks? In truth, SoftBank's cash
offer was extraordinarily generous, but it was also exceedingly fortuitous in
timing (though Masa later said he deliberately launched his bid in July, when
most bankers and rival predators were on their summer holidays).

Just three weeks before the ARM board agreed to SoftBank's terms, the British public voted narrowly in a referendum to leave the European Union, the most consequential foreign policy decision in half a century. Brexit spelled a messy, complicated divorce, disrupting the UK's entire political and economic relationship with the Continent. David Cameron announced he was resigning as Conservative Party leader and therefore also as prime minister. Sterling slumped. The ruling Conservative Party was convulsed by a bloody leadership contest. With the UK government in disarray, Jeremy Heywood played a central role in settling the fate of ARM Holdings.

Robey had arranged for a one-on-one meeting between Masa and Heywood ahead of SoftBank's bid for ARM being unveiled on July 18. Heywood was supposed to "look Masa in the eye," sizing him up as a suitable bidder and extracting promises about the future stewardship of Britain's top technology company. The cabinet secretary fancied himself as a negotiator from his days at Morgan Stanley, when he enjoyed one of those weighty-sounding but slightly meaningless titles like "global vice president of investment banking." But he was playing a weak hand—and he knew it. Having torched its relationship with Europe, the UK was in desperate need of friendly foreign investors. Relations with China had soured. The US was distracted by a divisive presidential election. Japan was a friendly face at a time of distress.

"If SoftBank had been an aggressive American company or a French buyer, there might have been a more negative reaction," says one SoftBank adviser, "but a Japanese company was different. There was no way shareholders or the government could turn it down."

On Wednesday, July 13, just before noon, as David Cameron was facing parliamentary questions on his last day as prime minister in the House of Commons, Masa entered the lacquered black door at 10 Downing Street. A study in Japanese humility, he told Heywood he wanted to build a long-term relationship with the UK government based on trust. He'd long admired ARM as a world-class technology company but would proceed with his bid only with the government's full support.

Heywood tested SoftBank's plans for future investment in the ARM business. What kind of sums were on the table? Over what time frame? Mindful of Brexit's economic impact, he also pressed for undertakings to boost the workforce. Above all, he wanted SoftBank to commit to ARM's headquarters in Cambridge.

Masa responded with a confident smile. More investment? Not a problem! More jobs? Naturally! In fact, he would double the workforce. (ARM executives had initially proposed an 80 percent increase, but Masa said doubling the number of jobs sounded far better.) When Heywood pressed for guarantees that Cambridge would remain as ARM HQ, Masa pledged that Cambridge's position was secure. ARM, he promised, would be at the center of SoftBank's "ecosystem."[14]

Heywood felt reassured that Masa's pledges would be set in cast-iron post-offer undertakings (POUs). At the end of the half-hour meeting, the man in effect running the country had negotiated the surrender terms for selling one of Britain's elite companies, a world-beater in an industry of the future.

Robey had also fixed a meeting for Masa with George Osborne that same day, not knowing that this would be his last as chancellor of the exchequer. Theresa May's first act as prime minister was to fire him and choose Philip Hammond in his place. A chastened Osborne received his visitor from Japan in his office overlooking St. James's Park and listened to his life story. It seemed a pointless exercise, though in retrospect not entirely futile. In 2021, after a stint as editor of the *Evening Standard*, Osborne joined Robey Warshaw as a rainmaker, with the prospect of earning several million pounds a year in advisory fees.

The meeting with Britain's new prime minister was more awkward. Masa had called May after she'd been elected Tory party leader on July 13, saying he had a "big gift" for her, a major investment in the UK when other business bosses were fleeing the country because of Brexit. Now he insisted on a meeting in Downing Street, seeing this as a chance to "build trust." The meeting took place on Monday, July 25.

Notoriously shy, May was prone to long, awkward silences. Seeking to break the ice, Chambers, accompanying Masa, praised the government's new industrial strategy: "I know what you are trying to do."[15] May assumed he was referring to Labour-style intervention in the economy and put on her Medusa face. The meeting ended soon afterward.

The sessions with City fund managers went more smoothly. Most were ecstatic with the all-cash offer of £17 a share. This was 40 percent over ARM's record share price and avoided their having to deal in volatile SoftBank shares.[16]

Not everybody was convinced. James Anderson, a star stock picker based at Baillie Gifford in Edinburgh, specialized in identifying tomorrow's tech giants, like Amazon, Alibaba, and Tesla. When Segars and ARM's finance director Chris Kennedy made the trip to Edinburgh to convince him to accept the deal, Anderson erupted in fury.

Fulminating at the loss of independence of Britain's national technology champion, he said: "Are you telling me I can't invest in public markets? Are you saying I can only invest overseas, in the US, or in private companies?"[17]

Anderson later complained about the "pornographic allure" of quarterly earnings and news headlines, declaring fund management in the UK was "irretrievably broken." Hermann Hauser tried to whip up a campaign, insisting the company he'd founded had a bright independent future. In a bid to shut him up, Masa called him on his mobile phone.

Hauser was in the middle of a ploughman's lunch at the Royal Oak pub in Barrington, Cambridge. Masa ran through his pitch on the internet of things and the coming "paradigm shift." The IoT would bring an explosion of connectivity, with a trillion devices talking to each other. ARM would supply the chips of choice.

Hauser said to himself: this man doesn't have a clue what he is talking about. The internet of things covered a multitude of applications. Lamps were not the same as cheap telephones or thermometers. Besides, there was more money in the next generation of data servers. When Masa repeated his promise to invest heavily and double the Cambridge workforce, Hauser was still not convinced. "His message was growth, growth, growth," he later said, lamenting that the UK had just signed away its standard-setting sovereignty in semiconductors, a step far more costly than the Brexit vote.[18]

On August 30, shareholders voted 95 percent in favor of the deal. Lord Myners, a City grandee and former government minister, bemoaned fund managers selling out at a high price at the expense of the long-term health of British industry. "It was a high valuation," said Myners, "but this is one of Britain's last wholly owned UK-based technology companies. Decisions will no longer be made in the UK and Cambridge."

Several City fund managers personally congratulated Rucker, though one added that ARM's loss of independence somehow "felt a shame."

On the face of it, the "system" worked. SoftBank made its four offers; ARM negotiated a mouthwatering price. The Takeover Panel's rules on bidding procedures were followed to the letter. The ARM board negotiated legal undertakings on employment, investment, and headquarters. The government was kept informed, avoided direct intervention, and ultimately gave its approval.

"Everyone played their role," said Rucker.[19]

Having earned more than £15 million in fees, Robey's verdict was equally sanguine: "It was as sweet an answer to a set of difficulties that you could possibly imagine."[20]

With the passage of time, views changed. In the Brexit chaos, the UK lost its flagship technology company to a foreign buyer. The government was so dazed that ministers merely went through the motions. The most expensive talent in London was mobilized to make sure that the tough questions about SoftBank's intentions were never asked. The official focus was on employment in the UK rather than the long-term stewardship of the company, or indeed where a newly configured ARM would list as a public company, whether New York or London.

From ARM's perspective, too, the deal was mixed. Masa was faithful to his word, doubling the workforce from three thousand to six thousand. He also invested in the internet of things, but the initiative did not go anywhere. From a financial standpoint, the doubling of the workforce did not lead to a doubling of revenue, but it did decrease the net profit margin and hit the share price. Within months of signing the ARM deal, and with Masa needing a lot of cash, Segars noticed that his boss's attention was wandering.

PART 5

HUBRIS

24

PROJECT CRYSTAL BALL

Masa was one year short of sixty, closing in on the last stage of the fifty-year life plan he had drawn up at Berkeley. He looked at the movers and shakers in Silicon Valley such as Facebook's Mark Zuckerberg or Tesla Motors' Elon Musk, and they were a generation younger. He was no longer the baby-faced prodigy who'd taken Japan by storm, drawing into his circle older men like Sasaki and Omori who saw in him a younger version of themselves. Now the man acclaimed as Japan's Bill Gates risked turning into a fossil and a bottleneck for growth.[1]

Masa had flirted briefly with the succession question when he recruited Nikesh Arora. It ended badly. Rather than handing over the reins at SoftBank, Masa had in mind something grander, a new global investment fund to invest in high-growth technology companies worldwide. The problem was he lacked cash, especially after ARM Holdings, his biggest-ever acquisition. Looking for inspiration, he turned to Rajeev Misra, whose network stretched from London to New York, the Middle East, and Hong Kong.

Misra likened his fellow Deutsche Bank alumni to a "band of brothers." One was Nizar Al-Bassam, a Saudi-born investment banker specializing in Europe and the Middle East. In the spring of 2016, frustrated with Deutsche cutting back its ambitions in emerging markets, Al-Bassam cofounded a London-based boutique advisory firm called FAB Partners, later rebranded Centricus. His partner was an ex–Goldman Sachs banker, Dalinc Ariburnu. Their idea was to set up a $20 billion fund that targeted high-tech start-ups, drawing on money from SoftBank and Middle East sovereign wealth funds.

Born in Dhahran, the son of a director of the giant Saudi Aramco oil company, Al-Bassam grew up in the "Aramco camps," fenced-in residential compounds modeled after the US suburbs. English was the primary language, and Al-Bassam went on to study at a private boarding school in Massachusetts and Colby College in Maine, a top liberal arts college. He was American and Saudi, a low-profile, charming networker whose only visible weakness was haute cuisine, preferably six or seven courses, served up at the finest restaurants near his office in London's Mayfair.[2]

Al-Bassam's focus was his homeland in Saudi Arabia, where deputy Crown Prince Mohammed bin Salman was spending hundreds of millions of dollars on consultants charged with writing a blueprint to reform its oil-dependent economy. Tall, thickset, with bulging arms, a large beak of a nose, and receding jet-black hair, the prince was still barely thirty. But few doubted he was the coming man. When Al-Bassam approached Misra and asked whether SoftBank would like to join future Gulf investors in his new venture, his old boss shot back, "You should be raising money for me."

Al-Bassam found Misra rough at the edges—the chain-vaping was particularly irksome—but he respected his brainpower. He saw the logic in Centricus abandoning its ambition to be a principal tech investor. Instead it would be a service provider to SoftBank, helping the Japanese tap into the big money in the Gulf petro-states and taking hefty fees in return.

When Masa heard about the plan to raise billions of dollars in Saudi Arabia, Qatar, and the United Arab Emirates, he immediately sensed the opportunity. Sovereign investors in the Gulf had all the money but few of the connections. He could assume his familiar role as a bridge, this time between the Middle East and Silicon Valley, the global hub of technological innovation and the world's premier center for venture capital. Bristling with excitement, he came up with a suitably grandiose name for his new venture: the SoftBank Vision Fund.

The Vision Fund wasn't unique simply because of its size and ambition but in the way it approached traditional methods of finance. Most orthodox financiers value companies by projecting their cash flow. Venture capitalists back promising start-ups before they even have cash flow to analyze. They take small stakes in "illiquid," loss-making companies and hold them for several rounds of financing in the hope of outsize returns.

Masa invented a new model: *he would be the capital market*. Rather than depending on disparate investors and going through the five- to seven-year venture capital cycle, his fund would exert overwhelming influence or effective control. He would have the most money, could back anybody, and would fund the next generation of high-tech companies. The closest analogy was the Rothschild family dynasty, the capital provider for the industrial revolution in the nineteenth century. It sounded megalomaniacal, but Masa was convinced he could make history, creating a global investment empire populated by visionary founders deploying cutting-edge technology and generating fabulous returns for himself, SoftBank, and his partners.[3]

On August 28, 2016, Masa's private plane touched down at 4 a.m. in Doha, Qatar, the first stop on a road show without precedent in the annals of modern capitalism. At stake was whether the rulers of Middle East petro-states would be willing to hand over billions of dollars to a Japanese businessman whom they barely knew or had ever met, in pursuit of a business idea they barely understood.[4]

Once best known for its pearl fisheries, Qatar had grown to become the world's biggest gas producer. The emirate operated a $230 billion sovereign wealth fund, the Qatar Investment Authority, which owned trophy assets such as Harrods and Claridge's hotel in London's West End and Paris Saint-Germain, the star-studded French football team.

On the plane ride from Tokyo, Masa went through a twenty-page slide deck under the code name Project Crystal Ball. The slides on his iPad contained a potted history of SoftBank, supported by its standout winners (Alibaba and Yahoo!). One big number stood out: SoftBank's internal rate of return (IRR), which measured the profitability of the company's investments. Masa claimed the IRR was a whopping 44 percent.

Masa's sky-high IRR number was based disproportionately on SoftBank's initial investment in Alibaba, which, while stellar, was hardly representative. Nor did it take into account the downside risk in an asset that made up more than 50 percent of SoftBank's portfolio by value. Misra himself was always uncomfortable with Masa's use of the 44 percent number, once correcting his boss in Hindi during a meeting with Prime Minister Narendra Modi.[5]

En route to the hotel in Doha, Masa suddenly and dramatically veered off script. Without forewarning, he announced that the investment fund target was no longer the originally planned $20 billion; not even $30 billion. The new target was $100 billion. By every known measure, $100 billion was a dizzying multiple compared to the average $2–5 billion raised every funding cycle by the top VC firms in Silicon Valley. It posed questions as large as the target itself: Where should such huge sums be invested, who was qualified to make such decisions, and how would the new Vision Fund operate? When al-Bassam protested that the $100 billion figure was unrealistic, Masa brushed him aside. "If I am going to do a fund, it has to be big enough to disrupt the whole technology world."[6]

When Masa dropped his $100 billion bombshell during a presentation to the Qatar Investment Authority that morning, it drew polite smiles. His next pitch was over lunch with the former Qatari prime minister and QIA chief Hamad bin Jassim Jaber Al Thani, one of the richest men in the world. Known by his initials, HBJ was a man who saw a business deal in everything he did. The British tabloids labeled him the man who bought London, citing the QIA's ownership of the Shard, Harrods, and the InterContinental Hotel on Park Lane. He took cuts on many lucrative deals, at times landing in hot water with regulators. But he was also a generous donor to philanthropic causes. In 2022, *The Times* reported that HBJ had handed over €3 million in cash to Prince Charles for his charities.[7] The money was in the form of €500 notes, stuffed into a suitcase, a duffel, and Fortnum & Mason bags.

Knowing HBJ's appetite for big deals, Masa proposed that the Qatari government put up $28 billion. He promised to match the sum using Soft-Bank funds, his own money and a contribution from Sprint. This was a stretch, but the numbers were large enough to delay lunch by an hour.[8] HBJ appeared impressed but asked pointedly: Why should I invest in the Vision Fund when the alternative is buying SoftBank stock? The logic being that if the Vision Fund was such a great idea, it would surely be reflected in SoftBank's share price. Masa glided over the answer. The meeting ended with HBJ hinting at a $3 billion investment.

Later that day, Masa abruptly announced he was heading back to Tokyo. He was due to accompany Japanese Prime Minister Shinzo Abe to the Eastern Economic Forum in Vladivostok, Russia, on September 2. Now he had more important business: he wanted a meeting in Japan with Mohammed bin Salman, then on a visit to China. On the return flight, Masa peppered Al-Bassam with questions about the history of Saudi Arabia, its culture, and the character of the prince. Masa's appetite for knowledge was insatiable. He'd long since given up reading books (though he claimed to have read hundreds while bedridden in hospital with hepatitis B), preferring instead to consume well-chosen articles or, even better, listen to experts. That night he kept Al-Bassam awake for all but one hour of the ride to Tokyo.

At Haneda Airport, a minibus stood waiting, curtains drawn to maintain secrecy about Masa's travel schedule, a personal obsession. The vehicle was fitted with three or four passenger seats usually reserved for Masa's closest aides, known as the samurai. He always traveled discreetly, dispensing with the ostentatious security detail favored by some Silicon Valley executives. That day, the exhausted party drove straight to Soft-Bank headquarters in the Shiodome Building, where the Conrad hotel occupies the twenty-eighth to thirty-seventh floors. Al-Bassam showered, changed his clothes, and went straight to Masa's office. Masa, looking as fresh as a spring chrysanthemum, greeted his visitor with a single instruction: *get me a meeting with MBS.*

Al-Bassam worked his iPhone all day, scrolling through his Saudi Aramco contacts, leaving messages but eliciting no response. The banker fell asleep on his bed, only to wake up at 6:30 a.m. with the phone vibrating on his chest. It was Yasir Al-Rumayyan, head of the Public Investment Fund (PIF), Saudi's multibillion-dollar sovereign wealth fund.

A keen golfer, Al-Rumayyan was well traveled, a suave banker in his mid-forties with a twinkle in his eye, a man who knew how to spend as well as to earn big money. He promised to see Masa in four hours. The session went well, Al-Rumayyan promising to raise SoftBank's investment proposal with the deputy crown prince. A follow-up meeting with Khalid Al-Falih, the cerebral head of Saudi Aramco, also went well. But the Saudi minister of commerce Majid Al-Qasabi proved a harder nut to crack.

"You have three weaknesses," he said sternly: "You are a one-man show; you went from hero to zero to hero. How do we know you don't go to zero again? Is your track record just from a few deals?"

Masa shot back: "How many people come back after losing 98 percent of their wealth?"

The frosty atmosphere gradually eased. After seventy-five minutes, both men were hugging and taking photographs together. The Saudis were falling under Masa's spell.

On September 3, under lights and flashing cameras, Deputy Crown Prince Mohammed bin Salman and Masayoshi Son posed for photographs at the Geihinkan Akasaka State Palace. The bulky, bearded prince, in formal dress, gesticulated with his left hand toward the assembled journalists. Masa, smart-casual, wearing a beige jacket, white shirt, and navy-blue trousers, looked suitably deferential.

In the meeting, a complex power dynamic played out. Masa was ostensibly in the weaker position. He needed the money. He was also starstruck by MBS's ostentatious display of wealth, expressing astonishment at how he and his immediate Saudi entourage had landed in Tokyo in not one but two A380 jumbo airliners.[9] Yet Masa also knew how to play on the young prince's insecurities, especially his fear of missing out on a once-in-a-lifetime investment opportunity. For his part, MBS grasped that backing the Vision Fund would brand him as a man of the future, strengthening his claim to the Saudi throne, in succession to his ailing father, King Salman.

At the end of their encounter, MBS approved in principle a $45 billion investment in the Vision Fund, a colossal sum that dwarfed any single contribution to a venture capital fund by a factor of ten or more. The Saudis were not merely cornerstone investors but copartners, as they saw it. They wanted clear rules about how and where their funds were disbursed, with the ability to walk away. They didn't want to come across as "dumb money"—precisely the impression created a year later when Masa boasted to a Bloomberg interviewer that he had raised $45 billion in forty-five minutes.[10]

Masa's off-the-cuff comment offended the Saudis and would come back to haunt him. But hubris knew no limits in those days, because raising money appeared to be as easy as turning on a tap. In the first serious sitdown with the PIF to talk about the Vision Fund, Alok Sama delivered a warning to Al-Rumayyan: "You are a limited partner. You are not the driver, you are in the back seat of the car."

Al-Ramayyan got up, put on his jacket, and stormed out of the room. He did not come back to the negotiating table for several days.

Shortly after his breakthrough with the Saudis, Masa flew to Abu Dhabi, the richest and most powerful member of the United Arab Emirates (UAE). There he visited Crown Prince Mohammed bin Zayed, the de facto ruler. A former helicopter pilot prone to long silences and impassive stares, MBZ was a modernizer but no democrat, a severe man vigilant against security threats from neighboring Iran or radical Islam within.[11]

Masa played on these concerns, explaining that the Vision Fund would hold a stake in ARM, the company at the center of developments in artificial intelligence, and OneWeb, the low-orbit satellite company providing high-quality broadband internet services. The impact on security would be immense, he argued.

In the future all doors would have chips in them. Cars would have three hundred chips. Even the fish tank in the crown prince's room would store data and emit data, like a Fitbit device. The person controlling the sensors could discover whether a door was open, whether it was closed, as well as the temperature inside the room. All this added up to a new world of remote, around-the-clock surveillance. The crown prince listened raptly.[12]

Masa's next key meeting was with Khaldoon Al Mubarak, forty-one, head of the Mubadala sovereign wealth fund. A graduate of Tufts University outside Boston, fluent in English, Al Mubarak attracted the ruling family's support after his father, a diplomat, was assassinated in Paris. He was an astute investor who exuded a breezy confidence, known in Abu Dhabi as Mr. Fixit. Not only was he chairman of Manchester City football club, Abu Dhabi's trophy sporting asset, he was also in charge of the $46 billion project to build Yas Island, a tourist destination off the UAE that hosted the Abu Dhabi Grand Prix.

Under his direction, the emirate's sovereign wealth fund steadily expanded its risk profile. Compared to the more conservative Abu Dhabi Investment Authority (ADIA)—in those days, more like a giant pension fund—Mubadala had a "special-forces feel." Investment managers were prepared to take risks in pursuit of returns, whether an oil refinery, an aluminium smelter, or a loss-making semiconductor chips foundry. The SoftBank Vision Fund looked like a similar strategic investment opportunity.

Soon after this visit, Masa received good news: the UAE was ready to hand over $15 billion, one-third of Saudi's contribution but still bringing him substantially closer to his $100 billion target. He went on to tap other friendly sources for money. Apple, normally one of the hardest-nosed investors, chipped in $2 billion, a sign of enduring loyalty going back to the iPhone partnership. Sunil Mittal was asked for $2 billion but politely declined. Masa's next call was Bill Gates, no longer in charge at Microsoft but actively running his own charitable foundation.

When Gates called and asked if Masa would put $150 million into his planned $1 billion Breakthrough Energy climate initiative, the Japanese immediately volunteered a donation. "I will do the full $150 million," said Masa, "but you have to do me one favor."[13]

Gates assumed his old friend was trying to wangle an invite to play at Augusta National Golf Club. He was wrong. Masa wanted $2 billion for the Vision Fund. Gates declined, explaining that he would rather invest directly in hot internet start-ups. Masa was disappointed but kept his word, sending Gates a $150 million check for his Breakthrough Energy fund.

On Friday, October 14, 2016, Masa arrived in Riyadh to announce the launch of the Vision Fund with Saudi Arabia as a strategic partner. Their goal was to become the biggest investor in the technology sector in the world, but also to support the Kingdom's Vision 2030 strategy to develop a diversified economy "beyond petroleum."

Many details regarding the operation of the Vision Fund still needed to be ironed out. Were the Saudis as the biggest contributors a copartner, or was this a one-man show, as Alok Sama had provocatively suggested? The Gulf Arabs were already investing in US technology companies, so how would conflicts of interest with the new fund be managed? In the near term, none of this seemed to matter because the numbers alone grabbed business headlines around the world.

Three weeks later, Donald Trump, real estate mogul, reality TV host, and born-again populist, defeated Hillary Clinton in the US presidential election. While liberals and Democrats wrung their hands, Masa was sanguine. Anyone was better than Barack Obama, whose administration had blocked SoftBank's efforts to merge Sprint with T-Mobile. Trump, by contrast, was the best friend of big business.

Masa sounded out prospects for a meeting at Trump Tower, the future president's gaudy headquarters on Fifth Avenue, near Central Park. Sheldon Adelson, the Las Vegas billionaire casino owner and Trump's single biggest donor, provided the introduction. Twenty years on, Adelson was still grateful that Masa had stepped in to buy his declining Comdex exhibition business at an insanely generous $850 million price, allowing him to borrow even greater sums to finance a global gambling empire.

Ahead of his meeting with the president-elect, Masa was prepped by Adelson and Steve Schwarzman, the private equity billionaire and boss of Blackstone. Both counseled him to emphasize that SoftBank was investing in America, playing to Trump's vanity. Masa listened carefully. Then, armed with an iPad and his ever-present magic pen, he took a seat in Trump's private office on the fifty-third floor of Trump Tower.

"Here is my positive vision for your administration," he said. "I am promising fifty thousand jobs with $50 billion of investment in the US."[14]

The words "Sprint" and "T-Mobile" never crossed Masa's lips, though he did make a reference to being let down by the Obama administration. He then outlined a multimillion-dollar commitment to the US made by Foxconn, the electronics company based in Taiwan. Foxconn had made a fortune manufacturing the Apple iPhone and happened to be a longtime business partner of SoftBank, Masa explained.

Trump grew visibly excited. "This is so good, we should tweet this. Do you think we should tweet this? Absolutely!"

Reince Priebus, Trump's incoming White House chief of staff, said maybe it would be a good idea to do some due diligence. Like which state the factory would be in.

"Put the factory in any state," Trump replied.

Masa barely got past the first page of his slide deck. Trump was already tweeting out the good news in real time.

At the end of the meeting, Trump retreated to his adjacent bathroom suite. Just as he was about to apply a comb to his hair in front of the mirror, he spotted Masa waiting dutifully outside. Trump knew that when big news was about to break, the little details counted the most.

He motioned to Masa and offered his best combing tips, apparently oblivious that the SoftBank boss was seriously thinning on top. Taking a comb to his head, Trump brushed backward in a brisk sweeping movement before lightly patting down his dyed blond hair—a well-rehearsed routine to look his best in front of the cameras. Finally, the president-elect inserted a Stars and Stripes into his own lapel button. Both men straightened their ties, both Trump red, and descended in an elevator to the foyer.

Trump trotted out Masa's line about fifty thousand new jobs and $50 billion investment in the US. Masa beamed into the TV cameras but grew flustered when one of the American reporters confused him with Terry Gou, the Foxconn boss. "No, no, no," said Masa. "I am Masayoshi Son, and SoftBank is not a bank."

Soon after, Al-Bassam's iPhone lit up with texts from Riyadh. "What is Masa doing?" said the man from the PIF. "This is our money!"

Terry Gou of Foxconn was similarly caught off guard. "What the fuck are you doing?" he said, wondering how his company had been set up with a huge US investment commitment. "I've had Beijing on the line."[15]

Masa was good at making promises, even better at spending other people's money. That day he felt ready to listen to the wildest ideas. Earlier, on his way to Trump Tower, he'd invited a tall young Israeli with long black hair to make a sales pitch in the back of his car. Within minutes, he had written a check worth $4 billion to an office-space-leasing company that promised to conquer the world.

The young messiah was Adam Neumann. The company's name was WeWork.

25

CRAZY GUY

On December 6, 2016, Masa was due to visit WeWork's headquarters in the Chelsea neighborhood of New York City. As usual, he was running late, and his meeting with president-elect Trump loomed large. The planned two-hour HQ tour turned into a twelve-minute walkabout. Unabashed, Masa invited WeWork's founder, Adam Neumann, to join him in the back seat of his SUV for a ride to Trump Tower, thirty-eight blocks north.[1]

Neumann brought along a printout of his pitch deck setting out his vision of a new world of work: cool, high-tech office space with cushions, Pelotons, and plenty of free booze, with each location selected using state-of-the-art-technology. Masa waved it all aside. Pulling out his iPad, the ever-present traveling companion, he sketched the outlines of a $4.4 billion investment to be cofinanced by SoftBank and the new Vision Fund. Even the perma-bull Neumann was left momentarily speechless by the size of SoftBank's commitment.

Half an hour later, Masa emailed a photo of the digital "napkin contract." It was a blur of lines laying out a global partnership, with Neumann's scrawled signature in blue ink beside Masa's in red uppercase. The SoftBank investment implied a valuation of $20 billion for WeWork, the same as Hilton Hotels. Only Uber and Airbnb, the new hotshots on the US start-up stage, had done better.

At thirty-eight years of age, Neumann had landed on cloud nine. SoftBank's fresh injection of cash would help create a real estate giant worth billions. Even better, he'd be worth $1 billion on paper. As his executive team later exchanged hugs and high fives, Mark Schwartz, the ex–Goldman Sachs banker soon to join the WeWork board, issued a note of caution.

Masa runs hot and cold, he warned. Right now, he's running hot on WeWork. Watch out, if he starts running cold.[2]

Masa first spotted Adam Neumann in January 2016, at an event called Startup India in New Delhi. Star billing went to Prime Minister Narendra Modi. But Neumann, a Jesus-like figure standing six feet five inches tall, with sculpted cheekbones and flowing black hair, stole the show.

For most of his life, Adam Neumann had battled against the odds. He was dyslexic; his doctor parents had divorced when he was seven years old. He enrolled in the Israeli Naval Academy, graduated officer school, served on a missile boat in Haifa, and then dropped out. Accounts of his military service differed. He informed some friends that he was a wayward flunky; others were told he commanded a warship in the Persian Gulf.[3]

That day in Delhi, Neumann talked about India's spiritual heritage as if he'd spent a lifetime in the subcontinent. Why was everyone talking about raising money, valuations, and the risk of a bubble? "That is not the goal. The goal is finding something that you truly love," he oozed. "Make sure it has intention behind it. Make sure it's going to make the world a better place."

In the evening, Masa was dining at the home of Sunil Mittal when Neumann waltzed in half an hour late. Ignoring the security guards, he said he'd been searching for the right address. Tempted to give up, he gambled on the biggest house on the block.[4] That was Adam Neumann: apparently sincere, outrageous, bordering on reckless. Like Masa, he operated on a different planet, where everything was possible and money was no big deal, especially if it was someone else's.

"Masa thought Adam Neumann was the Second Coming [of Christ]," says Jordan Levy, the New York venture investor who'd just left SoftBank. "Elon Musk, Jeff Bezos, and Bill Gates, all rolled into one."[5]

Masa's multibillion-dollar pledge to WeWork fitted a pattern of seemingly irrational decisions to invest mind-blowing amounts of money on founders he'd barely spoken to. At one level, Masa's investment in We-Work marked a "transformational moment," a display of unshakable confidence in his own judgment and the founder's potential. Such moments are the stuff of venture capital, which employs a high-risk, high-reward model. In industry parlance, it is called a "moon shot."

But in Masa's case, deeper psychological forces were at work. His approach to business and life in general was that if he could visualize something, it must be true. But this approach also left him susceptible to fellow dreamers, individuals with giant egos who talked about building business empires and world domination. The closest analogy, a SoftBank colleague says, is Ronald Reagan and his unshakable belief in the "Star Wars" missile defense system.

At the height of the Cold War, Reagan thought his Strategic Defense Initiative (SDI) could force the Soviets to the negotiating table and eventually rid the world of nuclear weapons. Experts told Reagan the space-based missile shield was unfeasible. But Reagan refused to listen. In Reagan's mind, seeing was believing. Masa applied the same yardstick to megalomaniacal founders like WeWork's Neumann. No matter that they might be charlatans or spendthrifts, the key was that they dared to dream, and they aimed high.

In the real world, Adam Neumann was little more than a middleman, renting office space wholesale and up-charging for flexible leases, cool design, and the provision of services such as the internet, reception, and mailroom.[6] To those who wondered what made WeWork different from any other real estate company, Neumann had a one-word answer: culture. He sold Wall Street a fantasy of joyous communal living like the kibbutz in Israel with an entrepreneurial twist.[7]

In March 2017, Neumann traveled to Tokyo to celebrate SoftBank's $4.4 billion investment and divvy up the proceeds: some $3.1 billion for global expansion, with SoftBank using the balance ($1.3 billion) to acquire WeWork stock. For all Neumann's talk about profit with purpose, he stood to gain several hundred million dollars, one of the most lucrative sales of stock by any start-up CEO.

Once the paperwork was signed, Masa had a surprise in store. He retreated to his private dining room, where Cheng Wei, founder of Didi Chuxing, the number-one ride-hailing app in China, sat waiting. Didi had beaten its US rival Uber in a brutal price war. Having backed both sides, Masa was now promising a further $6 billion to power Didi's global ambitions. Adopting the role of father-mentor, Masa said Neumann had lessons to learn from the shoot-out in China.

"In a fight, who wins—the smart guy or the crazy guy?" he said, staring straight at Neumann.

"Crazy guy," said Neumann.

"You are correct," said Masa, "but you are not crazy enough."[8]

Some likened Masa's one-upmanship to "bro culture" inside Wall Street investment banks. Others said it was behavior more suited to the casino tables, although Masa insisted he'd given up gambling, having lost a small fortune while a Berkeley student on a visit to Las Vegas.[9] In the case of Adam Neumann, Masa's goading encouraged the WeWork founder's worst instincts. It was like feeding a monkey alcohol, says one leading Vision Fund investor at SoftBank. And yet, almost until the very end, Masa appeared oblivious of the risks he was running for SoftBank, his investors, and his own reputation. Was he naive or a victim of hubris, too stubborn to spot the impending disaster?

"Masa always followed the principle of not interfering. He will always trust people until they give him a reason not to," says Jordan Levy, who worked with him for nearly twenty-five years. "The mistake was to trust him [Neumann]."[10]

In the late spring of 2017, still hunting for backers to boost the coffers of the Vision Fund, Masa requested a meeting with Warren Buffett, the Sage of Omaha. Buffett had built Berkshire Hathaway over many decades into a well-oiled machine that gushed cash. Investors loved Buffett's home-spun wisdom, expressed every year in an annual letter to shareholders.

"When leverage works, it magnifies your gains. Your spouse thinks you're clever, and your neighbors get envious. But leverage is addictive. Once having profited from its wonders, very few people retreat to more conservative practices."[11]

These words sounded like a repudiation of Masa's whole career. But none of that seemed to matter when Masa and his party arrived outside Berkshire Hathaway's headquarters in Omaha, Nebraska, on a Sunday afternoon, June 25, 2017.

Buffett, then eighty-seven, a slightly hunched figure with thick spectacles and a crop of white hair, greeted the SoftBank party himself. Most were still recovering from the flight from Tokyo. Opening the doors of the tall glass building, the Berkshire boss gave his visitors a twenty-five-minute tour. Rajeev Misra asked how many people worked for him. Twelve, replied Buffett. He was managing $110 billion, just trying to earn a few basis points.

Buffett then invited the SoftBank team into his modest office, with a clean table and no clutter in sight. Emails, he explained, were printed out by his longtime assistant, Debbie, and he would write or dictate an answer. Asked who was responsible for doing investment analysis, Buffett replied that was his job: "I always give them an answer in forty-eight hours."[12]

Masa, never good at small talk, went straight to the point. He wanted Berkshire to back the Vision Fund. Opening his iPad pitch deck, he boasted about his standout investments led by Alibaba and Yahoo!. Buffett replied that he was an old-school investor who wasn't interested in debt. "I'm a cash-flow guy," he explained.

Misra quickly grasped that Buffett had no interest in putting money into the Vision Fund. Masa carried on regardless, trying to persuade Buffett to put money into debt-strapped Sprint. Buffett was politely diffident. The meeting lasted barely twenty minutes. On top of his twenty-five-minute tour of the Berkshire Hathaway HQ, Masa had flown six thousand miles for a forty-five-minute meeting that ended with a giant zero.

Masa's search for "permanent capital" took on fresh urgency in 2017–18 after he approached Swiss Re, the reinsurance giant. His idea was to take a minority stake, leveraging Swiss Re's top-notch credit rating to raise further capital for global tech investing—a cheaper alternative to the (relatively expensive) Vision Fund arrangement with its guaranteed coupon. Despite warnings that the Swiss regulators would never wear the proposal, Masa and Misra had several top-level conversations with Swiss Re chairman Walter Kielholz, who describes the exchanges as "bizarre." Masa explored a similar deal with Axa, the French insurance giant.

Another high-level meeting that came to nothing took place two months before the Buffett meeting when Masa held talks with Elon Musk about taking Tesla private, a move that would have required the electric carmaker saddling itself with billions of dollars of debt. Tesla was burning cash, roughly $8 billion in the previous four years. By and large, investors were comfortable, believing in Musk's vision of a new generation of electric vehicles replacing their gas-guzzling rivals; but employees and suppliers had to be paid, promptly.

Musk was an outsider, a native South African who'd made his first millions cofounding PayPal, a digital payments company. Like Masa, he had a titanic ego. Like Masa, he was ambivalent about running a public company and equally resistant to being answerable to anyone. The difference was that Masa had the Vision Fund. He wasn't short of cash.

In the meeting, the two men circled each other warily, conscious of their individual standing as billionaire futurists. The meeting did not go well. Masa was willing to provide several billion dollars, but he pushed back on Musk's demands for super-voting shares in the new private company. As always, Masa was sensitive to being diluted because it implied a loss of control and influence.

Yet control was fast becoming an issue for SoftBank in the US. Starting with his purchase of Sprint, Masa's aggressive acquisition strategy attracted the interest of regulators, notably the Committee on Foreign Investment in the United States (CFIUS), the shadowy interagency body set up to review the national security implications of foreigners investing in certain US companies. In 2017, when SoftBank Group, the Tokyo-based parent company, bought Fortress Group, Misra's former employer, and Boston Dynamics, the advanced robotics maker, both deals were held up by CFIUS.

"Half the people seemed to think we were a Chinese bank," said one Soft-Bank adviser. "Masa [in 2017] had his butt kicked and his clock cleaned."[13]

With regulators pressing SoftBank Group to settle for less voting power, Masa structured deals such that only a small proportion was stock with voting rights, while most of it took the form of nonvoting preferred stock. This is why Masa balked at Musk's demands on Tesla going private, though his opposition to being diluted was ironic given that this was precisely what would happen with his WeWork investment, with catastrophic consequences.

In April 2018, after his "smart-crazy" session in Tokyo, Masa ordered all SoftBank Vision Fund companies to gather in New York to meet Prince Mohammed bin Salman of Saudi Arabia, who was making an inaugural visit to the US. Masa was keen to impress the newly elevated crown prince, mindful that he was already plotting to launch a successor, SoftBank Vision Fund 2. Without more Saudi billions, his new scheme would struggle to get off the ground.

The royal audience was arranged at the Plaza, a bus ride from the Four Seasons hotel where the SoftBank party was staying. Neumann turned up and demanded to know when the meeting with MBS would take place. Frustrated at the waiting time, he demanded his fellow founders introduce themselves. Then he wondered aloud whether they should reopen their investors' agreement with SoftBank to secure better terms.

"Adam was like a trade union leader," says a SoftBank adviser. "We had to get him out of there." When Rajeev Misra got wind of the incipient insurrection, he informed Neumann that he would have to wait a minimum of six hours for the crown prince. The WeWork boss disappeared in a puff of smoke.

Neumann was always looking for more money from Masa but he was infuriatingly elusive when it came to oversight. Rajeev Misra in London, as well as Ron Fisher and Mark Schwartz in the US, found him impossible. Both were on the WeWork board, but Neumann had the voting power, and he was a crafty operator. "Adam played the observant Jew card," said a SoftBank adviser, noting that Fisher strictly observed the Sabbath, which left all parties incommunicado from Friday evening to Saturday evening.

In mid-2018, thanks to SoftBank's $4.4 billion investment, WeWork was enjoying explosive growth in revenues, albeit matched by eye-watering losses.[14] On a lightning visit to Tokyo, Neumann pitched Masa on a plan to dominate the entire real estate market from apartment space to brokerages. WeWork would become the go-to space provider for office space around the world. Intrigued, Masa asked for more work to be done. And so was born Project Fortitude, the code name for a plan megalomaniacal in its ambition.[15]

By Neumann's calculations, WeWork's revenue would rise from a projected $2.3 billion in 2018 to $101 billion in 2023. It would have fourteen million members, up from the current 420,000. Overall, WeWork planned to have one billion square feet of office space, twice the size of the Manhattan real estate market.[16] For this, he demanded a $70 billion investment—a sum that on its own would devour more than two-thirds of the Vision Fund.

Instead of showing Neumann the door, Masa rolled out the red carpet. Later, sitting alongside him in WeWork's offices in New York, Masa pulled up on his iPad a chart that showed a hockey-stick-like growth curve for WeWork's main business. By 2028, he wrote, the business would have one hundred million members and hit $500 billion in revenue. Then Masa magicked up a valuation, incorporating every conceivable source of extra revenue for associated services.

In yellow ink, he scribbled "$10 T" and underlined it twice. The value of the entire US stock market was about $30 trillion. In Masa's imagination, WeWork would be worth $10 trillion by 2028. Back in Tokyo, Masa's top executives were stupefied. These were "fake numbers," one complained, only to realize that Masa himself had been complicit in the one-upmanship. The entire exercise may have been just "Masa talk." The one person who took the numbers at face value was Adam Neumann.

After tense negotiations, Masa and Neumann settled on a plan. Soft-Bank Group would buy out all Neumann's existing investors for about $10 billion and put another $10 billion into WeWork, giving SoftBank ownership of most of the company. Neumann would remain as the sole largest shareholder outstanding. The deal amounted to the largest ever US buyout and investment in a US start-up. It required SoftBank to deposit $3 billion to set the deal in motion, and overall implied a valuation of $47 billion, a staggering figure.

Rajeev Misra and Mark Schwartz decided it was time to confront Masa. But when they registered their protest, Masa just smiled. Back in 1999–2000, the SoftBank board opposed his decision to invest $20 million in Alibaba. He, Masa, was the only one to believe in Jack Ma and his vision of a world-beating internet business. He went ahead, and SoftBank's investment turned into many tens of billions of dollars.

"As you all object, I am becoming more and more interested in this company," he told a senior SoftBank colleague. "I am looking at Alibaba, and only he [Adam Neumann] looks like Alibaba today."

As the top echelons of SoftBank fretted about WeWork and its crazy valuation, the mood inside Saudi Arabia's Public Investment Fund turned hostile. Executives had long complained about blurred lines between SoftBank and the Vision Fund. Both entities had put money into WeWork, but if things went wrong, the Saudis, as lead investors, were exposed. What would happen then?

Inside the Desert Kingdom, the crown prince had pulled off an audacious power play. In August 2017, he ordered the state security services to detain dozens of the richest businessmen and force them to disgorge billions of dollars of allegedly ill-gotten gains. Saudi VVIPs such as Prince

Al-Waleed bin Talal of Kingdom Ventures were detained until they agreed to hand over the money. When one top Saudi businessman was asked whether torture was used to encourage compliance, he replied, "There has been no torture—unless you mean the owner of the Four Seasons having to spend several weeks in detention at the Ritz Carlton."[17]

One year later, on October 2, 2018, a prominent Saudi journalist-dissident by the name of Jamal Khashoggi was murdered in Turkey. Though Khashoggi had murky ties with Qatar, a bitter rival of the Saudi regime, he was a recognized writer and critic who regularly contributed to *The Washington Post*. After being lured into the Saudi consulate in Istanbul, he was detained, drugged, and dismembered by a squad of hit men flown in from Saudi Arabia.

The killing turned into a public relations nightmare for MBS and his modernization program—and for Masa. Even though the crown prince denied all responsibility, the CIA later found him to be complicit in the grisly murder. SoftBank's main financial backer was compromised. Coming on top of the WeWork debacle, some members of SoftBank's board found SoftBank's Saudi connection repulsive, more evidence that Masa would do business with anybody. "He mixed clean and dirty water," said Uniqlo boss Yanai. "If you deal with the wrong people, it's a waste of time."[18]

Masa was put on the spot when invited to the annual PIF investment conference in Riyadh, the so-called Davos in the desert. Several board members advised him to stay away; others argued that boycotting the conference organized by the leading investor in the Vision Fund would do incalculable damage. In the end a compromise was reached: Masa went to Saudi Arabia but stayed away from the PIF event.

During this tumultuous period, Masa's biggest challenge was WeWork and the $47 billion valuation that he had rashly put on the company. If something went wrong, it could send SoftBank's share price into a tailspin. Much depended on the long-planned listing of SoftBank Mobile, the telephone business that Masa had built over the past fifteen years.

SoftBank Group had ¥18 trillion of interest-bearing debt ($180 billion)—in contrast to around ¥4.1 trillion ($41 billion) twenty years before. SoftBank Mobile's IPO was supposed to raise ¥2.6 trillion ($26 billion) by selling around one-third of the business.[19] Although the issue was oversubscribed on debut on December 19, 2018, it raised only $23 billion. The mobile unit's shares were initially down a disappointing 14.5 percent from the offer price. SoftBank's chief financial officer Yoshimitsu Goto warned Masa that shareholders would revolt further if the WeWork deal went ahead. The buyout had to be called off.

On Christmas Eve 2018, Adam Neumann was in Hawaii, surfing, readying for the deal to close and to begin his next chapter as a private company. His iPhone rang. It was Masa. The deal, he said, was dead. Neumann tried to persuade him to reverse course, but this time Masa was immune to sweet talk. Instead, he offered Neumann a consolation prize: a $1 billion investment, at a $47 billion valuation. WeWork would have to opt for a public offering on the stock market.

This was the equivalent of a Hail Mary pass. Going public would expose Neumann to scrutiny utterly foreign to his nature. It would also depend on investors' risk appetite. Masa was still the man with the cash, but he was starting to lose friends.

I HOPE YOU GO BUST

n normal times, Michael Moritz spent weekends in San Francisco taking a spin on his elite racing bike or contemplating the German Expressionists and postwar British masterpieces in his mansion in Pacific Heights. But these were not normal times. An intruder from Japan had turned his world upside down.

On the morning of Sunday, September 17, 2017, Moritz, the lean Welsh émigré who became a venture capital billionaire, finally exploded. "There is at least one difference between [North Korean dictator] Kim Jong Un and Masayoshi Son," he wrote in an email to Sequoia colleagues. "The former has ICBMs that he lobs in the air while the latter doesn't hesitate to use his new arsenal to obliterate the hard-earned returns of venture and growth equity firms."[1]

His email continued: "The formation of the Saudi Arabian-backed Vision Fund has completely changed the landscape of private, global technology investing and threatens to more than halve the returns of all venture and growth investors in tomorrow's most promising companies."

He concluded: "For Sequoia and its longtime Limited Partners, the presence and tactics employed by the Vision Fund present the greatest long-term threat to the health of our business since our formation in 1974. We can either accept this as the new world order or choose to address it. As Mike Tyson once said, 'Everyone has a plan until they get punched in the face.'"

At one minute past noon, Moritz pressed the "send" button. His "Freedom Fund" email was a call to action: a plea to his fellow partners at Sequoia, one of the top VC performers in the US, to raise $20 billion to counter the threat from the Vision Fund. And so began an arms race in the world of venture capital. Over the next four years, in the middle of a bull market for technology stocks, Andreessen Horowitz, Benchmark, Sequoia, Silver Lake, and Tiger Global deployed ever greater capital to compete with SoftBank's gargantuan war chest. The spending reached levels never seen before in Silicon Valley.

Viewed from the previously unchallenged venture capital world, there were several things unusual about the Vision Fund. The fund's focus was not on start-ups but "later-stage" companies. Another oddity was the way the Vision Fund was financed. Just over half the capital was in the form of preferred equity—a debt-like instrument that paid the owner a fixed return of 7 percent regardless of the fund's performance. In a typical VC fund, the Saudis and the UAE as Limited Partners (LPs) would never have received interest or dividends on unrealized returns, though they would have had priority on return of their capital. In this case, the LPs received a steady return on investment via the 7 percent coupon, with a further component to have more upside—a very favorable arrangement.

This led in turn to a paradox: despite its size, the Vision Fund was quite strained financially. First, it had to buy stakes in target companies at a time of historically high valuations; second, it had to finance the ongoing cash losses of these firms, above those met by the initial capital injection; third, it had to fund the coupon on the preferred stock award to the Limited Partners. Despite the notionally long fund life of twelve years, plus an optional two years, the Vision Fund and its investee companies in aggregate were burning up cash quite fast. From the outset, therefore, the pressure to crystallize profits—from divesting stakes—was far higher than in traditional VC funds. "We were always doing things in a giant hurry," recalls one former Vision Fund executive.

By far the biggest surprise was the man chosen to head the Vision Fund: Rajeev Misra. He had no track record in venture capital. Then again, if the game was about financial alchemy, Misra fit the bill. In his wilder moments, Masa confided that his dream was to raise not one, not two, but ten Vision Funds, each piled on top of the other. It sounded delusional, but Masa carried on regardless. The result, he claimed, would be $1 trillion under management, the most powerful asset management and venture fund in history. He would be the capital market. And he would be the richest person in the world.

What Masa missed—or deliberately overlooked—was that Misra was no manager. The Indian possessed a roguish charm, but he had little sense of time, his manner was often deliberately rude, and he was an inveterate schemer who viewed encroachments on his turf as a declaration of war. He was also seemingly incapable of writing down anything on paper, preferring to communicate by text, WhatsApp, or Signal.

Shortly after the Vision Fund was officially launched in May 2017, Misra toured the major Silicon Valley VC firms. He was accompanied by four or five colleagues, often fellow Deutsche Bank traders or investment bankers like himself. One partner at Andreessen Horowitz remembers Misra wandering in sockless, vaping an electronic cigarette, and behaving like he owned the place.

"I remember thinking: How did this happen?" said the VC partner. "All of these guys are full of shit."

Around this time, Bill Gurley, a six-foot-nine former college basketball star, remembers Masa muscling into a fundraising event for Uber, the ride-hailing firm. Gurley's VC firm Benchmark had led the Series A financing for Uber six years earlier. Masa snapped up a 15 percent stake, diluting Benchmark's position, but not before threatening to put his money into Lyft, Uber's chief rival in the US. Gurley likened such conduct to asking for protection money. Except the protection was not forthcoming. When Uber later diversified into food delivery, Masa invested $1.5 billion in DoorDash, the San Francisco–based competitor.

"You ended up owning less of the company and carrying more of the risk," Gurley recalled. "It was a horrific experience."[2]

Not all the deals were bad. Between 2017 and 2020, the Vision Fund had stakes in ARM, Coupang, Didi, DoorDash, ByteDance—the Chinese internet giant and founder of TikTok—as well as Guardant Health and Roivant Sciences. Both exits from Coupang and Didi produced excellent returns, but overall, says one Vision Fund adviser, "There were too many shitburgers."

By the end of 2016, Masa had assembled the world's biggest war chest. He had received commitments for $60 billion from Saudi Arabia and Abu Dhabi as part of his SoftBank Vision Fund, which, at $98.6 billion, had fallen just short of its original target. This hardly mattered because the mainstream media invariably parroted Masa and rounded up the figure to $100 billion. Now he was desperate to put his money to work. "He would often tell us: 'I want SoftBank to be the most valuable company in the world,'" says a longtime SoftBank executive. "He wants to be an emperor, not just a CEO."[3]

Masa envisaged a high-tech ecosystem spanning the globe with Soft-Bank sitting at the center. At the height of the dot-com bubble, he presided over a semblance of empire. At a cost of around $4 billion, he had accumulated minority stakes in more than two hundred internet companies in the four major continents, from Latin America to Europe, the US, and Asia. The dot-com crash obliterated his global vision; now, thanks to Arab billions, he had a second chance to reassemble an empire.

Yet the practical obstacles to success were real. Finding appropriate candidates for investment was hard enough. Doling out sums between $100 and $200 million implied Masa meeting hundreds of individual founders to check their credentials. Even with Masa's legendary stamina, which enabled him to work seven days a week, eighteen to twenty hours a day, often flying on his private jet through multiple time zones, that was a physical impossibility. Crucially, much larger sums—$500 million or more—were required to move the needle in a giant fund like the Vision Fund. The target companies couldn't be start-ups as such; they were later-stage companies, turbocharged for growth by the injection of SoftBank cash.

Misra's band of brothers relished flouting Silicon Valley conventions such as the "term sheet," a nonbinding agreement between founder and VC firm. Term sheets cover valuation, size of investment, voting rights, and anti-dilutive provisions—all vital considerations for the entrepreneur. Once signed, the founder-entrepreneur is legally obliged not to "shop the deal" to other investors. Nor, once signed, should the term sheet be renegotiated or "retraded." But the Vision Fund often took full advantage of its superior financial power. One case involved Light, an advanced camera developer cofounded by the former US Marine Dave Grannan, a veteran who served in Desert Storm and Desert Shield.

"My experience with the Vision Fund was like putting a three-year-old to bed," he said. "Every time you thought you were done, they started screaming for another cookie."[4]

Grannan, a Palo Alto–based serial entrepreneur, launched Light in 2013. His company developed pocket-size cameras for smartphones and other commercial applications. By the time the Vision Fund turned up in late 2017, Grannan was in Series D, a fourth round of funding. After initial contacts with Vision Fund executives, Grannan was summoned to Tokyo for a meeting with Masa on February 14–15, 2018.

The ex-Marine was excited to meet one of the world's most charismatic investors, but it turned out to be a big letdown. Masa asked a few perfunctory questions but appeared bored. The two men shook hands on a deal where the Vision Fund would invest $105 million. Grannan was dispatched back to the US to work on a term sheet.

On Monday, March 8, 2018, as he was pacing on a treadmill in the Bay Club gym in San Francisco, Grannan took a call from Akshay Naheta, a former Deutsche Bank trader and Misra protégé. The deal was off, Naheta declared. Grannan was stunned. So was the Light board, which included several Silicon Valley veterans. With only eight weeks of cash in the bank, Light was running dangerously short of working capital.

After frantic reworking of the numbers, Grannan was summoned back to Tokyo for a second meeting with Masa. It was scheduled for an hour and a half but lasted barely twenty minutes. This time, Masa said, SoftBank would invest $105 million in tranches only, in return for a near-30 percent stake in the company. Unable to turn to other investors because of the lockup clause, Grannan had to accept SoftBank's terms: "It was a horrible, horrible time."

Three months later, in July 2018, Light closed on the deal and secured an initial $40 million funding. Grannan was summoned again, this time for dinner at Masa's palatial home in Woodside, California. Terry Gou, the Foxconn billionaire and an early investor in Light, was present, alongside Rajeev Misra.

"It was the Masa and Terry show," says Grannan, who watched both billionaires vying to take the credit for backing Light. Masa and Gou went back more than twenty years to when the SoftBank boss was looking for a cheap manufacturer of set-top boxes for his satellite TV joint venture with Rupert Murdoch. In the intervening years, Foxconn had become wildly successful thanks to an exclusive contract to manufacture the Apple iPhone in low-cost factories in China. Gou's relationship with Masa was a case study in mutual dependence and one-upmanship.

For Grannan, the only good memory was when Masa insisted— astutely—that Light's futuristic, three-dimensional camera technology was more suited to business applications like driverless cars than consumer products like smartphones. In hindsight, that was the high point of their relationship.

In late July, Grannan received a text from Akshay Naheta, about whom more later.

Light was showing a shortfall on its projected revenues. This was hardly unusual for a youthful enterprise that had just had its business plan blown up, but Naheta flew into a rage.

"This is complete horseshit," his WhatsApp message ran. "You guys have zero integrity."[5]

And then came the words which Grannan kept as a bittersweet souvenir on his smartphone. Words that Grannan never believed would come out of the mouth of a venture capitalist.

"I hope you go bust."

Such cavalier attitudes were typical. The Vision Fund operated more like an investment bank trading day-to-day securities than a venture fund employing "patient capital" and nurturing long-term growth. The cutthroat culture derived partly from Rajeev Misra, but it was also embedded in the terms of remuneration, which Misra constantly complained about.

Most VC firms offer partners and fund managers "carried interest," also known as "carry." This is a performance fee in the form of a portion of future profits from an investment, usually amounting to around 20 percent. But Masa ruled that "carry" was too expensive and anyway unwarranted, given that he'd raised the bulk of the Vision Fund himself. As a result, Vision Fund managers were remunerated according to their own deals rather than overall team performance—a recipe for rapaciousness and internal conflict.

The single constant was the guerrilla warfare between Rajeev Misra and Marcelo Claure, who by now was looking for a bigger job than managing the Sprint turnaround. Each leaked against the other like defective septic tanks. In March 2018, a *Wall Street Journal* article detailed allegations of the honey trap aimed at compromising Nikesh Arora. One day later, Masa called a key town hall meeting at SoftBank's office in San Mateo, just outside San Francisco. Everyone was gossiping about the *Journal* article, but Masa ostentatiously put his arm around Misra and declared: "I'm so grateful to you. You are family."[6]

From that day on, Misra was untouchable. Meanwhile, Masa awarded Claure more titles than a Mexican general. He named him SoftBank Group's chief operating officer, head of SoftBank International, and later head of a new Latin American venture fund. Still not satisfied, the Bolivian demanded a place on the SoftBank investment committee scrutinizing Vision Fund deals but found himself blocked. Nor would Misra allow his Vision Fund staff to be held accountable by legal services or any group function working for Claure. His was an empire within an empire.

"The rivalry was endless, and Masa wouldn't intervene," says a top former SoftBank executive in the US. "He was drawn to Marcelo for his entrepreneurial skills and to Misra for his intelligence. But at the same time, there was some level of avoidance on Masa's part."[7]

Faced with his feuding barons and mindful that he had yet to address the matter of succession, Masa looked to strengthen his Japanese executive bench. One notable recruit was Katsunori Sago, a fortysomething ex–Goldman Sachs banker with Hollywood looks and a taste for sharp suits and designer jackets. After twenty-three years at Goldman, he had taken charge at Japan Post, custodian of the nation's savings with some $1.2 trillion of assets on deposit. The numbers sounded impressive, but Japan Post's portfolio was conservatively managed and stuffed with Japanese government bonds. The scope for adventure—"active investing"—was marginal.

When two Tokyo bureaucrats turned up asking Japan Post to join in a rescue of Toshiba, the Japanese electronics giant, Sago's hopes rose. The prospect of leading an all-Japan restructuring of an industrial champion appealed. But then the men in suits indicated that only a US private equity firm like Bain Capital or Blackstone had the expertise to lead the Toshiba rescue. For Sago, this admission was a national disgrace.

Then Masa made contact. The pitch over dinner in his private dining room was seductive: Why work at staid Japan Post when SoftBank had just launched the world's most dynamic venture fund? He could look forward to a multimillion-dollar pay package, a seat on the SoftBank board, and a shot at succession. Sago dismissed that last part of the offer. Founders talked a good game, but they were never serious about handing over the reins. Working with Masa was the big draw. So were the sums he could deploy and the multimillion-dollar compensation package.

Another top recruit at the time was Rob Townsend, an experienced corporate lawyer. In his new post as head of legal services for Soft-Bank International, he inherited the still-unfinished, board-mandated investigation of the honey-trap mystery allegedly orchestrated by Rajeev Misra. With Claure's blessing, Townsend hired his own legal firm and a corporate espionage agency. But soon he ran into brick walls. The victim, Nikesh Arora, had moved to a new job and wouldn't talk.[8] Misra was infuriatingly elusive when called upon to answer before the legal inquiry. Within a couple of months, Townsend's report was ready to present to Masa.

"It was a Marcelo Claure classic," says one former SoftBank executive: "rely on someone to do the heavy lifting and wait for the shit to hit the fan."

When the American lawyer entered the SoftBank boardroom with his legal team, he was stunned to see Misra sitting in the room. On hearing the report's criticisms, Misra "exploded," according to a person present. The shouting match went on for some time. Reluctantly, Masa agreed to prolong the internal inquiry, which reported that no laws had been broken, despite questionable ethics. Although investigators found "plenty of smoking guns," there was no conclusive evidence of Misra's hand in the honey trap. Masa stood by his man.[9]

On July 26, 2019, eager to maintain momentum, Masa pushed out a press release claiming that a host of top tech companies, including Apple, Foxconn, and Microsoft, as well as top Japanese financial institutions (Mizuho, Sumitomo Banking Corp, MUFG, and Daiwa Securities), were expected to participate in a Vision Fund 2. "Based on these memoranda of understanding [MOUs], the anticipated capital to be contributed to the Fund has reached approximately $108 billion."

The mainstream business media took the bait as Bloomberg trumpeted: "SoftBank CEO takes more control in new $108bn Vision Fund." *The New York Times* was equally gullible: "SoftBank unveils new tech fund to expand its sprawling portfolio."

Behind the scenes an argument raged over the wording of the release, with the Vision Fund's chief spokesman, the experienced PR man Gary Ginsberg, and senior compliance executives raising doubts about the accuracy of the wording. The MOUs were real but meaningless, and no outside money was in the end forthcoming. Masa may have believed his second Vision Fund would become reality, but suggesting it was a done deal was courting legal risk with the regulators. He was heedless of the danger, caught up in his own fantasy world populated by visionary founders riding the next technological wave, a world where he was the central figure dispensing billions in largesse.

The moment of maximum madness came in September 2019, when Masa staged a three-day extravaganza for all his one hundred–plus portfolio companies, lead investors, and friends. SoftBank took over the Langham Huntington, a five-star hotel in Pasadena originally constructed in 1907 and nestling in the shadow of the San Gabriel Mountains. No expense was spared. The day before the event, more than fifty trucks arrived bearing champagne and caviar.[10] Every piece of furniture was rearranged, every room catered to the taste of the VIPs present including Larry Fink, chairman and CEO of BlackRock, and senior representatives (though, significantly, not the bosses) of the Saudi and UAE sovereign wealth funds. John Legend, the singer, songwriter, and pianist, was hired to perform the lead act.

"If you had to pick a moment in the whole crazy story that was the Vision Fund, this is it," an ex–SoftBank executive remembered. "It was peak Masa."

The idea was to promote SoftBank as one happy family, a high-technology ecosystem where companies drew bountiful synergies from each member. Masa was still trying to drum up interest in a second Vision Fund. Nobody was listening. All they could talk about was the crisis at WeWork and the whereabouts of Adam Neumann. Masa had given Neumann star billing, but the wild-haired real estate broker had failed to show up. In his place was Masa's new favorite son, OYO Hotels founder Ritesh Agarwal.

At eleven the next morning, *The Wall Street Journal* published a story documenting Neumann's erratic lifestyle and questionable use of company funds, which began: "Adam Neumann was flying high. Literally." The article went on to describe the use of marijuana on a private jet bound for Israel. More was found stashed in a cereal box for the return flight to New York. When the Gulfstream's owner found out, he recalled the plane, forcing Neumann to take a commercial flight home.

Larry Fink, who had engaged in a fireside chat about good governance and high-tech investing with Masa the previous evening, was appalled. We-Work, he told friends, was uninvestable.

Over the next six weeks, Masa worked frantically with his top team to decide whether to rescue WeWork. On the face of it, $4 billion was not a huge deal in the context of a $98.6 billion fund, and something was sure to be salvaged should WeWork go bankrupt. But the precedent of SoftBank itself intervening to rescue a Vision Fund portfolio company broke every rule in venture capital. The whole point was that VC was a high-risk business; failure was part of the package.

In the middle of the storm, Masa flew to the Middle East to attend the inaugural Red Sea regatta, organized by the Saudi crown prince and featuring seventy of the world's greatest boats. Masa was not a boat person; he preferred private planes. But this was one offer he couldn't afford to turn down. MBS was SoftBank's most important partner, and Masa still had hopes of securing money for his Vision Fund 2.

Several SoftBank executives were unconvinced. From the start, the Saudis thought they were equal partners, entitled to preapprove deals and second-guess decisions. Yasir Al-Rumayyan, chairman of the Public Investment Fund, was especially prickly. He hadn't forgotten Alok Sama's jibe that he was a backseat driver. Al-Rumayyan wasn't royalty, but his entourage treated their boss like a prince, and he expected others to follow suit.

Masa's view was that the Saudis had rights as limited partners, including the guaranteed 7 percent coupon. SoftBank would honor the agreement, but they shouldn't ask for more. Some SoftBank colleagues said it was time to move on. "Why take money from people who make your life more difficult?" asked one. "You have enough money. You are a public company. Why do this again?"

Having signed up for his Red Sea cruise, Masa needed a suitable superyacht. The first option was *The Flying Fox*, Russian-owned and $5 million a week to charter. Masa balked at the cost. Then one of Rajeev Misra's staff had a brain wave: How about the *Queen Miri*, the $70 million boat owned by the casino magnate Sheldon Adelson and named after his wife, Miriam? With one eye on future customers, his old friend from Las Vegas came up with the goods: "You can have the boat for free," Adelson told Masa. "You only have to pay for the food, drink and crew."

One evening, as dusk approached, Masa was invited to join the crown prince snorkeling in the middle of the Gulf of Aqaba. Here on the continental shelf, where the water reaches depths of up to six thousand feet, the natural beauty of the subterranean world is breathtaking. That evening, the coral was the size of small trees and the fish drifting past were supersized. Only the presence of underwater guards, each wearing sonar pulse bracelets, betrayed the fact that this idyllic spot was shark territory.

As Masa floated on the surface of the water, buoyed by a special pillow-like snorkeling device supplied by the crown prince, he cut a helpless figure. He was out of his depth. All at sea.

27

THE GREAT ESCAPE

In mid-October 2019, WeWork blew up. Its valuation was cut from $47 billion to barely $8 billion, Adam Neumann was forced out, and the IPO was delayed indefinitely as SoftBank took control of the company. The deal involved SoftBank—not the Vision Fund—offering $9.5 billion, which covered new debt and recommitted equity, as well as a new tender offer to buy out Neumann and other shareholders. SoftBank ended up with 80 percent of a company on its knees.

A humiliated Masa withdrew from the public eye. As he nursed his wounded pride, he latched on to a $50 billion project to build a new capital of Indonesia, a futuristic city four times the size of Jakarta on a sparsely populated coastline on the island of Borneo.

Indonesia's President Joko Widodo, nicknamed "Jokowi," was the driving force behind the new "smart city." Called Nusantara after an old Javanese compound ("outer sands"), the city would replace Jakarta, which was polluted, overpopulated, and sinking into the sea because of an overextraction of groundwater. Citizens would pay a service charge to live in the superwired new capital, with a chunk of the money eventually ending in SoftBank's pockets.[1]

Masa, an amateur sketcher and painter, fancied himself an architect too. Working feverishly over the New Year, he showed colleagues several dozen pages filled with boxes, each containing the dimensions of boulevards, mosques, train stations, and everything else that belonged in a modern Asian city.

On January 10, 2020, Masa met with the Indonesian president and pledged further financial support. All SoftBank's family of companies would contribute to the city's high-tech ecosystem: ARM, Grab, even a revived WeWork providing office space. When asked where the funds would come from, Masa pointed to Lex Greensill, the Australian supply-chain finance entrepreneur backed by the Vision Fund.

Greensill, a former Queensland melon farmer, aspired to become a global fintech champion. With his four private planes, Savile Row suits, and the former British Prime Minister David Cameron on the payroll, he looked the part. Lex was the money guy, Masa told "Jokowi" on footage captured on Indonesian TV.

Are you good for $100 billion on the new Indonesian capital? Masa asked Greensill. "Yes, I'm good for $100 billion," came the reply.[2]

Rajeev Misra said his boss was crazy. Nusantara would not produce any revenue for five to seven years. There was no way SoftBank could borrow the billions needed up front. Why not bring in Goldman Sachs to help on the financing? Masa wasn't listening. He continued to peddle his new dream capital at the World Economic Forum in Davos.

Holed up in a chalet in town, he received a stream of VIP visitors, including Ivanka Trump. That was how he absorbed information and stayed "in the mix." During the week in Davos, Masa ventured outside only once, to attend a business dinner with President Trump, who, at that stage, looked odds-on favorite for a second term in office.

After Davos, Masa went back to Indonesia, this time accompanied by Tony Blair. The British ex–prime minister, now turned dealmaker and philanthropist, had joined the Japanese on a high-level government steering committee to bolster investor confidence in Nusantara. But Masa's interest was waning as financial pressures on SoftBank grew.

The WeWork bailout had to date cost SoftBank shareholders $9.5 billion, excluding Masa's generous offer to make the Saudi Public Investment Fund whole to cover their losses. By the end of 2019, SoftBank's overall reported total debt (consolidated gross debt) had reached a mind-blowing $177 billion. That made SoftBank one of the most indebted companies in the world, below giant carmakers Volkswagen and Toyota but above Ford Motor, Verizon, Apple, and General Motors.

The suspicion that something might be amiss had long exacted a toll on SoftBank's share price. Nothing infuriated Masa more than those investors who valued SoftBank's diversified group of businesses at less than the sum of its parts. This was the so-called conglomerate discount, which went back at least twenty years. "Why do they hate SoftBank?" a self-pitying Masa often complained to colleagues.

Conglomerates like SoftBank Group could save money on financing and administrative costs, but their sprawling nature also allowed them to hide or blur failures within the larger entity. By 2020, the group had evolved into a far more complex business, combining asset management, robotics, and a mobile phone business. And that was before taking into account the Vision Fund with its "spray and pray" approach to investing, likened by one American venture capitalist to Jackson Pollock.

In 2019, as SoftBank's share price stumbled along, the "conglomerate discount" widened to the point where some Wall Street investors agreed with Masa: SoftBank's stock was indeed undervalued. Among this group was Elliott Management, run by Paul Singer, a New Jersey–born lawyer with a bristling intelligence and a nose for sniffing out undervalued assets. Known as the world's most feared "vulture capitalist," Singer never shirked a public fight.

His most notorious spat was with the Argentine government, a fifteen-year legal campaign waged over lapsed sovereign debt payments. His fight led to the seizure of an Argentine naval vessel and, eventually, a $2.4 billion bailout. While other bondholders settled for pennies on the dollar, Singer walked away with handsome compensation.

Taking on SoftBank was a stretch, even for Elliott. Activist investors were unwelcome in Japan. Masa was the Big Boss, venerated by his staff and rarely challenged within the board. To win over Masa required Elliott to shift tactics. They needed to appeal to Masa's vanity, his financial self-interest, and his sense of personal injustice. And that meant tackling his bugbear: the conglomerate discount.

Elliott had traded in and out of SoftBank stock since 2004. They went short when bad news was brewing, and they went long when Masa made some market-positive news, like promising to stop buying stuff. Then again, Masa's promises were like St. Augustine's battle with sexual temptation. "Lord, make me pure, but not yet."

During its research, Elliott discovered some pleasingly reassuring facts. SoftBank Group's stakes in listed and unlisted assets amounted to $262 billion, of which Alibaba accounted for half, with Sprint and Soft-

Bank Mobile the other big contributors. After adjusting for liabilities, Elliott reckoned the firm was worth $220 billion. Yet the market valued SoftBank at $87 billion—a conglomerate discount of $133 billion, which was nearly the size of the market cap of McDonald's.

Elliott's conclusion was blunt: SoftBank was ridiculously complex, corporate disclosure was terrible, and transparency was an alien concept. The board was tame, the foreign-management team was a nest of vipers, and corporate governance was a shambles. Against that charge sheet, the stock was trading at least 50 percent below net asset or "fair" value. The case for SoftBank buying its own stock to inflate the share price ("a buyback") was overwhelming. With the right timing, any investor with a strong stomach could make a pile of money.

Elliott began buying bite-size chunks of SoftBank stock. Buying accelerated after the aborted listing of WeWork in late 2019 and the subsequent multibillion-dollar bailout. Soon the New York fund had built an equity stake of 3 percent in SoftBank at a cost of around $3 billion, making it one of the largest shareholders behind Masa. At this point, Elliott notified SoftBank—but not the wider market—that it had a significant shareholding in the company and would therefore like to meet the boss and his team in Tokyo.

The first session took place on January 31 at SoftBank headquarters. Masa sat at the head of the boardroom table, with around fifteen Japanese executives present, including Yoshimitsu Goto and Rajeev Misra. Led by Gordon Singer, Paul Singer's son, and the analyst Nabeel Bhanji, the Elliott team emphasized that SoftBank traded at a steep discount to the value of all the company's holdings. By contrast, Berkshire Hathaway, the conglomerate run by Warren Buffett, traded at an investment premium to its net asset value. At the mention of Buffett, America's legendary investor, Masa's ears pricked up.

"That is so unfair," he complained. "Why is that? You guys claim to be experts in capital markets. Explain that one to me?"[3]

Singer explained that Berkshire had a built-in "discount control mechanism." If the company's shares fell to a premium of less than 20 percent to book value, Berkshire would consider buybacks to boost the share price. Elliott went on to say that Berkshire had a top-class board that was gender-diverse and independent—an implicit rebuke of SoftBank's eleven-person, all-male board, which had only two independent directors, one of whom had resigned the previous month.

This was stretching the point. In fact, Berkshire's board contained a lot of wise old men, several of whom were Buffett's longtime friends. It also had dual-class shares favoring the founders, hardly an advertisement for top-class governance. The reason Berkshire traded at a premium was not that its structures were exemplary but that investors trusted the octogenarian Buffett and his nonagenarian partner Charlie Munger, who steered well clear of leverage. As Buffett said: "If you're smart, you don't need it; and if you're dumb, you shouldn't be using it."[4]

In the next slide, the Elliott team pointed to other iconic American businessmen like Bill Gates or Mark Zuckerberg, who had assembled strong boards, practiced sound corporate governance, and witnessed a corresponding strong share price. Masa bristled at the mention of his onetime hero and golf partner.

"These are one-business guys. Bill Gates just started Microsoft and Mark Zuckerberg started Facebook. I am involved in a hundred businesses, and I control the entire [tech] ecosystem."

Masa continued: "These are not my peers. The right comparison for me is Napoleon or Genghis Khan or Emperor Qin [builder of the Great Wall of China]. I am not a CEO. I am building an empire."[5]

The Elliott executives were half-stunned, half-amused. They'd brought along a case study of Berkshire Hathaway. Nobody had thought of including a slide show on Napoleon Bonaparte.

When news of Elliott's overtures broke in *The Wall Street Journal*, SoftBank's share price rose 7 percent, seemingly vindicating the hedge fund's strategy. Elliott followed up with Masa, sending him via email a summary of their presentation, though this time omitting all references to Buffett and Zuckerberg.

On February 11, Masa enjoyed some good news. A US judge approved the $26 billion takeover of Sprint by T-Mobile, its longtime rival. The merger allowed SoftBank to shed around $40 billion of Sprint debt and finally realized Masa's vision of creating a "third force" through consolidation in the US telecoms market. It was a stunning achievement, the result of patience, persistence, and a stubborn refusal to give in to the skeptics who said the megamerger would never happen.

Yet there was bad news, too. A coronavirus first detected in Wuhan, China, was spreading like wildfire across the globe. At an earnings presentation on that day, Masa ignored the threat and talked up SoftBank's prospects. The tide is turning, he declared as he stood next to a slide with a crashing wave drawing from the famed Hokusai woodcut. That same day, the World Health Organization announced it had a name for the new virus strain: Covid-19.

On March 10, Masa broke a three-year Twitter silence to say he was "worried" about Covid-19. He promised to offer one million free tests for the virus. People could take a nasal swab at home and mail it to a lab, which would test the specimen and send back the results. The plan was dropped after criticism that Masa was interfering in public health provision,[6] but, as during the Fukushima accident, Masa was ever keen to ride to the rescue in the wake of a natural disaster. His mood shifted to despair, and he ordered all SoftBank workers to stay home for a year, warning a colleague that in Japan several million people risked dying.[7]

Three days after his Covid tweet, Masa announced plans for a $4.6 billion (¥500 billion) share repurchase. This was at the lower limit of what Elliott was pushing for. The positive market reaction was correspondingly short-lived. Over the next five days world stock markets plunged as fears over Covid-19 spread, hitting tech stocks and especially leveraged SoftBank, which fell 32 percent.

For several years, since the launch of the Vision Fund, SoftBank had been piling up ever greater levels of debt; now came a reckoning. SoftBank was too fragile to cope with the shock of the pandemic. Credit markets were starting to sort the potential survivors from the likely victims, massively increasing SoftBank's borrowing costs. By the evening of Thursday, March 19, Tokyo time, the value of SoftBank's market capitalization had fallen to $51 billion, a 73 percent discount to its net asset value.

Masa himself was grievously exposed. To plow his own money into the Vision Fund, he had pledged about 40 percent of his SoftBank stock (around $5.7 billion) as collateral to borrow from nineteen banks, including Japan's Mizuho, Credit Suisse, Julius Baer, J. Safra Sarasin, and Liechtenstein's LGT Bank.[8] On another front, he'd pledged shares as collateral to help other beleaguered SoftBank entities, a familiar practice.

His new favorite start-up entrepreneur was the youthful Ritesh Agarwal, founder of the Indian hotel group OYO. Masa's intervention doubled the valuation of loss-making OYO to $10 billion from the original level that the Vision Fund had invested in. It was a lifesaver for Agarwal, but it spelled trouble for Masa. If SoftBank's shares remained in free fall, the banks would demand more collateral to safeguard their loans. In early 2020, these share-backed debt facilities were on a different scale, leaving him with serious margin calls.[9]

"I was peering over a cliff," he later admitted.[10]

The next day was a public holiday in Japan. Masa, through his financial advisers, got in touch with Elliott and delivered a stark message: given the level of the sell-off and the way the market had completely misunderstood the value of SoftBank, there was only one option—take the company private.[11]

Masa had discussed this option at times of stress, notably in the wake of the 2008 global financial crisis and in October 2014 when Sprint's share price tanked and the company's debt was overwhelming. The temptation to go private reflected his love-hate relationship with public markets. He liked playing the showman, lacing his quarterly presentations with cartoons and quaint references to Japanese history. But when things turned ugly, he had little interest in answering questions from pesky investors.

The next forty-eight hours were "incredibly intense," according to one Elliott insider. Three or four transpacific calls on Zoom took place on Saturday, March 21, where both sides explored how to go private. Elliott thought the idea was worth exploring because SoftBank was "super-undervalued." If they could put in money at that level, the fund stood to make big gains once the stock recovered.

Elliott pledged between $2.5 billion and $3 billion, based on its current shareholding, with $3 billion to $5 billion on top. Masa claimed he could lay his hands on $20 billion. He instructed his team to reach out to Abu Dhabi's fund Mubadala. They secured a rough commitment of between $5 billion and $10 billion. That left the Japanese banks, though the working assumption was that the three biggest banks, MUFG, Mizuho, and SMIC, had maxed out after extending tens of billions of dollars of loans to SoftBank.

The final funding gap came down to around $20 billion, with an overall $50 billion to $60 billion of equity in the new private company that also required funding. However, none of these gargantuan numbers took into account the huge premium to pay other SoftBank shareholders, plus fees and taxes. After half a day of back-and-forth, Goto impressed on Masa that the leveraged buyout (LBO) was simply too difficult and time-consuming. A disappointed Masa contacted New York.

"I am not going to be able to figure this out in time, so what do you think I should do instead?"

Elliott said the menu was the same they had served up at their first meeting in Tokyo. Sell assets, do $20 billion of share buybacks, and change the board. That Saturday, SoftBank withdrew from talks to further fund One-Web, the global communications network powered by low-orbit satellites. Shortly afterward, OneWeb went into bankruptcy. SoftBank also walked away from a previously agreed $3 billion deal to buy shares from WeWork investors, including Adam Neumann and Benchmark Capital. Late on Sunday night, New York time, as the final wording of Elliott's statement of support was being drafted, SoftBank's share price started to move. Something had leaked, though the precise size of the buyback was still unclear.

On Monday, Masa announced $41 billion of asset sales and $18 billion of buybacks to a receptive stock market. It was a far bigger package than recommended. Nabeel Bhanji was impressed. Normally, CEOs do less than what Elliott pressed for. Masa did the exact opposite, unveiling the largest-ever stock buyback in Japan. Even in the middle of a crisis, Masa was still writing history.

"These guys recommended this," Masa boasted, "and I did more."

In fact, SoftBank timed the share repurchases in a specific way. Rather than setting preannounced dates for buybacks, the firm came in and out of the market for nearly six months. Because the denominator was sinking, Masa's own personal shareholding in SoftBank increased from 25 percent to 30 percent. "The psychology was powerful," said one Elliott admirer. "He backed himself with his own money."

On Monday, May 17, SoftBank announced an annual loss of $12.5 billion (¥1.35 trillion), the highest ever. During an investor call Masa defended his record, noting that Jesus Christ had also been criticized and misunderstood. He made the comment after analysts pressed him about whether there was a gap between the public's view of SoftBank and his own vision. The Beatles were also not popular when they started, he added.[12]

In fact, the tide really had turned this time. Two months earlier, coinciding with SoftBank's share buyback plans, the world's central banks announced emergency measures to respond to the Covid-19 economic shock. By lending freely to American financial firms, purchasing low-yield bonds and underwriting the value of some American junk debt, they eased the strains in global credit markets. All around the world the measures helped restore confidence in companies that had gorged on debt and might otherwise have had serious problems in rolling over their liabilities—of which SoftBank was Exhibit A. SoftBank's borrowing costs tumbled back to normal levels, and over the next six months its share price tripled in value.

Masa had pulled off yet another Great Escape. But in that very moment of liberation, the old restlessness returned. He complained his ambition was too low. Sure, he was ready to humor the Americans for as long as it took to restore investor confidence. But selling down assets and buying back shares was humdrum stuff. When one Elliott executive mentioned that the SoftBank share price cratered because of investor concerns about another crazy Masa buying spree, his SoftBank counterparts offered a collective shrug.

"He likes to be at the tables," said one.

As stock markets continued to rally, Masa grew increasingly impatient. He was right all along about the power of Big Tech. It was time to double down.

28

THE WHALE IS STILL HUNGRY

S ometime in early 2019, sitting in Takiya, one of his favorite tempura restaurants in Tokyo, Masa was holding forth about how lucky he was to live in an age where business tycoons ruled the world. Most worked in niche markets like electric cars, search, or social media. But he, Masa, had a global vision that connected everything within a high-tech ecosystem. Like Alexander the Great and Napoleon, he said, without a trace of irony, he had the luxury of having no serious competitors.[1]

When Masa made that hubristic claim, he was still top dog. He'd raised the biggest venture capital fund the world had ever seen. Everyone wanted to meet him; no one could afford to turn down his money. Then, in the blink of an eye, came the collapse of WeWork, the coronavirus pandemic, and SoftBank's brush with corporate death.

Twelve months on, Masa was desperate to mount yet another comeback. His plan was to shift into public markets with a focus on Big Tech stocks such as Amazon, Facebook, Google, Microsoft, and Netflix. He was at least seven years late to the party, but the fact that the man he chose to lead his new investment venture was Akshay Naheta, one of the least trusted people inside SoftBank, was an even greater surprise.

Tall, dark-eyed, his jet-black hair immaculately coiffed, Naheta was blessed with Bollywood looks. He was street-smart, suave, and oozed ambition. His twin passions, horse riding and Formula One racing, suggested a high tolerance of risk. "He was very bright," said a close SoftBank colleague, "and a very dangerous young man."

Naheta arrived, aged thirty-five, at the Vision Fund in January 2017, one more mathematically trained Indian recruit who had graduated with stellar grades at college in the US. After completing a master's in computer science and engineering at MIT, he joined Deutsche Bank, where he worked in New York, London, and Hong Kong. His next move was to set up his own asset management firm in London, in which Misra took a personal stake. When Naheta asked him to extend his commitment, Misra invited him to join the Vision Fund.

"Forget my rollover, that is a given," Misra said. "We [SoftBank] have all the money in the world."

Misra, fifty-six, saw Naheta as a young man in his own image: industrious, quick-witted, with a similar furtive approach to business. Both men obtained and used information adroitly to advance or protect their position inside SoftBank. Masa, too, was drawn to the young Indian. Naheta was a fellow outsider.

Born in Mumbai to a family of antique jewelers, he was a Marwari, a subgroup of the Jain caste known for their moneylending and trading skills. Like Masa, Naheta had broken with tradition, abandoning a tight-knit family for an education in the US. He had gone one step further, entering an interracial marriage with Emily Montgomery, a white American daughter of philanthropists.

In his first year at the Vision Fund, Naheta veered between hunting for investment targets and seeking out trading opportunities. One such bet involved Nvidia, the California-based producer of the next generation of AI-driven computer graphics chips. SoftBank had acquired a stake in December 2016 for $2.8 billion, which was transferred to the Vision Fund nine months later for a similar sum. Calculating that the shares were undervalued, Naheta accumulated a $4 billion stake in Nvidia involving a hedging strategy known as a "collar." While the strategy limited large upside gains, it also protected the investor against large losses.

As he predicted, Nvidia's shares rose on the back of strong earnings only to tail off, leaving SoftBank with substantial losses. Naheta's derivative trade cushioned the blow, but Masa was furious, pounding the desk with frustration. Although markets bounced back, Masa issued a sell order. In hindsight, he should have held on, because Nvidia shares rallied strongly.[2] Still, Naheta was able to present his bosses with a $3 billion check, and he made sure everyone knew about the windfall. "Akshay was very long on Akshay," says a SoftBank shareholder.

His next investment, involving a Munich-based payments company called Wirecard, appeared equally adroit. Acclaimed as Germany's fintech champion, Wirecard enjoyed the support of gullible German retail investors and an equally credulous political establishment. For a time, it was worth more than Commerzbank, a mainstream German bank. But on January 30, 2019, *The Financial Times* raised multiple questions about its revenues. Wirecard shares fell 40 percent, wiping several hundred million dollars off the company's valuation.

Wirecard CEO Markus Braun, a blowhard Austrian with a taste for black turtlenecks in the Steve Jobs style, convinced the German regulator Bafin to investigate. Braun claimed—with no evidence—that the *FT* was colluding with short sellers to destroy his company. Bafin duly ordered an unprecedented three-month ban on short-selling Wirecard stock and opened a criminal complaint against the *FT*.[3]

As the end of the short-selling moratorium approached, Wirecard was desperate to head off another attack and therefore needed buyers. Naheta calculated the upside potential was substantial. Initially, Masa was skeptical. Wirecard was an investment in public markets. The Vision Fund targeted private markets. But Naheta said he'd looked Markus Braun in the eye and decided: "He's for real."

In case the Austrian wasn't all he was cracked up to be, Naheta set conditions for his proposed $1 billion, five-year convertible bond. He required an unqualified audit by EY, Wirecard's auditors; an independent assessment by Sullivan & Cromwell, the Wall Street law firm; an investment-grade rating from Moody's; and, finally, approval for the deal by Wirecard's shareholders.

The hedge looked bulletproof, but Masa still passed, viewing the Wirecard trade as a distraction. Instead, he allowed Naheta to proceed in a personal capacity, along with top SoftBank executives and Mubadala, the UAE sovereign wealth fund. When news leaked, Wirecard shares rose 8.5 percent, later as much as 20 percent. The promise of a "strategic partnership" between SoftBank and Wirecard brought relief for Markus Braun at the (then) height of his troubles—and a handsome windfall for the SoftBank investor group.

By the time the SoftBank-backed bond floated in September 2019, Naheta had off-loaded the risk to Credit Suisse, which repackaged it into complex securities bought by private European banks and other institutional investors. Naheta and friends, including Misra, various senior Soft-Bank executives, and Mubadala, made more than $60 million. They'd merely arranged or "underwritten" the deal before the securities were passed on. Incredibly, they hadn't even put up a penny in cash.

Nine months later, on June 25, 2020, Wirecard imploded. Braun and his team were unable to account for €2 billion of cash missing from its balance sheet. The company's COO Jan Marsalek fled the country, escaping via private plane to Belarus to a hiding place believed to be in neighboring Russia. No amount of financial sophistry could save the company. Naheta sent out a tweet within sixty seconds, castigating the accountants EY for failing to spot the fraud.

That was Akshay Naheta. Quick to take the credit, even quicker to disappear at the first whiff of trouble.

By midsummer 2020, world stock markets had rallied strongly, along with SoftBank's share price. The Covid-19-induced crisis inside SoftBank was over, thanks to a steady sell-down in assets, including a portion of SoftBank's stake in Alibaba. Masa now had up to $50 billion to spend. Knowing his boss was eager to juice the SoftBank deal machine again, Naheta presented a plan over Zoom to "monetize" the group's balance sheet.

In his mind, this meant taking a more disciplined approach to buying and selling assets, including managing SoftBank's stake in Alibaba, accounting for more than half of its overall portfolio and therefore a potential risk on the downside. He also argued that SoftBank should exploit its unique banking relationships. Because SoftBank took the highest risks, it ended up paying the highest fees to banks. It was time to capitalize on "the Masa imprimatur," reducing fees and squeezing more value out of deals.

Naheta's pitch drew a polite yawn in Tokyo. Masa was fixed on the public markets, where tech stocks were on a tear. He had identified what he called the "P-30," a portfolio of top tech companies in the US and China. His other favorite acronym was: "TAFAANGs," meaning China's Tencent and Alibaba, followed by Facebook, Apple, Amazon, Netflix, and Google.

On the face of it, these tech champions had little in common beyond their stratospheric valuations. Tencent and Alibaba were based in communist China and increasingly under scrutiny, while the FAANGs conducted business in a free market economy, despite concerns about concentration of power. But Masa had long coveted holding stakes in Big Tech in America.

Back in early 2018, when Masa felt flush with Vision Fund cash, he summoned top executives to Tokyo and announced his intention to buy 5 percent stakes in each of the FAANGs. As an investment strategy, it made little sense. He would have no control and little influence compared to founders with dual-class shares like Amazon's Jeff Bezos. Besides, the absolute cost was eye-watering: $125 billion. If the market got wind of SoftBank's intentions, then the stock price would rise in anticipation of SoftBank buying, making the exercise even more expensive.

That evening, the FAANGs discussion continued over dinner in Masa's private quarters at SoftBank. When a Vision Fund executive pointed out that no consortium of banks would be willing to lend Soft-Bank that kind of money, Masa suggested spreading the trades over several months, $25 billion a time.

"Masa, you will be the Don of all the top companies in America," gushed one Japanese executive.

"No, not the Don, I will be the Godfather," Masa shot back. "No drugs. Only women."[4]

The off-color joke drew gales of laughter. The exception was the lone woman in the room: Mino, SoftBank's longtime chief translator.

Fast-forward to summer 2020: having decided against taking SoftBank private, Masa wanted his new investment vehicle for investing in public markets up and running. He called it SB Northstar, based in the Cayman Islands to minimize tax liabilities. Naheta was asked to move from London to Abu Dhabi, again for tax reasons. For some SoftBank executives, the pending appointment was courting danger. Akshay Naheta was smart, but he was a publicity hound. Fawning profiles appeared in the Indian media. Even a future job promotion appeared in Bloomberg, which brought a dressing-down from Misra. He was too conniving by half.

That said, Naheta was right about Adam Neumann and WeWork's flawed growth model. He was right to spot the potential of ARM, the UK chip designer languishing in the SoftBank portfolio. And he was right about the untapped value in Nvidia, though Masa was already pushing for an ARM-Nvidia merger that would create a colossus in advanced chip design.

The management of SoftBank's portfolio of companies (separate from the Vision Fund) was undisciplined. True, Yoshimitsu Goto and his team were experts in capital raising and managing relationships with the banks. Yet the portfolio's value, starting with SoftBank's stake in Alibaba, was at any time somewhere between $150 billion and $200 billion. As Elliott Management had pointed out, the value of the portfolio was not reflected in SoftBank's share price—hence the so-called conglomerate discount.

These portfolio companies were "orphans," neglected by Masa, who always focused on the next big thing. Naheta was also bothered by his boss's insistence that SoftBank's internal rate of return had to be 40 percent when he was constantly flipping assets. For all Masa's talk about a three-hundred-year company, his use of IRR meant that holding on to investments was not rewarded but penalized.

In mid-June 2020, Masa further informed the SoftBank board about his new investment strategy, saying he wanted to manage the firm's liquidity more effectively, using "excess funds" to invest in "world-class public companies" with a high-tech exposure. Two weeks later, after the annual general meeting, the board approved the strategy, along with Masa's role as a coinvestor.

In early July, a special directors' committee (a subgroup of the board including Masa, Goto, Japanese external directors, and Ron Fisher) further approved the public equities trading strategy, along with the name of the investment vehicle (Northstar); its new CEO (Akshay Naheta); and its (unusual) equity funding based on SoftBank loaning its own Alibaba stock, supported by a coupon payment.

SoftBank insists that at all stages Northstar's activities were discussed and approved by the board. But whether the risks were properly understood is another matter. Fisher says the matter was discussed, but "probably not enough." Another SoftBank insider involved says: "There was disclosure at the board as required under Japanese law, but not consistent with the level of disclosure and debate for most non-Japanese companies of the size and scale of SoftBank."

Expecting 40 percent returns from overpriced, high-performing tech companies was high-risk, bordering on delusional. Moreover, Masa's many charts predicting the irresistible rise of Big Tech share prices over the next decade were based on the previous ten-year bull market. This broke a cardinal rule in investing: past returns are no indicator of future performance. Initially enthusiastic about his big promotion, Naheta told Misra that he was minded to resign from Northstar.

"Don't be stupid," replied Misra. "If you resign, you won't get paid."

That settled it.

On August 10, well after Northstar's trading was underway, external members of the SoftBank board received an email from an anonymous whistleblower that laid out multiple concerns about the risks in Northstar's trading strategy and the level of disclosure to shareholders.

"You as independent board members must conduct a formal review of the investment activities set out here to avoid criminal prosecution as per violations of regulations of the SEC and Tokyo Stock Exchange," the email began. It went on to accuse Masa of misleading shareholders and the board for personal gain, claiming that his activities were "opaque and unethical."[5]

The whistleblower said Northstar's trading strategy bore no resemblance to the publicly stated commitment to investing on a conservative basis in liquid stocks and government bonds to manage SoftBank's $40 billion cash pile. Sharpening the criticism, the whistleblower pointed to Masa's role as a coinvestor, with his 33 percent stake alongside SoftBank's own 67 percent holding in Northstar.

First, Masa was investing personally, creating a potential conflict of interest. Second, he was borrowing billions from SoftBank to pay for his holding and therefore his trading. This was an asymmetric risk: Masa could make potential gains of tens of billions of dollars without any material downside, but the risk to SoftBank was up to $60 billion, the whistleblower claimed. Describing "rogue behavior" and a serious breach of corporate governance, the memo concluded: "It is akin to gambling the company's money on a leveraged long-term bet on the stock market."

This was all true, but Masa saw matters differently. His economics were the same as SoftBank's. They both stood to win or lose, depending on Northstar's performance. But in Masa's case, if the fund's worth went to zero, he would have to find cash from somewhere, assuming—and it was a big assumption—that he would be forced to make good. "It was a compliance nightmare," admits one former insider.

The whistleblower's email set off a firestorm at the top of SoftBank. The board asked its top lawyers, including Rob Townsend, to look into the allegations, bolstered by two independent Japanese law firms, Mori Hamada & Matsumoto and Anderson Mori & Tomotsune. The following day, August 11, Masa went on a previously scheduled earnings call with major shareholders, investors, and analysts.

After a rambling introduction, he announced the formation of a new investment management subsidiary. This vehicle, he said, would be investing in top tech stocks and would use derivatives to hedge the risk, just as SoftBank had done with the Nvidia trade. At no point did he mention the name Northstar. There was another conspicuous omission. SoftBank's new trading strategy placed the company in the same camp as any large, beat-the-benchmark asset managers. This was a world away from inspired Alibaba-style bets or building businesses that had made Masa rich and famous.

In the next two weeks, SoftBank's external board members received two more emails from the whistleblower, one threatening to go to the media. This prompted a cursory press release giving more details about SoftBank's trading but still without naming the vehicle. On August 31, a group of SoftBank executives, including Masa, Misra, Fisher, and Goto, held a call to discuss Northstar's progress. The mood was self-congratulatory: in paper terms, SoftBank was up $7 billion. But Naheta, calling from Abu Dhabi, pleaded tearfully that it was time to stop. To carry on risked wiping out the gains and, more seriously, piling up billions of losses.

Misra laughed, saying it was impossible to lose that amount of money that quickly. Besides, Akshay was the designated genius in managing risk. Masa resolved to stay the course. And so he plowed on regardless. SoftBank estimates the paper loss in this period at $2 billion; others knowledgeable about the trades put the figure much higher. Even using the conservative lower number, in a matter of weeks, SoftBank's investment strategy had witnessed a negative swing amounting to at least $9 billion in the middle of a bull market.[6]

How was that possible?

Masa was a momentum investor, carried away by Big Tech's stellar performance over the previous decade. Big Tech was, of course, the big winner in the first year of the pandemic, once central banks came to the rescue in the wake of the Covid pandemic. In August 2020, the value of Apple reached $2 trillion, more than the combined GDP of forty-eight African countries, including Nigeria and South Africa. But as usual, Masa was a market follower incapable of pacing himself, says a close colleague.

Furthermore, the trading strategy followed by Masa the sorcerer and Naheta the apprentice was flawed. Contrary to widespread belief, Soft-Bank (and Masa with his own money) was not pursuing a pure "long" bet on the FAANGs. In fact, Masa and Naheta were creating a complex portfolio consisting of actual stocks, credit transactions, and derivatives that included buying call options on listed shares, selling call options, and selling futures contracts.

By buying billions of dollars of call options—equity derivatives that give the purchaser the right to buy a stock at an agreed price—Northstar helped trigger a "melt-up" in some tech stocks. Market players who were initially betting on a market correction (i.e., a short) rushed to buy when prices of derivatives did not fall. In August alone, Tesla's share price shot up 74 percent while Apple rose 21 percent, Google's parent Alphabet 10 percent, and Amazon 9 percent.

Misra, himself no stranger to large derivative bets, believed that the Northstar trading strategy might have worked over time. The problem was that it risked staggering near-term losses and head-spinning volatility, especially if market sentiment shifted after the melt-up. For a publicly traded company, this was impossible. Shareholders and the market would have lost confidence. "You cannot take the noise," he warned Masa.

On September 4, 2020, *The Financial Times* revealed that the mystery buyer with the giant appetite for Nasdaq derivatives was SoftBank. While SoftBank refused to give any details about the fund, who was running it, or the precise size of the losses, the *FT* quoted someone familiar with the trades who said that many at Tokyo headquarters were getting nervous.

"People are caught with their pants down, massively short," said the person, who warned that Masa was still determined to pursue his multibillion-dollar bets on Nasdaq derivatives: "This can continue. The whale is still hungry."[7]

When Elliott Management representatives asked Naheta what on earth was going on, he replied: "I am the world's largest hedge fund."

With the identity of "the Nasdaq whale" now exposed, markets went short, believing that SoftBank could not sustain its massive positions. Elliott questioned Masa about the size of the losses at Northstar. The internal hedge fund's notional exposure to tens of billions of dollars was significant given that it was almost one-third of SoftBank's $100 billion market cap. In polite but firm terms, their message was: this is not your core business, it is excessive, and it has nothing to do with what you said you were going to do.

Masa was noncommittal. "I understand. Thank you."

From this moment Elliott began to quietly sell down its position.[8] The WeWork debacle was bad enough; the Nasdaq whale episode was confirmation that Masa was never going to change. He was a one-man show, and the SoftBank board was either too ignorant or too meek to challenge him. The departure of Uniqlo's Tadashi Yanai in December 2019 and Alibaba's Jack Ma in June 2020, both of whom were prepared to speak up, highlighted flaws in SoftBank's corporate governance.

When the independent Japanese law firms concluded that there were "no legal issues" regarding Northstar or Masa's own involvement, others still felt uncomfortable. Shortly afterward, three top SoftBank executives resigned: Gary Ginsberg, global head of communications and formerly Rupert Murdoch's top spokesman; Rob Townsend, chief legal officer; and Chad Fentress, chief compliance officer.

The breakup in the top ranks of SoftBank was about to begin. An exodus of executives, including Marcelo Claure, Rajeev Misra, and Katsunori Sago, would take place over the next year as Northstar's trading was scaled back drastically. It was a wild gamble gone wrong for which Masa later took full responsibility, refusing to blame Akshay Naheta directly.

"He's a smart guy, he's very capable," Masa said. "He was *largely* [italics added] making transactions based on my direction. So if anybody should be criticized it's me. . . . They were just executing my strategy and my strategy was bad with the timing and so on."[9]

As the Northstar strategy unraveled, Masa spoke of a winter storm enveloping SoftBank and the global economy. The coronavirus pandemic disrupted global supply chains, reminding the West about the dangers of dependency on China, where many believed the virus had originated.

For more than a quarter of a century, SoftBank had been a leading beneficiary of China's opening to the rest of the world. Alibaba was the golden goose that had laid a multitude of eggs. The country's steady progress toward a market economy was no longer guaranteed. The ascent of Xi Jinping, the most powerful leader since Mao, heralded the revival of the communist state, the propagation of a virulent nationalism, and the reclaiming of the commanding heights of the economy, especially technology.

"Masa never cared about politics," says a close colleague, "but the arrival of Xi changed everything."

29

BLIZZARD

Throughout 2021, trapped inside his Tokyo mansion, fearful of contracting the Covid-19 virus, Masa found solace in painting. In the early hours, he sketched French beaches and Van Gogh–style landscapes and portraits. One young woman in white looked suspiciously like Daisy Buchanan, the charming but fickle character in *The Great Gatsby*, F. Scott Fitzgerald's novel about unrequited love and the failure of the American Dream.

Masa too lived in a gilded age when money was cheap, the gap between rich and poor widened, and plutocrats called the shots. In the good times, he hopped onto his private plane and jetted around the globe meeting princes, presidents, and tech titans.[1] The pandemic brought Masa's world to a shuddering halt. Forced to communicate by email and Zoom, his circle grew smaller. He was no longer in the mix. "The pandemic was terrible for Masa," confided a close colleague.[2]

Masa felt the absence of Jack Ma, Alibaba's founder. Although they'd grown somewhat apart—Ma chafed at Masa's high-handedness in board meetings[3]—the two multibillionaires enjoyed a unique relationship. Jack was forever indebted to Masa, who'd stuck with him whenever he'd needed cash, never wavering in his belief that Alibaba would turn into one of the world's great tech companies. Masa respected Ma as a great innovator and leader. Nothing would ever change that.

The rally in tech stocks pointed to blowout SoftBank earnings for the full year ending March 2021. But the numbers flattered to deceive. Masa was still nursing several billion dollars of losses at Northstar. His second Vision Fund was up and running, but the blue-chip investors had stayed away. Vision Fund 2 was all SoftBank money, an initial $38 billion down payment that fell far short of the original $108 billion target for the fund.

The good news was that credit was still in ample supply, thanks to central bank interventions to counter the pandemic. But Masa was no longer the go-to source of funds for promising tech companies. "He's pillaged every source of capital on every continent," joked Mike Moritz, the Sequoia veteran. "The only assets he has not looted are pemmicans in Antarctica."[4]

Inside SoftBank, discipline around investment decisions collapsed. Masa started rating senior Vision Fund managers according to the number of deals struck. He later shared the results in a "naming and shaming" exercise with peers. Several top managers resigned in disgust, including Deep Nishar, the highly rated ex–Google and LinkedIn executive operating on the West Coast. Another top manager likened his own Vision Fund experience to "a fire in a dumpster truck."

Meanwhile, the power struggle between Misra and Claure continued unabated. A senior Japanese colleague likened their contest to *sansukumi-ken*, the medieval Japanese hand game equivalent of rock paper scissors, featuring a frog, snake, and slug. You never knew whether Claure was the frog, Misra the snake, or whether they were both slugs. The one certainty was that both believed they were entitled to more money. Masa, who abhorred confrontation, hoped the matter would go away.

"I like them both," he complained disingenuously. "Why can't they get along?"

Masa's solution was the "treaty of Tokyo." In future, he decreed, his top two executives would divide equally whatever money they made. To that end, after the successful Sprint-T-Mobile merger, he gave his blessing to SoftBank lending Claure and Misra each $500 million to allow them to buy T-Mobile stock. This generous handout was on top of a loan of $250 million to each of them to buy SoftBank Group stock, part of an employee incentive plan.[5]

Claure was still aggrieved. His achievements—pulling off the grand telecoms merger, placing postmerger a record amount of T-Mobile stock in the market, stabilizing WeWork by cutting costs and installing a new chief executive, managing the SoftBank portfolio companies—were real. In his view, Misra's Vision Fund was an inverted pyramid of promises.[6]

Masa found the Bolivian's voracious appetite for money irritating. At no point did it occur to him that their relationship was based on mutual exploitation. Nor that he'd made a financial promise that he'd meant in all sincerity at the time, but one that he could not deliver upon now. Not for the first time it would end up costing SoftBank dearly.

Rajeev Misra understood that Masa was transactional by nature. Masa wasn't much interested in people. Half a dozen at most; the rest were mercenaries. The approach suited Misra and his band. In the six years since he joined SoftBank, the Indian had accumulated hundreds of millions of dollars in remuneration, mainly the purchase of stock in SoftBank and related companies, thanks to loans from SoftBank itself.

Misra was so rich he could afford to be generous, allocating $35 million in T-Mobile stock he was going to purchase to Ron Fisher and $15 million to Rob Townsend, both of whom were leaving SoftBank and had contributed to the successful Sprint turnaround and merger with T-Mobile. If things got sticky, he reasoned, it was always good to have friends.

Nevertheless, there were limits to Masa's largesse. He told Claure that he could not meet his payout demands because any sum more than $50 million in aggregate would have to be disclosed to SoftBank shareholders. A public stink in Japan was inevitable. Frustrated, Claure and Misra came up with a creative solution. If both stepped down from the board, there was no need to disclose any numbers.[7] If anybody asked awkward questions, the reshuffle of the top team could be presented as a necessary rebalancing of executive and nonexecutive board directors. All in all, a model of sound corporate governance.

On November 9, 2020, SoftBank announced that Misra and Claure would leave the board, along with Yasir Al-Rumayyan of the Saudi Public Investment Fund and Katsunori Sago, the Japan Post recruit. Sago had already signaled he was leaving SoftBank. Fed up with the feuding, he took his family for a long break in Hawaii. Misra and Claure waited for their payout, only to be informed of a further delay. Although the two were no longer board members, they were still "officers of the company" subject to disclosure rules on remuneration.

Masa had Goto, his chief financial officer, pass on the bad news. He knew it would sit well with Japanese executives, who felt perennially underpaid compared to the foreigners. Goto was the ideal messenger: a trusted intermediary with an insane work ethic and an impressive capacity for drinking high-quality sake, usually with top representatives of the Japanese banks who'd lent SoftBank billions.

Thickset, with a sharp sense of humor, Goto was Mr. Reliable in Masa's Japanese entourage. He once observed that banking relationships in Asia were very different from the West. Corporate borrowers were like regular customers visiting the local bar every evening. When the drinking was done, you didn't pick up the tab straightaway. You paid at the end of the month, on time, in full. As things began to unravel at SoftBank, Goto was the coming man.

On May 12, 2021, SoftBank Group reported a record net income of $45.8 billion, but the figures were flattered by the sale of Sprint and proceeds from the blockbuster IPO of Coupang, the South Korea e-commerce giant. Masa promised to continue building his "factory of golden eggs," along with his usual promise to return to responsible ways. "Instead of being overwhelmed by the rise and fall of the market price like gambling . . . we will help more and more companies that use AI to redefine industries," he pledged. "Our group will make a rush of initial public offerings."

All this was said in apparent sincerity. Left unsaid was the 180-degree shift in SoftBank's investing approach. Instead of trying to place billion-dollar bets on potential unicorns, Masa had ordered dozens of smaller bets on tech-enabled companies with an AI component, real or imagined. The world's greatest venture capital fund had turned into a giant mutual fund.

There were other troubling signs. In late March 2021, Greensill Capital filed for bankruptcy. Less than two years before, after a $1.5 billion investment from the Vision Fund, Greensill had been valued at $3.5 billion. Now it was a lemon. Lex Greensill was in fact nothing more than a new face in the age-old business of factoring. He took supplier invoices and turned them into short-term assets that he put into funds, similar to money market funds, that investors could buy. These funds were sold through intermediaries, notably Credit Suisse. (Somehow the hapless Swiss bank[8] always ended up in the mix.) In Greensill's case, the money from investors helped pay returns to investors. It looked like a Ponzi scheme.

SoftBank Group was an investor in Greensill through the Vision Fund, but it was also pouring hundreds of millions of dollars into Greensill-related Credit Suisse funds via a separate corporate entity.

Thus, SoftBank was not only Greensill's largest shareholder but also a major lender. To all intents and purposes, this was a serious conflict of interest. When challenged, Masa appeared as perplexed as the crusty Maryland state senator and bar owner who'd just introduced a bill banning the sale of cheap booze by competitors: "How does this conflict with my interest?" he asked an inquiring reporter.[9]

Blowups like Greensill were becoming routine. In 2021, Katerra, the California-based construction company founded by Michael Marks, an ex–Tesla executive, filed for bankruptcy. Masa had touted Katerra as the future of the building industry, earning it a place alongside favored members of the SoftBank family such as OYO Hotels and WeWork. Both SoftBank and Greensill had poured money into Katerra, which at its peak employed eight thousand workers.

Masa brushed off these failures. He thought he was reliving the dot-com movie, but Covid had ripped up the script. The shock to global supply chains triggered a burst of worldwide inflation, which in turn triggered higher interest rates and higher borrowing costs, especially in the US and Europe. Once market sentiment shifted, Masa and SoftBank were highly indebted, highly leveraged, and dangerously exposed.

The geopolitical context had shifted too. Donald Trump's "America First" foreign policy had rapidly escalated into across-the-board confrontation with China. Trump accused Beijing of cyber espionage, theft of intellectual property, Iran sanctions-busting, and military adventurism in the South China Sea and against Taiwan. Democrats and Republicans were united in the belief that America had been taken for a ride.

Despite the seesaw markets, the Covid-induced crisis, and the huge losses at Northstar, SoftBank was still the largest technology investor in the world. Vision Fund 1 had deployed almost $100 billion of capital, Vision Fund 2 had more than $30 billion to spend, and the Latin American Fund had $5 billion to invest in companies in the region. Masa had made a lot of people rich quickly, even if the jury was out on the tech companies themselves as sustainable business propositions.

In geopolitical terms, however, SoftBank was "in the middle of the bull's-eye." The US ranked as the number-one investment in terms of dollars spent for SoftBank Capital and the Vision Fund, followed by China. But SoftBank was overly dependent on Alibaba financially—

at times it accounted for more than 50 percent of its market value—and overexposed politically because of its Chinese base. Masa's other vulnerability was SoftBank's long-term commercial relationship with Huawei, the world's dominant telecoms equipment supplier and bête noire of the US government.

"We became a topic of conversation in Washington," says a SoftBank insider. "Masa found himself in an awkward place."

SoftBank's founder had long struggled with geopolitics. He favored the Big Man theory of history. Put him in the same room as a strongman, and he could strike a deal. In this sense, he was little different from President Trump, who relished the idea of negotiating peace with Vladimir Putin or Kim Jong-un of North Korea. Masa saw himself as the bridge between the West and Asia and was a leading investor in China for more than a quarter century. The SoftBank Vision Fund portfolio had invested hundreds of millions in China's leading tech companies such as ByteDance, owner of TikTok, and Didi Chuxing, the ride-hailing app. Masa felt he had every right to feel secure, but he failed to understand that President Xi was a break from the past.

Masa was not alone. Even Jack Ma miscalculated. Back in October 2020, Ma had delivered a speech criticizing Chinese financial regulators, accusing them of a "pawnshop mentality" suffocating economic growth and stifling innovation. Ma had made similar criticisms in private, but this time he chose to make them public at the Bund financial summit in Shanghai, an annual conference attended by communist bigwigs, regulators, and big business.

Ma called for a credit-based system rooted in Big Data, led by Alibaba itself. None of the assembled nomenklatura missed the point: Ma was speaking on behalf of Ant Financial, Alibaba's mobile-payments affiliate, due to list shortly on the Shanghai and Hong Kong stock exchanges. Ant's valuation was widely expected to exceed $300 billion, the biggest IPO of all time, creating a giant payday for Ma, who'd stepped down as Alibaba's CEO in 2019 but remained a major shareholder.

Within days, Ma and his lieutenants were summoned for a dressing-down at the China Securities Regulatory Commission. Government regulators followed up with the suspension of the Ant Group IPO and a record

$2.75 billion fine for antitrust violations. The cancellation of the IPO cost Ma close to $37 billion, making his speech the most expensive critique in history. In time, the bill would rise even higher as Xi cracked down on China's $4 trillion tech industry and its plutocratic leadership. The collateral damage spread well beyond the Chinese mainland. Along with Jack Ma, the most prominent non-Chinese victim was Masa himself.[10]

In the late spring of 2021, as investors digested President Xi's assault on the technology sector, Alibaba's share price began to drift downward. The knock-on effect against SoftBank was severe because it still held around one-third of Alibaba stock. In the past, Masa had opposed selling down his stake. He was always more eager to buy than to sell. And the older he got, the more stubborn he became.

On May 21, Masa received another warning to mend his ways when Yuko Kawamoto, a McKinsey alumna, corporate governance expert, and sole woman on the SoftBank board, resigned. She'd lasted barely a year, before accepting an outside appointment as Commissioner, National Personnel Authority. In an exquisitely diplomatic letter, Kawamoto set out her differences.

"Having lost none of the spirit of a venture company in its formative years, SBG [SoftBank Group] engenders excitement as a dynamic, swift-acting company," she wrote, adding: "Sometimes, therefore, rules come after the decisions are made, and some might say the company has some weakness in that regard. In reality, however, the employees are professionals in their respective fields."

However, SoftBank acted with such speed that "in some cases" the rules and systems were not checked in time. Short-circuiting discussion inevitably meant that the process was simplified and "there might be a lack of sufficient explanation."

To SoftBank insiders, this sounded like a reference to Northstar. The sting came in the tail. Masa was a unique talent and SoftBank was a unique company in Japan, Kawamoto declared, but it was time for more accountability and oversight. SoftBank also needed a succession plan. To Masa's credit, he authorized the resignation letter to be published in full on SoftBank's website. But, aged sixty-three, he was in no mood to retire. Nor was a successor obvious. When pressed on governance reforms like installing a proper audit committee, he avoided giving a firm no. He would simply say: "Not now" or "Not the time."[11]

As market sentiment turned against SoftBank, Masa rediscovered his love affair with ARM Holdings, the microchip designer. He'd staked everything on merging ARM with graphics chipmaker Nvidia to create "the world's premier computing firm for the age of AI." But he missed the fact that governments from the US to Europe and China had grown wary of Big Tech's concentration of market power.

Masa was about to enter what he described as a blizzard. Whether the snowstorm was a natural disaster over which he had no control or whether he'd wandered into the storm of his own accord was left unclear. But in the next six months he was like a polar explorer who had lost his bearings on the ice sheet.

On January 27, 2022, SoftBank announced the departure of Marcelo Claure, the man Masa once regarded as a son. According to *The New York Times*, the Bolivian wanted $2 billion in compensation. The SoftBank press release tried to smooth over the ructions, but the reality was a spectacular falling-out. Claure acknowledged Masa had offered him "unlimited trust," but he felt cheated in terms of the money he believed was owed to him. This was no "napkin contract"; in fact, the ten-year employment agreement was worth up to $10 billion.

Almost two weeks later, on February 7, SoftBank announced it was abandoning the planned ARM-Nvidia combination in the face of regulatory opposition. From Yahoo! Japan to Japan Telecom to Vodafone Japan to Sprint-T-Mobile, Masa had cajoled regulators and rivals into giving him almost everything he wanted. Now he was living in a world where the powers that be could say no, though in Sprint's case, with the help of Marcelo Claure, he had ultimately prevailed after a seven-year fight.

On February 24, Russian forces invaded Ukraine, sending energy prices shooting skyward, turbocharging inflationary pressures in the wake of the Covid pandemic. The democratic West, led by the US, pledged support for President Zelensky's government in Kyiv. China stood by Russia, having pledged "a friendship without limits" during a Xi-Putin summit in Beijing just before the invasion. In a world divided, Masa was increasingly under pressure to take sides.

On March 16, 2022, the Federal Reserve approved a 0.25 percentage point rise in interest rates to 0.5 percent, flagging a further six hikes over the rest of the year. The Fed move belatedly recognized that inflation was here to stay. After three decades of cheap, some said "dumb," money, the return of inflation fundamentally challenged SoftBank's strategy of debt-fueled growth through acquisition.

The extent of Masa's personal liabilities was complicated. On one side, he'd long secured financing from SoftBank, pledging his own shareholding, usually around one-third of the company, as collateral. But he also had personal borrowings from a multitude of banks worldwide, with assets ranging from houses to paintings and planes offered as security for the loans. Depending on the state of financial markets and his access to cash, Masa could either repay or roll over the loan repayments schedules. If SoftBank stock fell, then he faced the threat of a margin call to repay the money.

Only a tiny handful of people knew the extent of Masa's borrowings. An intensely private man, he was equally secretive about his assets. His real estate empire stretched from Kyoto and central Tokyo to Woodside, California, as well as the huge house near Sprint's HQ in Kansas. These properties were intended to impress as well as entertain VIP guests, each designed and furnished with meticulous attention to detail.

Ron Fisher had known Masa for more than thirty years, dined in the best restaurants around the world, and watched his napkin routine dozens of times, but he still wasn't aware of the precise nature of his wealth or liabilities. And if he had half a clue, he wasn't saying. Like many who worked closely with Masa, Fisher never said a bad word about his boss. He was loyal to a fault. It wasn't just the millions he'd made himself, though the money helped; it was his love for the man, his creativity, his passion, even his occasional displays of naivety, like falling for Adam Neumann.

Katsunori Sago, briefly a putative successor to Masa, initially experienced the thrill of working for someone so spur-of-the-moment compared to the stultifying hierarchy of corporate Japan. For three years, Sago spent two to twelve hours a day with Masa, watching a natural entrepreneur in action. Often it was like working for the world's biggest start-up, an organized chaos featuring "Masa games," where colleagues would dream up dozens of ways to value the SoftBank portfolio in twelve or eighteen months, two years, or even twenty years. The obsession with making tons of money was exhilarating and utterly exhausting, but in the end it left Sago-san with a strange, empty feeling.

On May 12, 2022, a somber Masa walked onstage to deliver news of SoftBank's annual results. This time, there were no flying unicorns, no golden eggs, not even a reference to Napoleon. Instead, he began his presentation with giant letters painted in white against a deep blue backdrop: they spelled *mamori*, meaning defense.

Masa took personal responsibility for the giant losses. He'd done the same all his life, refusing to blame others for his misfortune. But all his talk about switching to defense and responsible investing rang hollow. Colleagues and investors had heard it all before. The difference this time was that Masa's own margin of maneuver was shrinking, fast. His 17.25 percent stake in the SoftBank Vision Fund 2 was wiped out, and he was nursing huge losses from the Latin American Fund as well as Northstar. Overall, he was on the hook to SoftBank for up to $5 billion, according to *Financial Times* calculations, which did not take into account further loans owed to international banks.[12]

On July 7, SoftBank announced internally that Rajeev Misra was launching a new $7 billion fund backed by Abu Dhabi investors, called One Investment Management. How this news squared with his own responsibilities at SoftBank Group or indeed the Vision Fund was unclear, but Masa emphasized that his top lieutenant was staying on, albeit with modified responsibilities. Two months later, the financial magician was gone.

Masa tried everything to persuade Misra to stick with SoftBank. But his financial consigliere was set on leaving. His sole concession, partly on the urging of the Saudis and Emiratis, was to continue in his role as "key man" managing the Vision Fund. As ever, Misra was playing the politics astutely, nurturing his relationships with the Gulf Arabs but keeping channels open to Masa.[13]

On November 11, Masa shuffled onstage to make his regular earnings call to analysts and journalists. His demeanor was unusually grave. Then came a dramatic announcement: this would be the last time he'd give any quarterly updates on trading or strategy. From now on, Yoshimitsu Goto would be the public face of SoftBank. The CFO paid tribute to Masa as one of the great entrepreneurs of his generation, not just in Japan but in the rest of the world. The problem, he said, was that his boss played several roles at once: entrepreneur, visionary, and CEO: "We have been asking him to do too much."

Goto meant every word. But SoftBank without Masa wasn't SoftBank. He would be back.

EPILOGUE

ate one afternoon in October 2023, as the sun slipped down over Tokyo Bay, Masa was sitting in his private office at SoftBank headquarters, at the head of a wooden table almost as long as Vladimir Putin's in
the Kremlin. He was recounting the low point of his career, a year earlier,
when he announced he was disappearing from public view.

"What a shitty life!" he exclaimed. "You know, on my Zoom call, I see
my face often on the video screen, and I hate looking at my face. What an
ugly face. I'm just getting old. And maybe I'm finishing my life as an entrepreneur in the next limited number of years, but what have I achieved?
What have I done? This is just a mediocre, shitty life. I have done nothing
that I can be proud of."[14]

There was a trace of self-pity about Masa as he contemplated aloud
his own mortality. His beloved white teacup poodle Marie had passed
away in the summer. Mitsunori was battling stage-four cancer in a Tokyo hospital. Masa visited his father every day, and every time Mitsunori
peppered him with questions about his latest investment plans. Even on
his deathbed, the pachinko king was eager to know where his son was
going to place his next big bet.

Artificial intelligence remains the key to Masa's reinvention as an
entrepreneur-futurist. For a self-styled visionary, his record as an investor
in AI-related companies has until now looked fitful at best. Between 2017
and 2022, he mentioned "AI" more than five hundred times in quarterly
and annual results presentations. He claimed that AI would "redefine all
industries," unleashing the next wave of the information revolution. Yet
when it came to Open AI and its breakthrough product ChatGPT, the

fastest-growing app of all time, the lead investor was Microsoft. In October 2024, Masa finally got a look-in when he invested $500 million in a new $6.5 billion round of fundraising driven by Sam Altman, Open AI's CEO.

Part of the problem was timing. During the six years Masa raised and deployed money for SoftBank Vision Fund 1 and 2, the opportunities to invest in generative AI companies were few and far between. Aside from Open AI, these businesses were either small scale, early in development, or out of the public eye. During the Covid-19 pandemic, Masa was at a material disadvantage, grounded in Tokyo. In early 2022, when travel restrictions were finally lifted, with the exception of China, SoftBank was sandbagged by record losses.

On the other hand, Masa was always in a hurry, throwing money at tech-enabled companies rather than "Deep AI." Most galling of all, says one longtime collaborator, Masa would have been perfectly placed in 2022–23 had he conserved his firepower rather than splurging money on more than five hundred separate companies in the Vision Fund 1 and 2 portfolios. With company valuations beaten down by higher interest rates, Masa could have acquired stakes in promising AI-related businesses at bargain prices.

In hindsight, Masa admits, "Timing-wise maybe we were a little too early." He detects a parallel between the emerging AI revolution and the early days of the internet, when SoftBank handed out checks to dozens of companies with the dot-com moniker. Although many went under in the dot-com crash, a good number went on to be real businesses generating real profits. The internet, meanwhile, became seamlessly integrated into daily life, just as Masa expects AI will in the none-too-distant future.

Today SoftBank's portfolio includes China's ride-hailing Didi and internet giant ByteDance; food-delivery services like DoorDash and Grab; and automated robotic warehouses like Symbotic. These were the "first wave" of AI-related companies with "baby" applications. In 2024 Masa invested in next-generation AI companies such as the US medical data firm Tempus and the UK self-driving-car technology start-up Wayve. The emergence of ChatGPT, according to Masa, has changed everything. So-called generative AI points to a future he has long predicted: the moment when machines think faster, learn faster, and react faster than humans.

"It's like the Cambrian Explosion," he says, referring to the proliferation of complex animal species that began life on earth more than five hundred million years ago. In this new world, dozens of new companies will be born, with dozens of applications in areas like smart robotics, autonomous driving cars, and smart logistics.

Masa knows he has ground to make up, fast. The balance of power in the technology arms race rests not with SoftBank but with the "hyperscalers" like Amazon, Microsoft, Google, and Meta, who are deep into AI. These are the new East India Companies, businesses with global reach, vast stores of capital and world-class technology. For a brief period, thanks to the Vision Fund, Masa could match these behemoths in terms of capital. His dream was to create a pool of assets of $1 trillion or more, with annual returns of up to 30 percent. In the end, Vision Fund 1 produced single-digit returns and Vision Fund 2 a sea of red ink. The Northstar escapade ended in disaster. WeWork ended in bankruptcy, costing SoftBank up to $14 billion. The man looking to hit a home run was responsible for one of the biggest swings and misses in the history of investing.

"If we had the same $100 billion right now, maybe we would focus on generative AI-related companies. Now these are true AI revolution companies. We were probably five years too early. But I think my instinct on the direction is still correct."[15]

It's a familiar story: right instincts, wrong timing. Yet one of Masa's AI bets has paid off handsomely. Chip designer ARM can plausibly claim to be a global force in the age of artificial intelligence. Today, it is the company at the center of yet another Masa super-vision: a $64 billion plan to transform SoftBank Group into a sprawling AI powerhouse, including a foray into the development of artificial intelligence chips.

In May 2024, Nikkei reported that SoftBank was planning for ARM to set up an AI chip division. The goal was to build a prototype by 2025, with each chip able to process vast volumes of data. Mass production was to be handled by contract manufacturers such as Taiwan's TSMC and was expected to begin in the autumn of that year. SoftBank declined to comment, but the reports suggested an attempt to create its own vertically integrated AI ecosystem, from manufacturing chips to operating data centers and industrial robots and power generation.

Once again, Masa has confounded his critics and wrong-footed rivals. His self-enforced absence from the public eye was in hindsight a ruse. Rather than serving penance, Masa was plotting in Tokyo. He was also making secret trips around the world, visiting chip plants in Taiwan and the US and sounding out potential partners like Sam Altman and his former financial backers in the Gulf. In hindsight, there were clues about his thinking all along.

In the summer of 2023, Masa went all in on a public listing for ARM, hoping to extract an eye-popping return on his $32 billion investment seven years on. Maybe $100 billion, maybe more. None of his financial advisers knew whether he was serious or blowing smoke. The IPO market had been virtually closed all year. Investors still licking their wounds from the tech bust in 2021–22 were suddenly presented with the biggest IPO of the year on Wall Street, courtesy of Masa.

In mid-June, he bought out a 25 percent stake lodged in Vision Fund 1, a sweetheart deal for Gulf investors who had lobbied to cash in and boost their returns. The move effectively set a floor under the ARM IPO on September 14, 2023, where Masa and Jeff Sine in New York mobilized a host of international tech companies to subscribe. The numbers were not large by themselves (each contribution was kept under $110 million to avoid antitrust considerations); but the symbolism of Apple, Google, ADM, Intel, Foxconn, and Samsung signing up was potent. After being treated as a laughingstock, Masa was back in the Big Tech fold.

In early 2024, following more excitement about Nvidia and the impact of AI, ARM shares rocketed. Acquired for $32 billion in 2016, the UK semiconductor chip designer was valued at more than $140 billion eight years later. And SoftBank still owned 90 percent of ARM stock. ARM really was a gem, even if it still lagged behind Nvidia, which hit a $3 trillion valuation in June 2024. Having sold down his Nvidia stockholding in December 2018, Masa missed out many times over. His AI superchip venture marks an attempt to catch up with Nvidia in a market estimated at $30 billion in 2024, and expected to exceed $100 billion in 2029 and top $200 billion in 2032.[16]

As Chris Miller recounts in his book *Chip Wars*, military, economic, and geopolitical power rests on the foundation of computer chips. They power missiles, smartphones, and the stock market, but superchips are a scarce resource, and the world is overly dependent on Taiwan's TSMC as supplier. Hence the race to diversify supply, with China, the US, Japan, South Korea, and multiple other countries investing billions to establish their own capacity. Masa has inserted himself into a position where he can try to influence the battle to control the world's most critical resource: the microchip.[17]

In our conversation in Tokyo in October 2023, Masa recounted again his "Eureka moment" when he first saw the picture of a microprocessor in a computer magazine. He experienced a sensation similar to Robert Oppenheimer, the scientist who developed the nuclear bomb. "It was a mixture of sacredness, respect, amazement, dreaming, and passion," he remembered, "and I said, 'Oh my God!' My fingers and hands started to shake, and I started really crying and said, 'I have to be in this. I have to be in this revolution. I have to participate.'"

The broader case for Masa rests not only on his reputation as a giant risk-taker ("Good for the system," says one veteran investor, "just as long there are not too many Masas"), but also on his role as a techno-optimist. Today, it has become fashionable to view technology as a job-killer or a corrupting force, creating a world where disinformation is spread at scale and speed. The debate about generative AI threatens to move in an even darker direction. Tesla's Elon Musk has warned of a "Terminator future," where AI would remove the need for people to work. In the future, jobs would be all about "personal satisfaction." Masa continues to believe that civilization was—and is—built on technology. The AI revolution is no different. While he favors a degree of management and control, like traffic lights and speed limits for cars, overall he remains captivated by AI's undimmed potential.

"I'm amazed how capable it is already. But if you imagine it becomes ten thousand times smarter than today, it will be beyond what we can imagine right now. As I said, a fish can never understand ABC. A fish cannot understand human society. It is beyond their imagination. AGI [artificial generative intelligence] is going to be just like that. It's going to be beyond our wisdom," he said, his voice rising in excitement. "We will say, 'How could this happen? How can this be so smart? How can they predict this much?' It's like you're asking God or a fortune teller.

He tells you, and you don't know how they got the answer. I truly believe that this is coming within ten years."

Far from AI creating a dystopian world where humans are subservient to machines, Masa believes in a more benign outcome, with fewer boundaries of geography, nationality, age, sex, or religion.

"I think all the fish should live happily in the fishbowl. We have to respect each other," he says, "because something really big is coming. We cannot misuse it or misbehave with it. We shouldn't have stupid little fights. The geopolitics of ideology or language or sex, these are small differences between humans."

In a world characterized by nationalism, populism, and Great Power tensions, especially between the US and China, this can come across as wishful thinking. But Masa's optimism is tempered by realism. For example, he understands that SoftBank can no longer go shopping for assets in China: "We had to choose," he says, "and we chose the US, Europe, and Japan."

Toward the end of a two-hour conversation, I ask Masa how he would like to be remembered, bearing in mind that he has no intention of retiring anytime soon. A long silence ensues, perhaps as long as fifteen seconds, as SoftBank's founder and boss digests the question.

"One of the foundation stones of AGI. I may not be the full story of AGI, but one of the foundation stones of AGI," he says. "AGI is the only thing I care about. The only word I care about, those three letters *AGI*. And then it's going to be ASI [superintelligence]."

The answer is something of a letdown coming from a man who puts himself in the same category as empire builders like Napoleon or Genghis Khan. But Masa is apparently satisfied that making a lasting contribution to the AI revolution will be a fitting legacy. "I will pass away with a good smile."

Not bad for a concluding line in the Masa drama. But wait, all is not over. He reminds me that in his youth he aspired to be a painter. Having earlier shown me his own watercolors—a bridge in Paris, a Van Gogh-style sunflower landscape, a Japanese spa town—he asks whether I would like to see a portion of his art collection, hung in his private dining room adjacent to his office. Only VVIP guests are allowed into Masa's private quarters. In terms of Japanese protocol, the invitation ranks right up there, until I realize that I am about to experience directly a man practiced in the art of seduction.

Masa slides open two wooden doors to reveal a breathtaking scene: a vast open space with three rock pools and three trees, symbolizing spring, summer, and autumn respectively. Every leaf on the trees, every leaf floating in the rock pools is hand-painted to capture the seasonal colors. To every intent and purpose, the visitor might have been transported in this moment to Kyoto, where rock gardens, temples, and healing springs represent the finest of Japanese cultural heritage.

In Masa's make-believe world on the twenty-eighth floor of SoftBank's headquarters, Japanese art adorns the walls, including calligraphy from the Edo period. In one corner there is a Hokusai painting of an old man looking up in awe to the sky. Farther along, a framed photograph of one of Masa's favorite white teacup poodles. At the far end of the room lies the main dining area, featuring an immaculately laid table and three bottles of Masa's favorite Romanée-Conti wines placed on a serving counter to the side. Assuming the menu for the guests features his favorite sushi, bought at the Tokyo fish market early that morning, the cost of dinner alone must be around $50,000.

In the central area lies an elevated lacquered wooden platform where guests can converse on elongated sofas and take in a panoramic view of the Japanese garden. But there is a catch. The platform arrangement creates a very different perspective of the rock pools and trees. It's not exactly trompe l'oeil, but the effect is to alter one's sense of time, distance, and space. It's a subtle reminder that in life there are many levels of reality, many shades of truth; perhaps a hint that what you see is not always what you get with Masa.

Alongside the bravado, the extraordinary wealth, and the manifest waste lie courage, creativity, and a capacity to effect change. As part of a despised minority, he rose from humble origins to challenge the might of Japan's corporate establishment. Time and again, he ventured where others feared to tread. He built a new business—software distribution— where none existed before. He secured loans from Japanese banks on the basis of a business plan rather than real estate. He bought valuable assets in America. He launched his own broadband and mobile phone business in Japan in the teeth of opposition. Against all odds, he brought off the Sprint–T-Mobile merger, creating a third force in the US telecoms industry and netting billions in returns. If hubris brought him tumbling down, not once, not twice, but three times, he never gave up.

In numbers alone, moreover, his wealth creation remains impressive. In mid-July 2024, before the sharp sell-off in the Tokyo stock market, SoftBank Group shares were trading at ¥10,380, which puts the media-tech company's market capitalization at ¥15 trillion ($97.7 billion). That amounts to a personal stake worth $28 billion. He also holds, indirectly through SoftBank Group, around 12 percent of SoftBank Mobile, a profitable business worth around $60 billion. Adding all his properties around the world and his stakes in SoftBank portfolio companies, his gross worth, absent borrowing, was probably somewhere between $30 billion and $35 billion—not bad for someone who grew up in a shantytown.

There is an old Wall Street adage—you make big money off a small base or small money off a big base. Masa tried to rewrite the script. He tried to make gargantuan returns off a gargantuan base. Yet SoftBank has never been about profits. It's always been about growth—and the moon shot. Even though he remains mistrusted by the Japanese establishment, Masa retains an extraordinary loyalty among Japanese retail investors and those institutional players who have had the stomach to stay with him on his wild ride, following the old lesson of "buying on the dip."

While it is true that Masa cannot touch the likes of Amazon, Google, and Microsoft, he is nowhere near out of options. He is a customer and supplier to the hyperscalers. His new chip-making venture involves billions of dollars of investment, drawing in Middle East money and partners from all over the world as well as SoftBank's own contribution. Once a mass-production system is established, the AI chip business could be spun off, realizing billions of dollars of value to its parent SoftBank.

Moreover, in September 2023, *The Financial Times* reported he was ready to put up $1 billion to develop "the iPhone of artificial intelligence," in partnership with Sam Altman and the former top Apple designer Jony Ive. This would be the first consumer device of the AI age, a landmark product to rival the smartphone.

Even if Masa has often sailed close to the wind, rumors of SoftBank going bust were always exaggerated. In Japan, it is probably too big to fail, its fate too intertwined with the Japanese financial system. Besides, Masa has for two decades operated proven assets like SoftBank Mobile and Yahoo! Japan that make real money. And finally, in addition to the new superchip venture, he is master of SoftBank's five-hundred-strong portfolio of companies, among which at some point in the future there may be another Alibaba or Nvidia.

He may not hold the aces, but Masa still has a seat at the top table.

ACKNOWLEDGMENTS

Embarking upon a biography is a daunting prospect, especially when the subject is a notoriously elusive character living several thousand miles away in Japan. In every respect, I owe a special debt to my Tokyo-based researcher Simon Angseop Lee, who accompanied me on every step of a three-year journey to complete the first Western biography of Masayoshi Son.

Simon dug deep into original Japanese source material, including public archives, Japanese-language biographies, and books on SoftBank. He was a diligent researcher and an expert guide around Tokyo's parks and historical places as well as the culinary hot spots in Kyushu, Masa's birthplace. As a fellow Korean Japanese, Simon was ideally suited to explain the hardship Masa endured as a start-up businessman in postwar Japan and the prejudice he continues to face today.

I met Simon in April 2021 through Professor Niall Ferguson, then teaching at Stanford University. At the time I was despairing of ever completing a book on Masayoshi Son. Over a sandwich lunch on campus, Niall recommended I hire a Japanese researcher—preferably a PhD student. Simon fell short on that count, but otherwise he hit the bull's-eye.

I owe a special thanks to friends who read early drafts of the manuscript. Patrick Foulis made numerous suggestions that illuminated the lead character and sharpened the narrative. In light of his editorial duties at *The Economist*, Patrick's contribution was generous and unstinting. Stephen Barber, my twin and a longtime student of Japan, was equally diligent in combing through the script for errors, both stylistic and factual. Bill Emmott, Haruko Fukuda, and Stanford's Professor Dan

Okimoto, a wonderful guide to Japanese corporate culture and history, were also kind enough to read the final draft.

I am also grateful to those patient souls who saw very early iterations and made many helpful comments: Richard Cohen in Los Angeles, Marcus Brauchli in Washington, DC, Michael Moritz in San Francisco, Jim McGregor in New York, Tom Stoppard in Dorset. I am particularly grateful to Richard, who advised me to make sure my subject was "present even when he was not in the room," and to Jim, who is a walking encyclopedia.

Gambling Man required traveling around the globe in Masa's vapor trail, leaving the author often stupefied with jet lag. I visited Japan five times in twelve months and California seven times in two years.

Along the way, I met many experts in finance, venture capital, and Japanese history. Professor Ilya Strebulaev of Stanford Business School and coauthor of *The Venture Mindset* was especially helpful in providing introductions to founders and financial backers and explaining the more arcane aspects of venture capital. And, of course, nonagenarian Professor Forrest Mozer, who over more than three years has been a constant source of information and insight about Masa's years at UC Berkeley and his first business ventures.

I am also grateful to Bradley Hope and Maureen Farrell, both Masa watchers who did groundbreaking reporting on SoftBank at *The Wall Street Journal* and *The New York Times*, for their generous help on sources and methods. In Tokyo, Hiroshi Kodama provided immensely useful background documentation on Masa's early career as revealed in his own investigative reporting for *Nikkei*. Thanks also to Tamzin Booth of *The Economist*, a shrewd SoftBank watcher.

During my research, I interviewed many people who had intimate contact with Masa, either during a twenty-minute audience or through more intensive collaboration over a number of years. There are too many to list individually, and many asked not to be named, in many cases because of their continuing commercial relationships with SoftBank.

I would like to thank Ron Fisher, a longtime US collaborator, for agreeing to several valuable interviews. Alibaba's Joe Tsai, Yahoo! cofounder Jerry Yang, and Bill Gates of Microsoft offered generous sitdown time. Rajeev Misra, Marcelo Claure, and Nikesh Arora were also very helpful. They had their differences while working for SoftBank, but they had one thing in common: a willingness to help this author better understand the character and business methods of one of the greatest risk-takers the world has ever seen.

I would also like to express my gratitude to two people who sadly passed away before this book was completed. Anshu Jain, former CEO of Deutsche Bank, spawned a generation of bankers and risk-takers, several of whom feature in this story. Despite his illness, he found time to see me in London and provide insights and introductions. Ben Wedmore, a longtime SoftBank watcher and analyst, offered a more critical eye.

It would be remiss of me not to thank SoftBank—in particular head of communications Take Nukii—for their assistance. Along with Mark Kornblau in the US, Take opened doors and provided valuable steers on tricky subjects. Without his cooperation, this project would have been much harder to complete. I would also like to thank Masayoshi Son for agreeing to sit down for four interviews in Tokyo and for allowing me to speak to his father, Mitsunori, at the family home in Tosu. All these sessions rank among the more memorable interviews I have conducted in my career as a journalist.

All reporters need a great editor, especially when stitching together a complex narrative involving dozens of characters and lots of numbers ending in zeros. In this respect, I am indebted to Stuart Profitt, my editor at Allen Lane. Stuart is one of the best editors in the world, a man who knows his historical references and is a stickler for accuracy. "Are we sure it was drizzling that morning?" must be one of the more penetrating questions an author must answer. Stuart was kind enough to read the manuscript not once, but twice. On each occasion, his suggestions improved the manuscript many times over.

I would also like to thank my agent Andrew Wylie, who was always available, always supportive, and who never failed to deliver an honest verdict on my drafts. All errors, of course, are my own.

Finally, a special thanks to Dash and Francesca, who had to listen to their father talk endlessly about his book on visits to New York and Los Angeles. And to Victoria, who watched me working endlessly in my "cave" in the Surrey Hills. Without her patience and support, this biography would never have seen the light of day.

NOTES

PROLOGUE
1. Velfarre is an amalgam of Versace, Ferrari, and Armani.
2. *Nikkei*, February 7, 2000, Morning Edition, p. 16. For "Velfarre," see *Nikkei*, December 20, 1997, Evening Edition, p. 7.
3. *Nikkei*, February 7, 2000, Morning Edition, p. 17.
4. *Nikkei*, January 20, 2000, Morning Edition, p. 22.
5. "Japan's Web Spinners," Bloomberg, March 13, 2000.
6. Ibid.
7. *Nikkei Sangyō Shimbun*, February 22, 2000, p. 32.

1: ROOTS
1. Barak Kushner, interview with author, March 11, 2022.
2. Eiji Ōshita, *Son Masayoshi: Kigyō no Wakaki Shishi* (Kōdansha, 1999), p. 36.
3. Shinichi Sano, *Anpon: Son Masayoshi Den* (Shōgakukan Bunko, 2014), pp. 16, 64.
4. Mitsunori Son, interview with author, April 1, 2023.
5. Kim Yeong-dal, *Sōshikaimei no Hōseido to Rekishi* (Akashi Shoten, 2002), p. 88.
6. The precise death toll is fiercely disputed by Japanese and Koreans. Official Japanese accounts at the time severely minimized the casualties, while some Korean accounts put the figures as high as twenty-five thousand.
7. Sano, *Anpon*, p. 138.
8. John W. Dower, *Embracing Defeat: Japan in the Wake of World War II* (W. W. Norton, 1999), p. 21.
9. Mitsunori Son, interview, April 1, 2023.
10. Kushner, interview, March 11, 2022.
11. Mitsunori Son, interview, April 1, 2023.

2: PACHINKO
1. Tosu Shishi Hensan Iinkai, *Tosu Shishi, Vol. 4: Kindai-Gendai Hen* (Tosu Shi, 2009), p. 474.
2. Sano, *Anpon*, pp. 28–39.
3. Atsuo Inoue, *Aiming High: Masayoshi Son, SoftBank, and Disrupting Silicon Valley* (Hodder & Stoughton, 2021), p. 2.

4. Mitsunori Son, interview with author, April 1, 2023.
5. Dower, *Embracing Defeat*, p. 108.
6. Sano, *Anpon*, p. 115.
7. Ibid., p. 159.
8. Ibid., pp. 340-47.
9. Ibid., pp. 350-51.
10. Ibid., p. 28.
11. Masayoshi Son (Masa), interview with author, February 10, 2023.
12. Imperial Japan acquired Taiwan in 1895.
13. Ibid.
14. Hiroshi Kodama, interview with author, October 24, 2022.
15. *Nikkei*, November 8, 2017.
16. Using contemporary yen to dollar exchange rate, i.e., ¥360 to $1.
17. Mitsunori Son, interview, April 1, 2023.
18. Senior SoftBank official, who asked not to be named, interview with author, November 2023.
19. Masa, interview, February 10, 2023.
20. Nikesh Arora, interview with author, November 30, 2022.
21. Pachinko originally derived from the British game of bagatelle in penny arcades. In Tokyo, it was known as "pachi-pachi" and in Osaka as "gachinko." Both were onomatopoeias for the clinking sounds the machines made. Hence the portmanteau name: "pachinko." See Kazuo Sugiyama, *Pachinko Tanjō: Cinema no Seiki no Taishō Goraku* (Sōgensha, 2008), p. 40, and Emiko Suzuki, *Ten no Kugi: Gendai Pachinko o Tsukutta Otoko Masamura Takeichi* (Banseisha, 2001), p. 51.
22. Min Jin Lee, *Pachinko* (Apollo, 2020), p. 415.
23. *Fortune*, January 30, 2017.
24. Lee, *Pachinko*, p. 414.
25. A statue of a lion stands outside Mitsunori's home on the outskirts of Tosu.
26. Mitsunori Son, interview, April 1, 2023.
27. Ibid.
28. Masa, interview, February 10, 2023.
29. Koreans made up 85 percent of all resident aliens. The practice was abolished when the law was revised in 1993.
30. "Den Fujita, Japan's Mr Joint Venture," Obituary, *New York Times*, March 22, 1992.
31. Ibid.

3: AMERICAN AWAKENING

1. Inoue, *Aiming High*, p. 16.
2. I am grateful to Professor Dan Okimoto at Stanford University for these insights.
3. In addition to his passport, Son held an alien registration certificate from birth, with his Japanese alias, Masayoshi Yasumoto, written in brackets. Hence the fact of segregation.
4. Masa, interview with author, February 10, 2023.
5. Ibid.
6. Ibid.
7. Inoue, *Aiming High*, p. 18.

8. Masa, interview, February 10, 2023.

9. Taizō's autobiography, *Sonke no Idenshi* (Kadokawa Shoten, 2002), p. 85.

10. Inoue, *Aiming High*, p. 21.

11. Ibid., pp. 23-24.

12. Masa, interview, February 10, 2023.

13. Inoue, *Aiming High*, pp. 30-31.

14. Masa, interview, February 10, 2023.

15. Bill Gates, interview with author, July 8, 2022.

16. Tadashi Sasaki autobiography, *Waga Kōshisai: Kansha Hou'on no Ki* (Zaikai Tsūshin Sha, 2005), pp. 49-53.

17. Sano, *Anpon*, p. 120.

18. I owe this insight to Ben Tarnoff reviewing Walter Isaacson's biography of Elon Musk in the *New York Review of Books*, January 18, 2024.

4: LOST IN TRANSLATION

1. Mozer's invention appeared in the *Oakland Independent*, October 5, 1977.

2. Forrest Mozer, interview with author, October 29, 2021.

3. Ibid., April 8, 2022.

4. Masa, interview with author, February 10, 2023.

5. Hong Lu, interview with author, December 2, 2022.

6. Ibid.

7. Masa uses the long-standing mean exchange rate of ¥100 to $1 to get the $1 million figure. In 1978-79, the rate was around $1 = ¥200. So a more accurate figure would be $500,000.

8. Inoue, *Aiming High*, p. 69.

9. Mozer, interview and email exchange with author, 2022-23.

10. Henry Heetderks, email exchange with author, February 6, 2022.

11. Inoue, *Aiming High*, p. 45.

12. Lu, interview, July 26, 2022.

13. Ibid.

14. Ibid. And email exchange.

15. Masa, interview with author, March 29, 2023.

16. Ibid.

17. Mozer, interview, April 8, 2023.

18. SoftBank Group email exchange, February 2024.

19. Mozer, interview, August 10, 2022.

20. Taito was founded in 1953 by Misha Kogan, a Ukrainian Jew whose family had fled to Manchuria in the 1930s. Kogan went to Tokyo Imperial University during the Second World War. "Taito" is a contraction for "Far Eastern Jew."

21. Inoue, *Aiming High*, p. 59.

22. Lu, interview, December 2, 2022.

23. Inoue, *Aiming High*, p. 61.

24. Lu, interview, December 2, 2022.

5: SOFTBANK 1.0

1. *Ōru Taishū* (1/15 January 1981), p. 26.

2. Hiroshi Kodama, *Nikkei Business*, October 20, 2000, p. 177.
3. Masa, interview with author, March 29, 2023.
4. Ibid.
5. Ibid.
6. Kodama, *Nikkei Business*, October 30, 2000, p. 177, but Masa says it was a mistaken filing. See Inoue, *Aiming High*, p. 65.
7. Seiichirō Takita, *Son Masayoshi: Internet Zaibatsu Keiei* (Nikkei Bijinesujin Bunko, 2011), p. 64.
8. Inoue, *Aiming High*, p. 67.
9. Masa'aki Satō, *Honda Shinwa, Vol. 1: Honda Sōichirō to Fujisawa Takeo* (Bunshun Bunko, 2008), p. 55.
10. Juri Tsukui, ed., *Heisei no Ryōma Densetsu: Onshitachi ga Kataru Son Masayoshi no Sugao* (Genbun Media, 2011), pp. 94–95, and Sasaki, *Waga Kōshisai: Kansha Hou'on no Ki*, p. 212.
11. SoftBank Japan was owned jointly by Unison World in the US and MRI. See *Nikkei Sangyō Shimbun*, October 6, 1981, p. 4.
12. Inoue, *Aiming High*, p. 69.
13. Masa, interview, March 29, 2023.
14. Masa, *Harvard Business Review* interview, January–February 1992.
15. The exchange rate is ¥220 to the US dollar.
16. Email exchange with SoftBank Group, February 17, 2024.
17. Inoue, *Aiming High*, p. 206.
18. Tsukui, *Heisei no Ryōma Densetsu*, p. 96.
19. Heetderks, email exchange, February 24, 2022.
20. Inoue, *Aiming High*, p. 118.
21. Hiroshi Kodama, *Gensōkyoku: Son Masayoshi to SoftBank no Kako Ima Mirai* (Nikkei BP, 2005), pp. 67–69.
22. *Cinderella Boy* was a popular manga at the time. *Shūkan Asahi*, February 26, 1982, pp. 162–63.

6: MIRACLE CURE

1. *Nikkei Sangyō Shimbun*, May 20, 1982, p. 9; March 29, 1983, p. 27.
2. Kodama, *Gensōkyoku*, p. 74.
3. Inoue, *Aiming High*, p. 83.
4. Masa, interview with author, March 29, 2023.
5. Ibid.
6. At an exchange rate of ¥260 against the US dollar.
7. Lu in an email exchange suggests Masa siphoned off profits from the US video games to pay back the loan. Kodama, *Gensōkyoku*, p. 88.
8. SoftBank Group email exchange.
9. In Kodama's taped interview, Masa said "a couple of bank transfers" had been made before he stopped the scheme (December 21, 2000).
10. Sano, *Anpon*, p. 214.
11. Kodama, *Gensōkyoku*, p. 80.
12. Ōshita, *Son Masayoshi*, pp. 240–41; Sano, *Anpon*, p. 223; Kodama, *Fantasia*, p. 81.

13. Kodama, *Gensōkyoku*, pp. 81-82.
14. Gates, interview with author, July 8, 2022.
15. Ibid.
16. Ibid.
17. Ōshita, *Son Masayoshi*, pp. 242–47.
18. Takita, *Internet Zaibatsu Keiei*, pp. 175-80; *Sūkan Gendai*, July 9, 1983, p. 30.
19. Masa's notebook from 1982, copy provided by Kodama.
20. Lu, interview with author, December 2, 2022.
21. Inoue, *Aiming High*, pp. 89-90.
22. Ibid., p. 90.
23. Masa, interview, March 29, 2023.
24. Ōshita, *Son Masayoshi*, pp. 248-351.
25. Dan Okimoto, interview with author, March 17, 2023.
26. Inoue, *Aiming High*, p. 104.
27. Sano, *Anpon*, pp. 225-28.
28. Ibid., p. 218.
29. Ibid., pp. 228-29.

7: MR. GATEWAY

1. Bobby Kotick, interview with author, January 17, 2023.
2. Ibid.
3. Ibid.
4. *Nikkei Sangyō Shimbun*, June 1, 1988, p. 7; August 29, 1988, p. 7; September 26, 1988, p. 7.
5. Ted Dolotta, *Wartime Vignettes: A Boyhood Memoir of World War II and of Its Aftermath* (Uniflow Press, 2017).
6. Inoue, *Aiming High*, p. 108.
7. Ron Fisher, interview with author, May 24, 2022.
8. Takita, *Internet Zaibatsu Keiei*, pp. 233-34.
9. Fisher, interview, May 24, 2022.
10. Masa, interview with author, March 29, 2023.
11. In fact, Koreans had been able to naturalize under their ethnic name since 1984, thanks to a revision in Japan's nationality law and a change in naturalization procedure successfully pushed by *zainichi* Koreans. See Minozkumei o Torimodosu Kai, ed., *Minozkumei o Torimodoshita Nihonseki Chōsenjin* (Akashi Shoten, 1990), pp. 200-201.

8: PAPER BILLIONAIRE

1. Paul Sheard, interview with author, January 23, 2024.
2. Kodama, *Gensōkyoku*, pp. 123-24, 136.
3. Ibid., p. 126.
4. Ibid., p. 129.
5. Ibid., p. 126.
6. Shigeru Ishii, *Yamaichi Shōken no Shippai* (Nikkei Bijinesujin Bunko, 2017), p. 93.
7. *Nikkei*, February 3, 1992, Morning Edition, p. 17.
8. Kodama, interview with author, February 9, 2023.

9. Kodama, *Gensōkyoku*, p. 124; Sano, *Anpon*, p. 257.

10. Sano, *Anpon*, p. 256.

11. Kodama, *Gensōkyoku*, p. 133.

12. Sano, *Anpon*, p. 258.

13. Kodama, *Gensōkyoku*, p. 141.

14. Mitsunori Son, interview with author, April 2, 2023.

15. Fisher, interview with author, May 24, 2022

16. Ibid.

17. Jordan Levy, interview with author, April 28, 2002.

18. Ibid.

19. Masa, interview with author, March 29, 2023.

20. *Nikkei Sangyō Shimbun*, July 27, 1994, p. 7.

21. *Nikkei*, July 23, 1994, Morning Edition, p. 13.

22. *Gekkan Keieijuku*, December 1994, pp. 24-27.

9: WHAT DOES IT TAKE TO WIN?

1. Jeff Sine, interview with author, September 29, 2022.

2. Steve Rattner and Peter Ezersky, interview with author, July 28, 2022.

3. Dirk Ziff, interview with author, July 8, 2022.

4. Obituary, *New York Times*, January 12, 2021.

5. Ibid.

6. Ōshita, *Son Masayoshi*, p. 350, and Massachusetts court case: https://casetext.com/case/adelson-v-adelson.

7. Jason Chudnofsky, interview with author, March 1, 2023.

8. Ibid.

9. Ibid.

10. Yoshitiko Kitao, email exchange with author, October 4, 2022.

11. Masa, interview with author, March 29, 2023.

12. Albert Alletzhauser, *The Fall of the House of Nomura: The Inside Story of the Legendary Japanese Financial Dynasty* (HarperCollins, 1999), pp. 236-40.

13. Ibid.

14. Kitao, email exchange, October 4, 2022.

15. By comparison with "Big Bang" deregulation in New York and then London, Tokyo was more measured.

16. Ibid.

17. Ōshita, *Son Masayoshi*, p. 419.

18. *Nikkei*, March 17, 2011.

19. Fisher, interview with author, May 24, 2022.

20. Under the scheme, employees later had to take out loans to pay for the options. (See Chapter 12, "Whistleblowers.")

21. Interview with senior banker, who asked not to be named.

10: YAHOO!

1. Sebastian Mallaby, *The Power Law: Venture Capital and the Art of Disruption* (Penguin Books, 2022), pp. 154-59.

2. Ibid.

3. Masa upped his game, funding Japanese scholars to attend elite American colleges as well as supporting the Schwarzman Fellows program for overseas students studying at Tsinghua University in Beijing. Okimoto, interview with author, March 17, 2023.

4. Eric Hippeau, interview with author, June 7, 2022.

5. Jerry Yang, interview with author, April 26, 2022.

6. Mallaby, *The Power Law*, pp. 154-59.

7. Inoue, *Aiming High*, pp. 117-19.

8. Yang, interview, 26 April 2022.

9. Michael Moritz, interview with author, August 15, 2022.

10. Ibid.

11. Ibid.

12. Mallaby, *The Power Law*, p. 156.

13. Moritz, interview, August 15, 2022.

14. Ibid.

15. Taizō Son, *Sonke no Idenshi* (Kadokawa Shoten, 2002), pp. 146-50.

16. An unlikely savior appeared in the guise of Michael Ovitz, the Hollywood superagent turned Disney executive. He says Masa was willing to off-load his Yahoo! stake for $250 million. Sensing a bargain, he flew back to Los Angeles to pitch the idea to Disney boss Michael Eisner, who rejected it out of hand (interview with Michael Ovitz, July 9, 2023; see also *Who is Michael Ovitz?*, Michael Ovitz, 2018, p. 345). Levy, interview with author, October 31, 2022.

17. Fisher, interview with author, May 24, 2022.

18. John Tu, interview with author, March 10, 2023.

19. Gary Rieschel, interview with author, September 15, 2022.

20. The details of the initial deal and earn-out figure are featured in Kōichi Yoshida, *Naibu Kokuhatsu: SoftBank Yuganda Keiei*, p. 142 (see Chapter 12).

21. *Wall Street Journal*, August 19, 1996.

22. *Nikkei Business*, August 26, 1996, p. 12.

23. Tu, interview, March 10, 2023.

11: MURDOCH

1. Harold Evans, *Good Times, Bad Times* (Weidenfeld & Nicholson, 1983), pp. 154-67.

2. John McBride, interview with author, May 9, 2023.

3. Ibid.

4. Barry Diller, interview with author, August 16, 2021.

5. McBride, interview, May 9, 2023.

6. Ibid.

7. Sine, interview with author, October 9, 2023.

8. McBride, interview, May 9, 2023.

9. Ibid.

10. Ibid.

11. Kazunori Nakagawa, *Nijū Rasen: Yokubō to Kensō no Media* (Kōdansha, 2019), p. 261.

12. Okimoto, interview with author, March 17, 2023.

13. Sheard, interview with author, January 23, 2024.

14. SoftBank Group press release, October 20, 2000, https://group.softbank/news/press/20001020.
15. SoftBank Group press release, March 1, 2000, https://group.softbank/news/press/20020301_0.

12: WHISTLEBLOWERS

1. Yoshida, *Naibu Kokuhatsu*, p. 2.
2. *Nikkei Business*, October 13, 1997, p. 32.
3. Levy, interview with author, April 27, 2022.
4. Yoshida, *Naibu Kokuhatsu*, p. 70.
5. Ibid., p. 123.
6. Ibid., p. 88.
7. According to SoftBank Group in February 2024, "The stock compensation plan was not directly related to SoftBank under Japanese accounting rules, and therefore not recorded in SoftBank financials."
8. *Kinyū Business*, February 1999, p. 32.
9. In email exchange with SoftBank, February 6, 2024.
10. Yoshida, *Naibu Kokuhatsu*, p. 106.
11. Kotick, interview with author, January 17, 2024.
12. *Los Angeles Times*, October 27, 1997.
13. Ibid.
14. Fisher, interview with author, May 24, 2022.
15. Interview with author, source asked not to be named.
16. *Los Angeles Times*, May 25, 1995.
17. Ibid.
18. *Nikkei Business*, November 17, 1997, p. 6.
19. Ben Wedmore, interview with author, February 21, 2022.

13: BUBBLE MAN

1. Jim McGregor, interview with author, April 29, 2023.
2. Brad Feld, interview with author, June 12, 2023.
3. Rieschel, interview with author, September 14, 2022.
4. Fisher, interview with author, March 24, 2022.
5. Bill Ford, interview with author, September 28, 2022.
6. Moritz, interview with author, August 23, 2023.
7. Ann Hance, interview with author, June 12, 2022.
8. Masa, interview with author, March 29, 2023.
9. John Burbank, interview with author, December 6, 2021.
10. Stephen Barber, email interview with author, October 23, 2023.
11. "Master of the Internet," Forbes.com, July 5, 1999.
12. Sheard, interview with author, January 23, 2024.
13. Takashi Arimori, *Ginkō Shōmetsu*, Vol. 1 (Kōdansha Plus Alpha Bunko), p. 255.
14. *Nikkei Sangyō Shimbun*, February 25, 2000, p. 1.
15. Yoshitaka Kitao, email interview with author, October 4, 2022.
16. Levy, interview with author, October 31, 2022.

14: THE CRASH

1. Duncan Clark, *Alibaba: The House That Jack Ma Built* (HarperCollins, 2016), pp. 123-24.
2. Duncan Clark, interview with author, February 14, 2022.
3. Mallaby, *The Power Law*, p. 230.
4. Joe Tsai, interview with author, August 9, 2022.
5. I am grateful to Porter Erisman for many insights into China in the 1990s.
6. Masa, interview with author, March 29, 2023.
7. Interestingly, Masa equates economic modernization with civilization.
8. Hangzhou, with its fabled lake, later served as Alibaba's headquarters.
9. Ōshita, *Son Masayoshi*, pp. 494-96.
10. Lu, interview with author, July 26, 2022.
11. Ibid.
12. AERA, May 17, 2010, p. 16.
13. Masa, interview with author, October 10, 2023.
14. Rieschel, interview with author, September 14, 2022.
15. Ibid.
16. *Shūkan Asahi*, May 5, 2000, p. 16417; *Asahi Shimbun*, May 8, 2000, p. 12.
17. Ibid., December 27, 2000, p. 8.

15: BROADBAND REVOLUTION

1. Inoue, *Aiming High*, p. 141.
2. Sir Peter Bonfield, interview with author, September 17, 2021.
3. Inoue, *Aiming High*, p. 136.
4. *Nikkei*, March 25, 2000, Morning Edition, p. 9.
5. Sine, interview with author, September 29, 2022.
6. Sachio Semmoto, interview with author, February 7, 2023.
7. Shinsuke Furuya, "Hitotsu no Sekai," in Haruhito Takeda (ed.), *Nihon no Jōhō Tsūshin Sangyō Shi* (Yūhikaku, 2011), pp. 170-74.
8. Inoue, *Aiming High*, p. 143 and passim.
9. Takashi Nawa, interview with author, February 9, 2023.
10. Masa, interview with author, March 29, 2023.
11. Takashi Arimori, *Net Bubble*, Bunshun Shinsho, October 2000.
12. Tadashi Yanai, interview with author, October 18, 2022.
13. The third musketeer was fellow SoftBank board member Shigenobu Nagamori of Nidec, the electronics manufacturer.
14. Ibid.
15. Yang, interview with author, April 26, 2022.
16. Ibid.
17. "Fat Pipe Dream," *Wired*, August 1, 2003.
18. Ibid.
19. Steve Schwarzman, interview with author, June 7, 2022.

16: GOLDEN GOOSE

1. Tsai, interview with author, August 9, 2022.
2. Clark, *The House That Jack Ma Built*, p. 161.

3. Tsai, though SoftBank, declined to confirm the numbers.

4. Tsai, interview, August 9, 2022.

5. The pocket translator episode was different. Professor Mozer thought he had a gentleman's agreement. Masa believed he had promised nothing specific and therefore had not broken his word.

6. *Nikkei Sangyō Shimbun*, May 26, 2004, p. 3.

7. William Esrey, interview with author, January 6, 2023.

8. Ibid.

9. Interview with senior SoftBank Vision Fund executive.

10. Tsai, interview, August 9, 2022.

11. Yang, interview with author, April 26, 2022.

12. I am grateful to Rik Kirkland, formerly with *Fortune* and McKinsey, for his insights.

13. Yang, interview with author, April 22, 2022.

17: MOBILE MAN

1. Inoue, *Aiming High*, p. 153.

2. NTT Communication, *Fū'unji*, pp. 29-30.

3. Docomo was NTT's mobile unit. *Shūkan Economist*, December 12, 2006, p. 18.

4. Bill Morrow, interview with author, March 16, 2023.

5. Vittorio Colao, interview with author, March 15, 2023.

6. Rajeev Misra, interview with author, February 3, 2023.

7. Arun Sarin, interview with author, March 3, 2022.

8. Misra, interview with author, December 17, 2023.

9. Misra pointed out that the loan could be hedged with derivatives, thus reducing the risk. Anshu Jain, interview with author, September 9, 2021.

10. *International Herald Tribune*, October 21, 2006.

11. Longtime Masa associate, who declined to be identified,

12. Inoue, *Aiming High*, pp. 156-57.

13. Masa's slogan makes more sense in Japanese because their units go from 1,000 to 10,000 to 100m (1-sen, 1-man, 1-oku). Ibid.

14. *Nikkei Sangyō Shimbun*, November 1, 2006, p. 3.

15. Ibid., January 9, 2007, p. 3.

16. Ōshita, *Son Masayoshi Hiroku* (East Shinsho, 2015), pp. 231ff.

17. Carl-Henric Svanberg, interview with author, June 16, 2023.

18: STEVE JOBS TO THE RESCUE

1. Sine, interview with author, May 11, 2023.

2. Masa, interview with author, October 10, 2023.

3. Ibid.

4. Walter Isaacson, "The Real Leadership Lessons of Steve Jobs," *Harvard Business Review*, April 2012.

5. Masa, in his interview of October 10, 2023, offers similar versions of the Jobs encounter as in his interview with David Rubinstein for Bloomberg TV, October 11, 2017; see also Sano, *Anpon*, passim.

6. Masa, interview, October 10, 2023.

7. Ibid.
8. Walter Isaacson, *Steve Jobs* (Simon & Schuster, 2011), pp 466-67.
9. Masa, interview, October 10, 2023.
10. Ibid.
11. ITmedia Business Online, June 13, 2008.
12. Fisher, interview with author, January 31, 2023.
13. Ministry of Internal Affairs and Communications, *Denki Tsūshin Jigyō ni okeru Kyōsō Jōkyō no Hyōka 2012*, September 2013, p. 8, https://www.soumu.go.jp/main_content /000247827.pdf.
14. Masa, interview, October 10, 2023.
15. Ibid.
16. Longtime senior SoftBank executive, who asked not to be named.
17. Takashi Sugimoto, *Son Masayoshi 300 Nen Ōkoku eno Yabō* (Nihon Keiji Shimbun Sha, 2017), p. 463.
18. Ibid., p. 464.
19. Two separate SoftBank sources off the record.
20. Sugimoto, *Son Masayoshi 300 Nen Ōkoku eno Yabō*, p. 319.
21. *Nikkei Asia*, January 17, 2021, https://asia.nikkei.com/Business/SoftBank2/Force -behind-SoftBank-Vision-Fund-is-44-year-old-chief-of-staff.
22. SoftBank Earnings Results Analyst Meeting for FY2007, May 9, 2008, Presentation Material, p. 39; SoftBank Earnings Results Analyst Meeting for FY2008, May 1, 2008, Presentation Material, p. 38.

19: THIRTY-YEAR VISION

1. Sine, interview with author, October 9, 2023.
2. Masa, tweet, April 9, 2010.
3. SoftBank's corporate logo—a two-line design—derives from the flag of Kaientai, an enterprising shipping company founded in 1865 by Masa's hero, the visionary samurai Sakamoto Ryoma.
4. Both friends were speaking off the record.
5. Inoue, *Aiming High*, pp. 114ff.
6. Sugimoto, *Son Masayoshi 300 Nen Ōkoku eno Yabō*, pp. 96-97.
7. Former senior SoftBank executive, off the record.
8. *Wall Street Journal*, March 29, 2001.
9. Author has original planning document; also see *Daily Mail*, March 8, 2017, on iceberg basements.
10. *Shūkan Asahi*, August 26, 2011, p. 27; *Shūkan Post*, February 8, 2013, p. 152.
11. Sine, interview, October 9, 2023.
12. Inoue, *Aiming High*, p. 130.
13. *Shūkan Asahi*, August 26, 2011, p. 27.
14. Office Kurio, *Shutoken Meisaku ni De'aeru Bijutsukan Annai* (Mates-Publishing, 2018), p. 76.
15. Sine, interview, October 9, 2023.
16. *Shūkan Post*, February 8, 2013, p. 152.
17. VIP guest, off the record. A dozen other visitors have described the house and its interior.

18. Sugimoto, *Son Masayoshi 300 Nen Ōkoku eno Yabō*, p. 115.
19. Richard Layard's influential book *Happiness: Lessons from New Science*, was published in 2005. Bloomberg, September 27, 2018.
20. *SoftBank Shin 30-Nen Vision*, p. 103.
21. Masa, interview with author, October 10, 2023.

20: FUKUSHIMA

1. *Shūkan Asahi*, March 16, 2012, p. 96
2. Y. Funabashi and K. Kitazawa, "Fukushima in review: A complex disaster, a disastrous response," *Bulletin of the Atomic Scientists* 68, no. 2 (2012): pp. 9-21.
3. Ibid.
4. Ibid.
5. Ibid.
6. In 2006, Governor Sato was elected to office after his namesake and predecessor, Eisuku Sato, was ousted from office and later convicted of bribery charges. Afterward Sato wrote a book, *Annihilating a Governor* (2009), claiming the accusations were politically motivated on account of his dealings with whistleblowers who had highlighted more than twenty safety lapses at the Fukushima plant. Largely ignored at the time, the book became a bestseller after the 2011 disaster.
7. Masa, interview with author, October 10, 2023.
8. Sugimoto, *Son Masayoshi 300 Nen Ōkoku eno Yabō*, pp. 471-74.
9. Ibid.
10. Ibid., p. 475.
11. Ibid., pp. 476-77.
12. *Asahi Shimbun*, May 27, 2011, Morning Edition, p. 3.
13. *Nikkei*, June 15, 2011, https://www.nikkei.com/article/DGXNASFS15033_V10C11A6PE8000/.
14. *Nikkei*, June 28, 2011, https://www.nikkei.com/article/DGXN-ZO31176890Y1A620C1M10800/; *Nikkei*, June 12, 2011, https://www.nikkei.com/article/DGXNASFS12006_S1A610C1000000/; *Asahi Shimbun*, July 28, 2011, Morning Edition, p. 4.
15. *Nikkei*, November 16, 2011, Morning Edition, p. 7.
16. "A Timeline of Son's Trip to the Disaster Site," provided by SoftBank.

21: SPRINT

1. Masa, quoted in *Hollywood Reporter*, October 6, 2011.
2. Sine, interview with author, October 9, 2023.
3. Sunil Bharti Mittal, interview with author, September 8, 2022.
4. *Wall Street Journal*, October 12, 2012.
5. Sine, interview with author, May 11, 2023.
6. Ibid.
7. Fisher, interview with author, October 11, 2022.
8. *New York Times*, March 11, 2014.
9. Marcelo Claure, interview with author, March 8, 2023.
10. Ibid.

11. Ibid.
12. Ibid.
13. Ibid.
14. *Wall Street Journal*, August 11, 2015.
15. Ibid.

22: TWO INDIANS ARE BETTER THAN ONE

1. In 2020, under pressure from a creaking WeWork, Masa secured a $92 million loan using the Woodside property as collateral (*Financial Times*, January 14, 2024).
2. Arora, interview with author, November 29, 2022.
3. Ibid.
4. Misra, interview with author, February 3, 2023.
5. Ibid.
6. Jeffrey Katzenberg, conversation with author, July 13, 2023.
7. Michael Lynton, interview with author, December 5, 2022.
8. Levy, interview with author, October 31, 2022.
9. Ibid.
10. Tadashi Yanai, interview with author, October 19, 2022.
11. Arora, interview, November 29, 2022.
12. Masa says he was introduced to DRC by the boss of Oracle Japan, who had a famed wine cellar.
13. Reuters, August 19, 2016.
14. Len Blavatnik, conversation with author, June 24, 2023, in Italy.
15. "SoftBank's Rajeev Misra Used Campaign of Sabotage to Hobble Internal Rivals," *Wall Street Journal*, February 26, 2020, and "SoftBank Probes Who Was Behind Smear Campaign Against Top Executives," *Wall Street Journal*, March 16, 2018.
16. "SoftBank's Rajeev Misra Used Campaign of Sabotage," *Wall Street Journal*, March 27, 2018.
17. Yanai, interview, October 19, 2022.

23: SMASH AND GRAB

1. Hermann Hauser, interview with author, March 16, 2022.
2. James Ashton describes how gifted computer architects Sophie Wilson and Steve Furber drew inspiration from two Americans who had just invented a new architecture called RISC (Reduced Instruction Set Computer) in *The Everything Blueprint, Processing Power, Politics and the Microchip Design That Conquered the World* (Hodder & Stoughton, 2023).
3. Sine, interview with author, April 21, 2022.
4. Simon Segars, interview with author, April 26, 2022.
5. Ibid.
6. Stuart Chambers, interview with author, February 23, 2022.
7. William Rucker, interview with author, May 19, 2022.
8. Segars, interview, April 26, 2022.
9. I owe this delicious detail to Jeff Sine.
10. *Shropshire Star*, June 20, 2019.

11. Two former senior Whitehall officials, speaking off the record.
12. Rucker, interview, May 19, 2022.
13. Alok Sama, interview with author, May 23, 2022.
14. Masa, interview with author, October 18, 2023; senior SoftBank adviser off the record.
15. Chambers, interview, February 23, 2022.
16. The problem was where to park the cash. ARM had long been a go-to tracker stock; now it was going private, there was no comparable tech company to fill the gap in their portfolios.
17. As reported to author by a former ARM executive, who didn't wish to be named, on January 24, 2023.
18. Hauser, interview, March 16, 2022.
19. Rucker, interview, May 19, 2022.
20. Simon Robey, interview with author, July 13, 2022.

24: PROJECT CRYSTAL BALL
1. Fisher, interview with author, November 12, 2022.
2. Bradley Hope and Justin Scheck, *Blood and Oil* (John Murray, 2021), pp. 121-27.
3. I am grateful to Steve Schwarzman for the historical analysis of capital markets.
4. Hope and Scheck, *Blood and Oil*, p. 125.
5. Senior SoftBank executive, speaking off the record.
6. Mallaby, *The Power Law*, pp. 346-47; Saudi source, speaking off the record.
7. "Prince Charles Faces Inquiry into Sheikh's €3m Charity Cash," *The Times*, June 27, 2022.
8. SoftBank adviser, speaking off the record.
9. The Saudi delegation was five hundred strong and arrived in thirteen planes. Misra, interview with author, July 29, 2023.
10. Masa, interview with David Rubinstein, October 11, 2017.
11. Description based on author's two private meetings with MBZ several years earlier.
12. Account based on a person present at the meeting, speaking off the record.
13. Gates, interview with author, July 8, 2022.
14. This account was provided by a person present who spoke off the record.
15. Two sources speaking off the record confirm the exchange.

25: CRAZY GUY
1. Eliot Brown and Maureen Farrell, *The Cult of We: WeWork and the Great Startup Delusion* (Penguin Random House, 2021), pp. 166-67.
2. Ibid.
3. Reeves Wiedeman, *Billion Dollar Loser: The Epic Rise and Spectacular Fall of Adam Neumann and WeWork* (Hodder & Stoughton, 2020), pp. 16-17.
4. Sunil Bharti Mittal, interview with author, September 8, 2022.
5. Levy, interview with author, April 28, 2022.
6. Brown and Farrell, *The Cult of We*, pp. 212-13.
7. *Jewish Currents*, November 5, 2020.
8. Brown and Farrell, *The Cult of We*, p. 216.
9. Masa, interview with author, October 18, 2023.

10. Levy, interview with author, October 31, 2022.
11. Warren Buffett, letter to shareholders, 2011.
12. Warren Buffett, interview and email exchange with author, July 17, 2023.
13. Two former SoftBank executives confirmed the serious problems in Washington pre-2018.
14. In 2017, WeWork had lost $883 million, despite having some $886 million in revenue. In 2018, the company managed to lose $1.9 billion on some $1.8 billion of revenue.
15. Brown and Farrell, *The Cult of We*, p. 167.
16. Ibid.
17. Senior Saudi business executive, speaking off the record.
18. Yanai, interview with author, October 19, 2022.
19. SoftBank says the group holding company is not legally or morally obligated to repay the debt of its subsidiaries. Therefore, a fair measure of SoftBank Group's financial stability is loan-to-value based on net debt on a standalone basis. Given the complex, interconnected structure of SoftBank Group debt, more conservative analysis prefer to look at consolidated debt. This measure is mainly used in the book.

26: I HOPE YOU GO BUST
1. Moritz, interview with author, August 15, 2022.
2. Bill Gurley, interview with author, December 1, 2022.
3. Former senior SoftBank executive, speaking off the record.
4. Dave Grannan, interview with author, March 16, 2023.
5. Dave Grannan showed the author the text on his iPhone.
6. "SoftBank Probes Who Was Behind Smear Campaign," *Wall Street Journal*, March 26, 2018, and "SoftBank's Rajeev Misra Used Campaign of Sabotage," *Wall Street Journal*, February 26, 2020.
7. He was speaking off the record.
8. Arora had become CEO of Palo Alto Networks in June 2018.
9. Several people in the room, speaking off the record, have confirmed the account of the meeting.
10. Alexi Mostrous, "The Curse of SoftBank," Tortoise Media, October 23, 2019.

27: THE GREAT ESCAPE
1. Duncan Mavin, *The Pyramid of Lies* (Pan Macmillan, 2023), pp. 158-64.
2. Ibid.
3. The account of the meetings between Masayoshi Son and Elliott Management is based on several sources who spoke on condition of not being identified.
4. Warren Buffett on CNBC, *Squawk Box*, interview, February 26, 2018.
5. A person present at the meeting speaking off the record.
6. PCR tests were later adopted in Japan.
7. Senior former SoftBank executive speaking off the record SoftBank's.
8. Kana Inagaki and Leo Lewis, "SoftBank: Inside Two Weeks of Turmoil That Squeezed Masayoshi Son," *Financial Times*, April 5, 2020.
9. Ibid.
10. Masa, interview with author, October 18, 2023.
11. The following is based on multiple sources speaking off the record.

12. Robert Smith and Kana Inagaki, "Jesus Christ Was Also Misunderstood, Masayoshi Son Tells Investors," *Financial Times*, May 18, 2020.

28: THE WHALE IS STILL HUNGRY
1. A person present at the Tokyo dinner who asked not to be named.
2. In June 2024, thanks to AI fever, Nvidia joined the elite club of US companies with a $3 trillion market capitalization. In retrospect, having sold down his 4.9 percent stake, Masa missed out on a second Alibaba.
3. Author was *FT* editor at the time and intimately involved in the Wirecard reporting and editing.
4. A senior SoftBank executive present at the meeting who asked not to be identified.
5. Author has seen the whistleblower emails.
6. SoftBank Group's consolidated financial report, published on February 8, 2024, for the nine-month period ended December 31, 2023, puts Northstar's cumulative loss since inception at ¥941.7 billion. That amounts to $9.41 billion at $1 to ¥100, and using the May 2024 rate ($1 = ¥153) at $6.15 billion.
7. "SoftBank Unmasked As 'Nasdaq Whale' That Stoked Tech Rally," *Financial Times*, September 4, 2020.
8. In June 2024 Elliott disclosed it had built a $2 billion stake in SoftBank. Once again, it identified the "conglomerate discount" and pushed for a share buyback to profit from its investment.
9. Masa, interview with author, October 18, 2023.

29: BLIZZARD
1. His private plane had the tail number N25TID, *T* standing for trillion and *D* for dollars.
2. Interview with Marcelo Claure, May 12, 2023.
3. Former SoftBank senior executive, speaking on condition of anonymity.
4. Pemmicans are pressed cakes of pounded dried meat mixed to a paste with melted fat, originally made by Native Americans and later adapted by Arctic explorers.
5. SoftBank says it provides stock options to regular employees as incentives. In the case of senior management who are board members, Masa believes the extension of loans to purchase SoftBank Group stock implies taking on downside risk too. All transactions were approved by the SoftBank Group board.
6. In November 2023, WeWork, whose office-leasing business model was crushed by the Covid lockdown, filed for Chapter 11 bankruptcy.
7. Three separate former SoftBank executives have given the same account of the board reshuffle.
8. UBS acquired Credit Suisse for a meager $3.2 billion in an all-stock deal on March 19, 2023.
9. Richard Cohen, veteran columnist at *The Washington Post*, told the author the story.
10. "Alibaba Founder Living in Tokyo Since China's Tech Crackdown," *Financial Times*, November 29, 2022.
11. Former senior SoftBank executive, speaking on condition of anonymity.

12. "Masayoshi Son Owes Softbank $4.7bn After Tech Rout," *Financial Times*, November 17, 2022.
13. Among One's first investments was putting $500 million into WeWork, which soon filed for bankruptcy. Misra's view was that the business concept was sound, but the Covid pandemic and working from home killed the office-leasing business.

BIBLIOGRAPHY

Alletzhauser, Albert. *The House of Nomura: The Inside Story of the Legendary Japanese Financial Dynasty.* HarperCollins, 1990.

Arimori, Takashi. *Net Bubble.* Bunshun Shinsho, 2000.

Ashton, James. *The Everything Blueprint: Processing Power, Politics and the Microchip Design that Conquered the World.* Hodder & Stoughton, 2023.

Brown, Eliot, and Maureen Farrell. *The Cult of We: WeWork, Adam Neumann, and the Great Startup Delusion.* HarperCollins, 2021.

Clark, Duncan. *The House that Jack Ma Built.* HarperCollins, 2016.

Dower, John W. Dower. *Embracing Defeat: Japan in the Wake of World War II.* W. W. Norton, 1999.

Evans, Harold. *Good Times, Bad Times.* Coronet Books, 1983.

Funabshi, Yoichi, and Kay Kitazawa. *Fukushima: A Complex Disaster, A Disastrous Response.* Sage Journals, 2012.

Goto-Jones, Christopher. *Japan: A Very Short Introduction.* Oxford University Press, 2009.

Harding, Christopher. *The Japanese: A History in Twenty Lives.* Allen Lane, 2020.

Inoue, Atsuo. *Aiming High: Masayoshi Son, SoftBank, and the Disrupting of Silicon Valley.* Hodder & Stoughton, 2022.

Isaacson, Walter. *Steve Jobs.* Simon & Schuster, 2011.

Yeong-dal, Kim. *Sōshikaimei no Hōseido to Rekishi.* Akashi Shoten, 2002.

Kodama, Hiroshi. *Gensōkyoku: Son Masayoshi to SoftBank no Kako Ima Mirai.* Nikkei BP, 2005.

Mallaby, Sebastian. *The Power Law: Venture Capital and the Art of Disruption.* Penguin Books, 2022.

Mavin, Duncan. *Pyramid of Lies: The Prime Minister, the Banker and the Billion-Dollar Scandal.* Pan Macmillan, 2022.

Miller, Chris. *Chip War: The Fight for the World's Most Critical Technology.* Simon & Schuster, 2022.

Michael Moritz: *Return to the Little Kingdom: Steve Jobs and the Creation of Apple.* Duckworth, 2004.

Min, Jin Lee. *Pachinko.* Hachette, 2017.

Nakagawa, Kazunori. *Nijū Rasen: Yokubō to Kensō no Media.* Kōdansha, 2019.

Nikkei Communication. *Shirarezaru Tsūshin Sensō no Shinjitsu: NTT SoftBank no Antō.* Nikkei BP, 2003.

Ōshita, Eiji. *Son Masayoshi: Kigyō no Wakaki Shishi.* Kōdansha, 1999.

———. *Rongo to Keiei: SBI Kitao Yoshitaka.* Vol. 1. MdN Corporation, 2022.

Sano, Shinichi. *Anpon: Son Masayoshi Den.* Shōgakukan Bunko, 2014.

Sasaki, Tadashi. *Waga Kōshisai: Kansha Hou'on no Ki.* Zaikai Tsūshin Sha, 2005.

Satō, Masa'aki. *Honda Shinwa, Vol. 1: Honda Sōichirō to Fujisawa Takeo.* Bunshun Bunko, 2008.

Seth, Michael J. Seth. *Korea: A Very Short Introduction.* Oxford University Press, 2020.

Shawcross, William. *Murdoch: The Making of a Media Empire.* Touchstone, 1993.

Sheard, Paul. "The Japanese Economy: Where is it Leading in the Asia Pacific?" Mari Pangestu and Li Gang Son (eds.). *Japan's Future in East Asia and the Pacific.* Australia National University, 2008.

Sugimoto, Takashi. *Son Masayoshi 300 Nen Ōkoku eno Yabō.* Nihon Keizai Shimbun Sha, 2017.

Suleyman, Mustafa. *The Coming Wave: AI, Power and the 21st Century's Greatest Dilemma.* Bodley Head, 2023.

Takeda, Haruhito. *Nihon no Jōhō Tsūshin Sangyō Shi: 2 Tsu no Sekai Kara 1 Tsu no Sekai e.* Yūhikaku, 2011.

Takita, Seiichirō. *Son Masayoshi: Internet Zaibatsu Keiei.* Nikkei Bijinesujin Bunko, 2011.

Tett, Gillian. *Saving the Sun: A Wall Street Gamble to Save Japan from its Trillion-Dollar Meltdown.* Harper Business, 2003.

Tsukui, Juri (ed.). *Son Masayoshi: Heisei no Ryōma Densetsu: Onshitachi ga Kataru Son Masayoshi no Sugao.* Genbun Media, 2011.

Vogel, Ezra. *Japan as Number One.* Harvard University Press, 1979.

Wiedmann, Reeves. *Billion Dollar Loser: The Epic Rise and the Spectacular Fall of Adam Neumann and WeWork.* Hodder & Stoughton, 2020.

Yoshida, Kōichi. *Naibu Kokuhatsu: SoftBank Yuganda Keiei.* Yell Shuppansha, 1997.

Yoshida, Tsukasa. *Son Masayoshi wa Taorenai.* Asahi Shimbun Sha, 2001.

Tosu Shishi Hensan Iinkai (ed.). *Tosu Shishi, Vol. 4: Kindai-Gendai Hen.* Tosu Shi, 2009.

INDEX

Verizon, 201, 202, 203
Vernet, Carle, 187
video games, 24, 35–36, 39
Vision Fund. *See* SoftBank Vision Fund
Vladivostok, Russia, 234
Vodafone/Vodafone Japan, 154, 162–170,
    173, 189, 206
Vogel, Ezra, 37

W
The Wall Street Journal, 94, 202, 214–215, 256,
    259, 267
Warner Music, 214
Warshaw, Robey, 224, 226
Warshaw, Simon, 223
The Washington Post, 249
Watanabe, Tsutomu, 108
Wayve, 298
WebFirst, 124
Webvan, 120, 124
Wedmore, Ben, 115
Wei, Cheng, 243
Welch, Jack, 124
WeWork, xii, 240, 263, 270, 273
    aborted listing of, 249–250, 266
    bailout, cost of, 264
    cost to SoftBank, 299
    crisis of, 259–260
    Marcelo Claure and, 286
    Masa on growth of, 247–248
    Project Fortitude, 247
    Saudis and, 248–249
    SoftBank investment in, 241–244
Wheeler, Tom, 202
whistleblowers
    allegations by employees, 107–115
    Northstar and, 279–280
*Whistle Blown: SoftBank's Crooked
    Management*, 107
Whitacre, Edward, 147–148
Whitman, Meg, 158
whole company securitization, 167
Widodo, Joko, 263–264
Wind Hellas, 215
Windows operating system, 62
Wirecard, 275–276
Wired (magazine), 148

WME-IMG, 211
Woodside, California, 171, 208, 220, 255
WordStar, 40
World Economic Forum, Davos, Switzerland,
    x, 132, 149–150, 264
World Health Organization, 268
World War II, 5–6
Wuhan, China, 268

X
Xi Jinping, 283, 290, 291

Y
Yahata steel plant, Kyushu, Japan, 14
Yahoo! BB, 141, 142, 143, 144, 148, 154, 155,
    165
Yahoo! China, 158
Yahoo! Japan, 92, 109, 133, 141, 165, 305
    eBay and, 151
    e-commerce sites and, 121–122
    Google and, 207, 208
    on the JASDAQ market, 114–115
    launching of, 91
Yahoo! US, 17, 189, 233, 245
    alternative to, 207–208
    Chinese state control and, 157
    founders, 87
    "Golden Triangle" between Alibaba,
        SoftBank and, 158
    investment in, 88–91, 92, 115, 120
    Masa's profit from, 92
    stock, 120, 145, 147–148
    value of, 124
    Yahoo! Japan and, 91, 115
yakuza (gangsters), 9, 15
Yalta conference (1945), 11
Yanai, Tadashi
    on doing business with Saudi Arabia, 249
    leaving SoftBank board, 282
    in Masa's impulsive and erratic behavior,
        147
    on Masa stepping down as CEO of
        SoftBank, 195–196, 217
    on Nikesh Arora, 212
    reason for joining SoftBank board, 146–147
    relationship with Masa, 146
Yangban class, Korea, 3, 7, 10

ABOUT THE AUTHOR

Lionel Barber is the former editor of *The Financial Times*. As editor, he interviewed many of the world's leaders in business and politics, including US Presidents Barack Obama and Donald Trump, Russian President Vladimir Putin, Chancellor Angela Merkel of Germany, and Indian Prime Minister Narendra Modi. Barber has cowritten several books and has lectured widely on foreign policy, transatlantic relations, and economics. He also served on the Board of Trustees at the Tate and the Carnegie Corporation of New York. He graduated in 1978 from St. Edmund Hall, Oxford University, with a joint honors degree in German and modern history and is fluent in French and German.